workhuman*

---*---

Explore the platform
workhuman.com

Experience the movement
workhumanlive.com

Also by Eric Mosley and Derek Irvine

978-0071817981

978-0071838405

Praise for *Making Work Human*

People are not the most important resource in your company. People are your company. Eric Mosley and Derek Irvine don't just believe this—they've led a powerful movement to help leaders build organizations that put people first. Their book isn't just a compelling case for why to do it—it's also a practical guide for how to do it.

> —**Adam Grant**, *New York Times* bestselling author
> of *Originals* and *Give and Take*, and host of the
> chart-topping TED podcast WorkLife

Powered by an incredible depth and breadth of research and case studies, this book is a call to action to every leader to invest in a human-centered culture rooted in gratitude, kindness, openness, and mutual trust. But it goes a step further and shares tangible suggestions for *how* leaders can do this right away, making it an invaluable must-read.

> —**Nataly Kogan**, creator of the Happier Method™
> and Happier@Work

Welcome to the new world of work. In this relentlessly practical book, Eric and Derek provide a disruptive blueprint for revolutionizing the culture of your workplace by making it more human. If you care about getting your team to reach its full potential, this is a must-read.

> —**Ozan Varol**, law professor at Lewis & Clark Law
> School and author of *Think Like a Rocket Scientist*

Making Work Human packages research and practical advice to help leaders foster a more positive culture. The strategies outlined in the book can help drive more sustainable performance and well-being.

> —**Christine Porath**, professor of management
> at Georgetown University and author of
> *Mastering Civility*

I've long thought we can make work better by making work about people. The Workhuman Charter of Workplace Rights champions that notion by challenging workplaces to become more responsive to human needs, but it goes beyond that. This charter isn't about helping people work better for the benefit of business; this charter is about helping people *be better. For the benefit of society.* Smart organizations know business performance will follow; if you do the right things, the right things will happen. But truly great organizations understand we exist for more. We have the power to change the world, and we can start by changing work.

—**Jason Averbook**, CEO and cofounder of Leapgen

Caring for your employees, as well as your customers, will translate into business success. *Making Work Human* shows the power of gratitude and human connection.

—**Tony Hsieh**, *New York Times* bestselling author of *Delivering Happiness* and CEO of Zappos.com, Inc.

The future of work is all about building strong, flexible teams and creating the frameworks and feedback loops for those teams to drive innovation. Eric and Derek make a compelling case for any company—whether a start-up or well-established business—to leverage a culture of gratitude and connection in a way that brings people together, improves performance, and delivers a better experience at work for all of us.

—**Kat Cole**, COO and president, North America at FOCUS Brands

If work is such a huge part of human life, shouldn't humanity be a huge part of working life? That's the powerful case that Eric Mosley and Derek Irvine make in this essential book. By showing appreciation, communicating with empathy, and recognizing people's achievements, business leaders can build an enterprise that combines profit and purpose.

—**Daniel H. Pink**, *New York Times* bestselling author of *When* and *Drive*

The concepts Eric and Derek set forth in *Making Work Human* are both wonderfully simple and groundbreaking. While many leaders espouse the importance of humanity at work, Eric and Derek are the first to offer concrete, proven strategies that help people and businesses thrive. They challenge each of us to reframe the employer-employee dynamic in order to pave the way for a healthier and more productive and sustainable future.

—**Cy Wakeman**, international keynote speaker, drama researcher, and *New York Times* bestselling author

How companies care for, coach, and connect people at work is the biggest opportunity for businesses today. *Making Work Human* is a must-read for any CEO or business leader who wants to bring out the best in all people and maximize potential.

—**Marshall Goldsmith**, *New York Times* #1 bestselling author of *Triggers*, *Mojo*, and *What Got You Here Won't Get You There*

MAKING WORK
human

MAKING WORK
human

HOW HUMAN-CENTERED COMPANIES
ARE CHANGING THE FUTURE OF WORK
AND THE WORLD

Eric Mosley & Derek Irvine

New York   Chicago   San Francisco   Athens   London
Madrid   Mexico City   Milan   New Delhi
Singapore   Sydney   Toronto

1 2 3 4 5 6 7 8 9   LCR   25 24 23 22 21 20

ISBN   978-1-260-46420-7
MHID   1-260-46420-2

e-ISBN   978-1-260-46421-4
e-MHID   1-260-46421-0

McGraw-Hill Education books are available at special quantity discounts to use as premiums and sales promotions or for use in corporate training programs. To contact a representative, please visit the Contact Us pages at www.mhprofessional.com.

CONTENTS

PART II BUILDING A HUMAN ENTERPRISE

FOREWORD

We are living through twin revolutions.

Over the past 15 years, we have been privileged to witness how much our lives can be changed by technology. But as the pace of change increased, we began to worry and to wonder: What was happening to humans in the midst of all this change? Where would humans fit into the future?

Simultaneous to the technological revolution was the birth and rise of positive psychology. The more we learn from advances in positive research, the more we are realizing that humanity is also on the brink of its own revolution, based in part on that technology. We have reached a point where society can no longer be enamored with mere productivity as it was throughout the twentieth century. In the past, more hours plus more technology yielded higher profit. Now we can't be asked to work longer hours with more stress and expect with any rationality to maintain performance for long. Instead, the technological revolution forced us to examine how we can make work human again. For only by increasing meaning, connection, shared purpose, optimism, and happiness, can we find a path forward and upward.

In 2015, I had the privilege of speaking about happiness at the very first Workhuman® Live conference in Orlando, Florida. The audience of 400 HR leaders and practitioners was small, but mighty. I joined a stellar cast of keynote speakers, including Arianna Huffington, Adam Grant, and Rob Lowe, tackling topics such as wellness, sleep hygiene, gratitude, and givers—not the typical topics you find at a business conference.

Yet it was clear even from that first gathering that Eric and Derek had tapped into a critical need—a need for a community of like-minded professionals to share ideas, research, and aspirations for making work more human. Human resources as an industry and as a profession needed a path forward in order to reclaim humanity and put people first. What I found to be incredible is that they were using technology, often reviled for getting in the way of happiness, as a tool for increasing gratitude and connectedness.

I continued to be involved in Workhuman Live as a speaker in 2016 and 2018, as the audience grew from hundreds to thousands. And during that time, I became more familiar with Workhuman as a company and leader in social recognition and continuous performance management. Eric and Derek built Workhuman with a simple premise: that giving and receiving gratitude would improve performance in any business. Thanks to the momentum of Workhuman Live and customers like Cisco, JetBlue, LinkedIn, Merck, Intuit, P&G, and more, that premise has become a global movement and community. I've seen this firsthand as I've collaborated with Workhuman on research studies on the connections between praise, retention, and employee happiness. I had the privilege of collaborating with the Workhuman research team to publish findings on the ripple effect of social recognition on employee performance and new hire retention at LinkedIn. It's a case study that has modeled out the enormous impact that more frequent recognition can have on employee performance, tenure, and impact, as you'll read about in this book.

With the advent of *big data*, we are now able to see humans so much clearer. We are no longer content just researching whether we can make a leader happier. Now we can find out how making leaders more positive or creative impacts an employee two degrees separated from them or how the optimism of an HR leader could impact a sales leader's client's optimism. This is *big potential*, the awareness that the majority of our happiness and success occurs in the intersection between the individual and his or her ecosystem at work or home. It's incredibly gratifying to see the once unlikely marriage of positive human values and big data analysis now empowering leaders to build the workplace of the future. Workhuman is leading this effort, building a new category of human applications that fundamentally change the employee experience. I'm grateful to be around to witness how more organizations are building cultures of belonging, purpose, meaning, happiness, and energy. For to ignore happiness at work is to ignore the greatest competitive advantage in the modern economy.

It takes a while for society to figure out how to deal with advances. What gives me so much hope is that companies are talking not just about profit and productivity, but they are focused on connectedness, mindfulness, happiness at home and at work, and diversity. What we are seeing is a return to being human at work. The laggards in the future will be the companies that ignore the value of an interconnected approach to happiness and success, and the leaders will be the ones that value humans the most.

And as the COVID-19 pandemic demonstrated, it also takes a while for society to figure out how to deal with adversity. In *The Happiness Advantage* I observed, "The most successful people see adversity not as a stumbling block, but as a stepping-stone to greatness." COVID-19 created enormous adversity, and the healthiest people and organizations responded with creativity (videoconferencing, work sharing) and compassion (considering how my social distancing helps your well-being). In fact, many of the healthiest organizations adapted with astonishing speed. And across the world we saw an outpouring of gratitude and respect for healthcare workers, first responders, and other essential workers.

At its core, valuing humanity in the workplace is about treating people with respect. It's valuing every single person who contributes to an organization's success. It's about equality and maintaining a certain standard of employee rights—no matter where an employee sits in the organization.

As our world becomes more connected, people are demanding more transparency in every facet of business, including how organizations treat their employees. What Eric and Derek have put forth in this book is a path forward and a strong call to action for truly progressive organizations to put a stake in the ground. To make a statement to investors, board members, shareholders, customers, and the world that their first priority is their people—and that success follows from there.

Each and every person has the right to lead a happy life at work. The methods shared in this book, backed by research and data, show a positive path forward for humans in the future of work.

Shawn Achor, happiness researcher
and *New York Times* bestselling author
of *Big Potential*

ACKNOWLEDGMENTS

This is our first book since Workhuman Live, our annual conference, began, and since then, so much has changed for people in the workplace—for the better. Everyone mentioned in this book is a maverick, pioneer, and leader who cares about making the modern workplace better for all people—so all of us humans can do the best work of our lives. The workplace now has even more influence than ever before to change our world and our lives, so we are truly grateful to all the contributors, as our collective efforts are helping advance the Workhuman movement and better the world we live in.

Our special thanks and gratitude to Doug Hardy, Kevin Mullins, Dan Miller, Lynette Silva, Jessica Klay, Chris Lee, Carrie Rogers, and Maureen Buxton, all of whom worked directly on the content and project management for this book, professionals in every way, without whom this would not have been possible. A special thanks for ALL who appear in the book and your quotes, your case studies, your ideas, your vision, your commitment, and your energy and passion. Thank you also to ALL our Workhuman® Cloud users and customers, ALL our fellow humans at Workhuman, and the many thousands of people we've met at Workhuman Live or who have been part of the movement from afar. Each of you has contributed to this incredible journey to make the workplace more human for all. You are the reason this book exists, and we dedicate it to each of you amazing humans.

This book also represents a remarkable journey of the past 20 years since Workhuman, the company, began. At that time, the workplace was in a very different place. The progress and potential of the workplace as a place for all was a mere glimmer of hope, lit by brave leaders who knew that an inclusive work environment was not only right for people but also smart for business. The past decade was an acceleration of this mindset, with each year seeing more impactful gains to benefit all people and the world as a whole.

Many may say we live in a divided world. That certainly may appear to be the case when viewing the superficial newsfeeds and television updates we encounter. But a wider view reveals incredible progress for employees and others around the world. Companies today have served as a unifying force and are creating stronger communities and more trusted environments than ever before. They have served as the last best place for people of all backgrounds and viewpoints to work together for a shared purpose.

As we look ahead to the next decade, we are overflowing with optimism. Continued progress won't be easy. It never is. Momentum is born out of movements and bold ambitions toward something greater. It is also unearthed from continued disruptive thinking and approaches about what is possible. Our future generations need not have the baggage of the past to restrict their thinking. Rather, they have the opportunity to create an even better world. To be their best selves. And to build upon the work and progress of great leaders. Thank you for joining us in this movement and for standing up for what is right. Continue to push forward. There's more work ahead. And the opening is right in front of us.

INTRODUCTION

On December 10, 1948, the United Nations General Assembly adopted the Universal Declaration of Human Rights. It's a brief and noble document, just as relevant today as it was more than 70 years ago. Among the rights listed are those in Article 23, which begins, "Everyone has the right to work, to free choice of employment, to just and favourable conditions of work and to protection against unemployment."

There are reasons to celebrate the world's progress since Eleanor Roosevelt led that effort to recognize basic rights for all. Extreme poverty has declined; basic education and healthcare are more widely available; and for all their flaws, modern business and nonprofit enterprises have raised the material well-being of humans at a scale beyond the most optimistic projections of 1948.

Now the time has come for those enterprises to adopt an additional charter that expresses the rights and aspirations of the workforce. We should recognize and declare the enduring, human-centered principles of business and nonprofit enterprises.

In 2020, just as this book was being completed, the world faced its worst health crisis in more than a century. COVID-19 spread globally with incredible speed, testing the resilience of people and institutions in ways people hadn't imagined. While we are still learning its lessons, even now we can reflect on the roles that business played and continues to play in the crisis.

There are plenty of standards by which to judge the broader impact of an enterprise on society, for example its environmental impact or the number of well-paying jobs it creates. In the COVID-19 crisis, we measured impacts in terms like lives saved, and jobs lost and restored. We saw the range of human capabilities, including heroic efforts by healthcare workers. We at Workhuman were moved to create a website (www.thankhealthcare.com) where anyone could thank healthcare workers publicly and we were overwhelmed by the massive outpouring of gratitude from around the world.

What's missing today is a doctrine of standards by which consumers and employees can recognize that a company is using its power to bend the moral arc of the universe just a bit more toward human values.

An awakening across business disciplines is bringing all our humanity to the workplace to create an environment where employees are more motivated, engaged, creative, innovative, and productive. More than a passing fad, this awakening is growing into a global movement and community of people, purpose, and passion that inspires more humanity to today's modern workplace—the Workhuman movement. It represents a cultural shift underpinned by extensive global research showing how companies can thrive by creating a positive employee experience. The mission of the Workhuman movement is to galvanize leaders worldwide to harness the transformative power of people for the next generation of people practices. We celebrate breakthrough organizations that meet the core human needs of employees and inspire them to do the best work of their lives—where people feel appreciated, respected, and empowered for who they are and what they do.

We propose an inclusive, evidence-based program to acknowledge and celebrate employers who support those rights. We call it the *Workhuman Charter of Workplace Rights*. We have created an objective, databased program to certify which employers support those rights. Like the Universal Declaration of Human Rights, the Workhuman Charter of Workplace Rights includes fundamental rights like equal pay for equal work, the right to a decent standard of living, and the right to time for rest and leisure.

Because the workplace has changed vastly since 1948, the Workhuman Charter of Workplace Rights includes additional rights made essential by developments in business, society, and technology. For example: Everyone's right to privacy includes the right to "switch off," or opt out of, the collection of personal data. Everyone has the right to a workplace respectful of mental and emotional safety in addition to physical safety. Marital or parental status cannot be a reason to discriminate among employees; neither can disability nor can genetic information. All people have a right to be respected and to express who they are—for example, their sexual or gender identity, cultural background, or religious beliefs. Sexual harassment, as well as other forms of harassment or intimidation, is not tolerated in the workplace.

The Workhuman Charter of Workplace Rights isn't only a list of prohibitions. Rather, it casts an aspirational vision of what a workplace can be:

- A place where people deserve to grow to their greatest potential through training, feedback, and rewards
- A place where people feel secure to express their views and ideas, with respect for themselves and others
- A place where people can use their talents and voice for good
- A place that supports environmental, social, and economic sustainability

We are asking enterprises to state their position on these rights and aspirations and share evidence that shows their support is real. Now businesses must recognize and fulfill these expectations for practical as well as moral reasons. Much of this book discusses those reasons. They begin with the tectonic changes shifting the business landscape today—changes that make our most human attributes more valuable to business than ever.

The Workhuman Charter of Workplace Rights grew out of our 20-year mission to make workplaces more responsive to human needs. Workhuman creates solutions and champions practices that make work a better place for people of all kinds. We have learned that there are specific practices through which organizations can become more human-centered, and this book is one part of our mission to spread the word about those practices.

We wrote the Workhuman Charter in 2019, as this book was being written. Our sense of urgency about the need for a charter, and a way to certify that companies are making progress in becoming more human, is told in greater detail in the final chapter. You can learn the latest about the Workhuman Charter of Workplace Rights at www.workhuman.com.

To understand *why* its time has come, we need to detail the reasons that enterprises of all types and missions need to pay greater attention to human values.

This Is the Human Decade

Everything is changing in the way work is managed, planned, and lived. Every business practice is being dismantled, disrupted, torn apart, and rearchitected in response to profound shifts in business, technology, and society. Ten years ago, ideas like "agile transformation" were the rarefied proposals of visionaries, but now entire multinational corporations are modeling themselves on its principles.

Not long ago, you learned a set of skills and developed them over the course of a career. Now you need new skills every couple of years to manage all the changes technology brings[1]—not just technical skills but new ways of finding, serving, and innovating for your customers. Disruption means if you don't manage these changes and build an organization that can thrive in the midst of uncertainty, you will be out of business.

The qualities that make us most human—connection, community, positivity, belonging, and a sense of meaning—have become the corporate fuel for getting things done, for innovating, for thriving in the global marketplace, and for outperforming the competition. Workhuman recognizes businesses that thrive by bringing humanity and social connection to the employee experience. Workhuman is the future of the workplace.

The Workhuman movement is out to change the world by changing work. We all spend so much of our time at work. Work has such an enormous influence upon our personal well-being, our state of mind, the teams we're on, and our families and friends because it affects our overall psyche. The quality of our work experience radiates outward to everyone and every place we touch.

We changed the name of our company* to embrace the new paradigm. Twenty years ago we said our mission was to help every person feel valued for who they are and what they do. We spent years rethinking and reinventing the practice of employee recognition, and one of our habits was to be customer-driven. In recent years, customers started to say, "We love working with you because your products and your conferences and even your sales pitches are uniquely about emotions and connections and positivity among employees. But there doesn't seem to be a single platform that brings all that together."

It dawned on us that we could be a partner to all our clients, providing solutions through social recognition that could promote a positive agenda for everything that humans bring to the workplace—diversity, performance management, wellness and mindfulness, civility, and equality. So we went back to work. That larger purpose became so deeply embedded in everything we do, that today we like to say, "We make work more human!"

The Three Pillars of Working Human

Workhuman began as a provider of social recognition software and services to business organizations. Since then, we've studied how the power of simple human appreciation can improve virtually every process and outcome in any industry. Our research partners conduct objective and searching studies to understand where and when recognition works. With them, we're building a global movement to make the workplace more human. And the evidence keeps mounting that the more human a workplace can be, the more likely it is to be successful.

To make a simple conceptual framework for all these activities, we coined a shorthand catchphrase describing three pillars to the future of

---

* Until 2019 Workhuman was named Globoforce.

continuous performance management and culture management. They are *THANK, TALK, CELEBRATE*.

THANK means expressing authentic appreciation for someone's work effort or positive behavior. It means taking a moment as an individual to drop the mask of formality that so many of us put on at work and simply note when another person has done a good job. THANK creates a positive relationship between individuals, and collectively it creates a culture of positivity throughout the organization. THANK is the foundation for a host of benefits for individuals and the organization, from greater engagement to lower turnover. It weaves gratitude, one of the most powerful human emotions, into the life of a company.

TALK includes all the ways in which we communicate in a modern workplace—e-mail, social media, apps like Slack—but especially we mean talking or writing one-to-one. It's the way employees grow and encourage one another toward common goals. TALK is how managers check in with performance goals or coach employees with information, insight, and skills training. TALK isn't just one-way—it means an open and deep dialogue between people and among teams.

CELEBRATE is the way we share what matters most to us. That might be a personal milestone, such as a wedding or a work anniversary, or it might be a shared accomplishment, such as completing a big project. CELEBRATE means we regularly pause to show our common concern for each other, affirming our common values and showing regard for one another.

THANK, TALK, CELEBRATE is our framework for bringing mountains of research and more than 50 million data points detailing behavior in the workplace into clear and memorable focus. Since a positive employee experience is the keystone of performance, we've given examples of the ways everyone can weave THANK, TALK, CELEBRATE into the daily flow of work.

The legendary management thinker Peter Drucker once codified the practice of management as performing three tasks: The first is to establish an institution's specific purpose and mission. The second is to make work productive and employees effective. The third is to manage the social impacts and social responsibilities of the enterprise.[2] This is as true for a church or a hospital as it is for a global enterprise or a corner store.

More than any other factor, what distinguishes greatness from mediocrity is how well people perform in service to those three tasks. Capital is vital, but start-ups almost always begin with little money. Technology is critical to success as well, but the greatest technology can't inspire people with a mission or choose which social responsibilities to serve. There is only one irreplaceable factor, and again Drucker clarified this, years ago, when he wrote, "A business enterprise (or any other institution) has only one true resource: people."

This is a book about that only true resource. We'll show how weaving THANK, TALK, CELEBRATE into the daily lives of your people will reinforce your organization's purpose, improve productivity, and even magnify the social impact of your business.

While we have always focused on human needs and emotions, recent advances in technology from artificial intelligence to robotics have accelerated the need for a more human workplace. At the heart of the modern business enterprise lies a seeming paradox: The more our machines and computers take over tasks once performed by humans, the more attention needs to be paid to the most human characteristics. Rather than diminishing humans in the workplace, technology is steadily increasing the value of our most human qualities.

Hard Data Meets Human Hearts

At Workhuman Live events you hear discussion of hard, quantifiable business goals that include terms like *imagination, courage, appreciation, gratitude, vulnerability, kindness, dedication, selflessness*, and *love*. What was once just the intuitive perception of "soft" human resources practitioners is now confirmed by the most data-centric researchers. And technologies that analyze the actions around THANK, TALK, CELEBRATE are revealing incredible insights, empowering organizations to thrive in a business environment that never slows down.

We listened to and learned from leading business thinkers like Gary Hamel and Brené Brown, organizational behavior experts like Adam Grant and Simon Sinek, social entrepreneurs like Amal Clooney and Tarana Burke, and a group of distinguished management and technology specialists too many to list. Over the years a surprising truth has appeared: The century-long battle between "quantitative," databased management and "qualitative," emotion-based management is over.

Business has reached a stage at which, given the choice between managing by data or by emotion, between facts and feelings, the answer is, *We don't have to choose.* Quantitative data analysis now promotes qualitative human aspirations. When we measure human activity and interaction in detail, we find insights that enable leaders to create organizations liberated from stifling bureaucracies. When we put control in the hands of employees, entrusted to work together with shared values toward a shared mission, they get the job done in ways more inspired and responsive than any command-and-control hierarchy. And when humans are encouraged, rewarded, and recognized for their unique gifts and contributions, all traditional goals, such as profits for a business or patents for a research organization or patient outcomes for a hospital, are realized.

The Moral Case Is the Business Case

Anyone making the case for a change in business practices (as this book does) faces the question, "Should I appeal to my reader's heart, head, or wallet?" The language of business suggests a quantifiable approach: Use financial data to make the case in material terms—increasing revenue, profits, and shareholder value. The thinking goes this way: If you can't explain the need for a more human workplace in the unsentimental language of balance sheets, your reasoning is weak or merely sentimental.

We reject the implicit belief that the head, heart, and wallet should be separate. Throughout this book you'll find ample data that proves a more human workplace is also a more successful workplace. But we will also argue that a more human workplace is a good unto itself. We believe that global business can occupy a place in society in which it does more than create profits that fuel prosperity. Even as political systems wrestle with the changes that technology and globalization have wrought, societies are looking to business leaders to pass on a better world to future generations.

Wharton's Adam Grant points out that when you make a business case for a moral purpose, people immediately start to compare it with the business case for everything else they could invest in. Thus, when we present the business case for investing a minimum of 1 percent of payroll in social recognition, that case should compare well to other programs. One way to look at it: One penny out of every dollar, given to the people to give to each other, is a small investment to increase productivity, retention, and an organizational culture you can be proud of.

We'll show throughout this book a compelling business case for social recognition. Social recognition brings documented bottom-line benefits like improved performance, greater employee engagement, lower turnover, and significant cost savings. It attracts, retains, and motivates talent. We'll also show how recognition can combine with cloud and data analysis technologies to give incredible new insights into the organization. We make that case because recognition should be justified using the same rules as for any other investment.

This isn't theory: Through 20 years Workhuman has recorded more than 50 million moments of recognition and gratitude among 5 million employees, and our research team has worked in partnership with others like the IBM Smarter Workforce Institute to analyze those interactions and their outcomes. We are learning through data how to connect measurable business outcomes to their causes in the motivation and dedication of employees.

But the Workhuman movement has another case to make, one that we feel is even more compelling. That is the moral case for bringing more humanity to the workplace.

A number of annual surveys identify companies and organizations as excellent workplaces. At the top of the rankings, employees uniformly say they are participating in a mission bigger than their own self-interest.

Great workplaces are about much more than pay and benefits, or promotion opportunities, or even fundamental needs like safety. They are about making the lives of their employees, customers, and communities better. They have cultures that inspire people, and as you read the surveys, you notice that the most inspiring companies are also among the most successful in such traditional terms as profits and shareholder value.

Even when they have been initially slow to address a problem, as in the case of privacy and data protection in the last few years, companies are structured to respond to social demands in a more agile way than government. Businesses have the potential to influence and then create change for the better, and putting more and more emphasis on serving humans inside and outside the company accelerates that power.

Wealthy business leaders have formed foundations that apply not only their money but unique expertise to relieve suffering. Bill and Melinda Gates fight malaria with data, and during the COVID-19 crisis, creative alliances formed among medical, business, and financial groups to find breakthrough solutions. Salesforce's founder Marc Benioff states, "The business of business is improving the state of the world," and Salesforce invites all entrepreneurs and their companies to commit 1 percent of their product, time, or resources to philanthropy. Foundations based on business fortunes have existed since the days of John D. Rockefeller and Henry Ford. What's changed is that today, many businesses weave social good into the core of their reason for being.

The Why and How of Working Human

This book is organized into two parts: Part I reviews the new realities of the workplace. We'll see how technology, globalization, new business models, and pervasive disruption in every industry call upon leaders to create a workplace that can attract and retain the best talent through cultures that THANK, TALK, CELEBRATE what is most human in us. We'll also see how employees find energy and engagement in a culture of appreciation and gratitude.

Part II focuses on the practical ways to use social recognition and data analysis to address the urgent challenges in the new organization—performance management, compensation and rewards, diversity and inclusion, and leadership itself.

At the end of each chapter, we suggest brief written exercises for you, the reader, to relate your unique experiences to the ideas we discuss. We urge you to do these exercises; our customers tell us they create an emotional as well as intellectual understanding of the concepts presented in this book. The exercises are in a box labeled "CONSIDER THIS."

Central to understanding the new realities of the workplace, and then doing something about it, is the expertise we at Workhuman have developed. For 20 years we have observed the ways that the practice of social recognition creates a culture of positivity and gratitude. As we expanded recognition's toolset to analyze organizational dynamics such as unconscious bias or hidden performance gaps, we saw that recognition could become more than a way to create positivity. It can discover hidden problems, and then, in practice, *social recognition is the solution for the problems it discovers.*

Again: *Social recognition is the solution for the problems it discovers.*

We'll describe the latest in social recognition—what it is, what it does, and why it's an unmatched tool for making work more human. We'll introduce a lot of data and ideas, but at its heart, the Workhuman movement can be stated quite simply. Not long ago, our research team asked employees across industries, "What is the one thing that you would change about your organization's culture?" The top response was that people want to foster a culture of appreciation for who they are and what they do—in short, mutual respect among the people of a company, from top to bottom. Similarly, when asked to choose one thing they wish their manager did more of, the top response was for the manager to show more appreciation.[3] A basic human need is to be seen and valued by others. At work, we need to know our managers see us, too.

Business leaders don't have to choose between head, heart, and wallet. Social recognition, powered by advanced data analysis, is the most practical-minded path to sustained performance in the long run. It also inspires the best in us. Our call for a more human workplace springs from a vision of a better way of doing business, a better society, and a better world.

MAKING WORK
human

PART I

HUMANS AT WORK

1 | The Human Enterprise

Inspiring Employees to Give Their Best

HUMAN MOMENTS

"My favorite recognition moment is the very first one we had at Baystate Health using our social recognition platform. It was from a physician who was recognizing a groundskeeper, to thank him for having an impact on the health and well-being of all our patients when they come through our doors and see the beautiful grounds that he's been keeping for many years. That moment was really profound because it brought two worlds together. In a healthcare organization a physician and a groundskeeper don't have a lot of connection points, but that recognition connected them, and it had a major impact on that groundskeeper. What might surprise you is that it also had a major impact on the physician. She learned that the moments she took to research the groundskeeper's name and recognize him, really mattered to him."

—Jennifer Faulkner, VP, Team Member Experience
& Talent Management, Baystate Health

Work might be the last, best place to realize our full humanity.

If that strikes you as unlikely, consider that the tectonic changes disrupting business are also buffeting nations, societies, families, and individuals. Polarization and tribalism shadow our political and social lives even as we are more connected than ever. Yet our businesses represent the coming together of diverse people around shared values and missions. Employees come to work with different backgrounds and beliefs, but they agree to share broad goals. And as a changing world requires businesses to become more diverse, employees can potentially reach across the chasms that modern tribal life has built.

We are at an inflection point in the way work is managed, planned, and even lived. Tidal waves of technology, globalization, and disruption require business leaders to redesign their organizations to be more agile, connected, and team-focused and less bureaucratic. Of necessity, organizations are rethinking jobs, and people are rethinking careers as a long arc of continuous learning, not just learning new skills but learning new roles, relationships, and ways of measuring progress. This is revolution, not evolution.

As we write, the COVID-19 pandemic is forcing everyone to rethink how they do their jobs, and the world economy is grappling with sudden, massive unemployment. Those with jobs are telecommuting or keeping social distance in the workplace. All the changes we knew about, and many more, are coming with unprecedented speed.

Humans are at the heart of this change. As business steps into a new world, we find that all the changes of the twenty-first century have returned HR to the most basic questions: *How can people work well together? Why would someone choose to work for this employer over that one? What can humans do better than machines? Once material needs are satisfied, what makes people work? What makes a meaningful life?*

The Edelman Trust Barometer, a global survey of trust in institutions of all kinds, found in 2019 that while trust is declining in government, public organizations, and think tanks, trust in corporations is going up. This is particularly true of corporations that authentically strive toward a higher purpose than profits. And while employees tend to trust their organizations generally, they give their highest levels of trust to their close team members.[1]

When people give their trust to employers and coworkers above others, they influence each other. Companies that recognize the power of peers to influence each other can improve their institutional relationship with all employees.

Kat Cole, COO and president, North America, at FOCUS Brands, oversees a portfolio of food service companies with wildly different brands and cultures, from the hip and healthy Jamba Juice to the indulgent Cinnabon. These are franchise businesses, with practical and legal limits to how much a leader can command change. So she has become expert at moving the company's 100,000 employees working in 62 countries toward common goals through understanding and steady influence.

"Just because we are a collection of companies does not mean we want to homogenize all the ways that people 'bring their human' to work," says Cole. "Certainly, there are things we consider universal, like treating everyone with respect, and we work to amplify or improve or accelerate those things in our brands. But everyone has different histories, and that affects their belief systems. What's going on in their lives today affects the business. It affects how they show up. So the first step is identifying unique cultures and honoring them."

A growing body of research now points to the benefits of a human workplace for creating positive employee experiences. According to research from IBM and Workhuman,[2] a human workplace is primarily characterized by opportunities for:

- Organizational trust
- Coworker relationships
- Meaningful work
- Recognition, feedback, and growth
- Empowerment and voice
- Work-life balance

We call this the *human enterprise*. It represents a new value proposition between employer and employee far beyond the traditional formula of work-for-pay, a model that only valued the efficiency with which people learned skills and carried them out in an assembly line. It means companies get the best out of their employees by satisfying more than basic needs like having a safe place to work. In the human enterprise, a culture that enables all employees to feel accepted, recognized, and rewarded for all their attributes will also be a culture where innovation and creative problem solving can thrive because it values continuous learning and growth. Instead of trying to *get* the best out of employees, human enterprises enable and inspire employees to *give* their best.

The most competitive companies are evolving in the direction of the most human qualities: inspiration, social connection, diversity, individual empowerment, emotional intelligence, and an aptitude for learning and adaptation. The least competitive companies cling to top-down, slow-moving hierarchies. They are in a race to the bottom, unwilling or unable to adapt their practices to an agile and empowered world. They are caught in a downward spiral, unable to attract the best talent and becoming steadily less competitive.

For centuries, leading companies have engaged in a systematic effort to identify what people do better than machines (and vice versa) and to allocate work accordingly. The power loom replaced the weaver. The steam engine replaced the horse. The adding machine replaced the abacus and the scratch pad, and the electronic calculator replaced the adding machine.

These were simple substitutions by today's standards. Lately, the changes no longer follow a straight-line, predictable evolution. The internet, cloud computing, and social media are augmenting human capability and changing it. Artificial intelligence is beginning to replace certain cognitive skills (pattern matching, memory recall, data gathering, and real-time analysis). "Brain work" increasingly means "working with the machines," bringing critical thinking, social skills, creativity, empathy, imagination, and other "right-brain" skills to decide what data to gather and what questions to ask.[3]

Josh Bersin, an expert on the future of work, recently wrote, "In an era when automation, AI, and technology have become more pervasive, important (and frightening) than ever, the big issue companies face is about people: how we find and develop soft skills, how we create fairness and transparency, and how we make the workplace more flexible, humane, and honest."[4]

> ## THANK TALK **CELEBRATE**
>
> "Everyone has different histories, and that affects their belief systems. So the first step is identifying unique cultures and honoring them."
> —Kat Cole, FOCUS Brands

Disruption Everywhere

Business is changing at a speed that was inconceivable a generation ago. A brief review of the most significant challenges points to why the human enterprise is coming to the forefront of organizational cultures.

Disruption has spread into every industry, enabling tiny start-ups to threaten large enterprises. The disruption might be a new technology, a new business model, innovative practices, or even a new customer experience. Disruptive companies are not necessarily more human, as the public embarrassments of companies like Uber demonstrate, but they force competitors to become more innovative and agile, and that can only be done by motivated employees.

The ever-increasing pace of change requires every organization to adapt quickly to new surroundings. This includes the exponential growth of mobile devices and the billions of sensors collectively called the *internet of things*, the unmeasurable growth of data storage and processing in the cloud, the acceleration of climate change, and the increasing mobility of people (and their skills). The effect on organizations is that they have to reconfigure to change as fast as change itself.

Hypercompetition is created by a global marketplace, technology transfer, and the power of data management to minimize costs. The dislocations created by hypercompetition are evident in the worldwide political and social reaction to it, from new trade barriers and agreements to legal regulation of internet giants like Facebook and Google.

Information is becoming a commodity. Search engines and infinite data storage mean that more than 4 billion people with internet access can acquire information, whether that's the price of corn, a CEO's salary, or the recipient of the Nobel Prize for Literature in 1995.[5] A recruiter can find radiation technologists in Denver, and her candidates can check which hospitals are rated best by their employees. Useful information is so abundant and inexpensive to acquire, that it is effectively a commodity. That means the value of information is more a factor of what you do with it than how much you pay to acquire it. What matters is asking the right questions and discovering the right relationships among data points.

Knowledge and talent are portable. Talented employees can move from employer to employer, using their skills and knowledge in a new context. A flexible workplace attitude is growing among global workers who might switch between work and nonwork cultures as easily as they switch between languages. A nondisclosure agreement or noncompete contract might protect a business for a limited time but cannot restrain employees from applying their raw talent somewhere new.

Diversity fuels innovation. If you want to create a culture of innovation, you need the widest possible range of knowledge, skills, and life experiences at hand. The creative collisions that spark innovation are fed by differences in your workforce, not just similarities. Put another way, how are your employees supposed to innovate if they all see each problem from the same perspective?

Innovation is the best survival strategy. Companies that innovate across product lines, methods, and business models avoid the race to the bottom because they adapt to changing conditions by creating a new environment in which they offer new value to customers. But because every product, process, or model is subject to duplication by competitors, innovation cannot be the job of just one team or a few persons. Companies that thrive today are creating a culture of innovation that reaches out to the furthest edges of their influence.

Thus, innovation becomes the work of everyone, all the time, every day. There is no single way to "do innovation." It is more a matter of culture than technique. It is the mindset that is endlessly curious and alert to conversations with customers, with vendors, with peers, and with the wider world. Innovation is the point where knowledge leaps into creativity and imagines something new. Companies must hire people who bring the gifts of their creativity and passion to work. Then comes the hard part: Companies have to nurture and liberate that creativity and passion.

The evolving business discipline called *agile* (not to be confused with Agile software development) is one response to the changed conditions. According to business consultant McKinsey & Company, an agile organization is "a network of teams within a people-centered culture that operates in rapid learning and decision cycles which are enabled by technology, and that is guided by a powerful common purpose to co-create value for all stakeholders."[6] Agile recognizes that every component of business, from customer preferences to investor demands, is subject to sudden change. An agile workforce unites around a common purpose; it is more diverse in background, thought, life experience, and desires. People who operate well in that environment want a wide and diverse array of rewards in addition to compensation. Working in such a flexible and ever-changing environment, employees expect an employer to recognize and reward their differences.

What does this mean for HR? The best workforce mirrors the best management in that it never descends to the stultifying "stability" of the old top-down, hierarchal organization. Instead, the best workforce is a dynamic, ever-evolving population of employees united by values and goals but also highly individual. They are adaptable and energetic. Wharton professor Adam Grant captures this attitude when he advises, "Don't hire for talent, knowledge, or skill. Hire for motivation and ability to learn."[7]

| Reclaiming Creativity

"When you take a group of children age 2 to 5, and give them a box of paper clips, they can probably think of 120 ways to use those paper clips. There's no bias, there's no preconceived perspective. It's just, hey, go figure this thing out.

"But over time, our ability to think divergently begins to decrease because we get fed a formulated belief set, based on categorizing experience, and then the kid in us becomes less creative and innovative. That's a subtle example of bias entering the system: Just the way you look at things and/or have been conditioned creates a different outcome.

"The same is true with diverse teams. If you come in with fresh thinking, if you come in without obstacles or limitations, then you're going to foster divergent thinking. And for sure divergent thinking leads to breakthrough thinking and greater results."

—Amy Cappellanti-Wolf, SVP & CHRO, Symantec

Technology's Paradox

The more our technologies replace human capabilities, the more they make what is most human, most valuable.

The current business environment changes so rapidly that the business lexicon has adopted the military term *VUCA*—volatile, uncertain, complex, and ambiguous—to describe it. In this VUCA environment, those who don't learn and change as fast as the environment will face extinction. The basis of competitive advantage has evolved beyond efficiency to include learning and innovation.

One result of global disruption has been the weakening of the top-down corporate model and the introduction of the gig economy. Business leaders for decades have sought to maximize efficiency, starting with computing and business processes and continuing with new workforce models, including reducing the number of full-time workers in favor of outsourcing, contingent workers, temporary hires, and partners. In the past 20 years, this continued with new time arrangements, virtual and temporary teams, distance working, and adaptable techniques like agile.

Among these changes, some jobs were redesigned to make the most of human advantages, thus making humans more productive.[8]

Some of the world's most admired firms took that idea in another direction. MIT professor Zeynep Ton, author of *The Good Jobs Strategy*, found that companies like Costco, Toyota, and Trader Joe's achieved stellar growth and profits by designing jobs that emphasized the human genius for social interaction and creative problem solving.[9]

The latest technological waves of robotics, big data, and artificial intelligence (AI) are causing simultaneous anxiety and enthusiasm in the business community. That always happens when big innovations come along. The three waves together are already changing how we think about work, and our challenge is to step back a bit, understanding that business leaders have an opportunity—and an obligation—to harness new technologies in businesses that enhance our human rights and conditions.

Professor Daniel Kahneman, whose work on judgment, decision making, and behavioral economics was recognized with the Nobel Prize in Economics, believes that robots will steadily improve their power to decode human interactions and read human expressions in vocal or body language.[10] But that won't make them human—it will make them advanced expressions of the programming built into them. If that programming includes human biases (sexism, racism, or ageism, for example), they might perpetuate and even deepen problems embedded in an organization. Confirmation bias, the human tendency to focus on information confirming one's predetermined beliefs, might be built into a system intended to be objective.

It's impossible to predict what AI will look like in 10 years, but we can describe this early stage in its development as quickly doing narrowly defined tasks that require a huge amount of data. For example, AI in social media can identify the faces of your Facebook friends, which requires matching incredible amounts of image data, but it cannot yet understand your relationship to even one of those friends in the way you understand it. To do that, it needs a separate data set, for example, examining all the communication between you on Facebook; but even that is only a tiny subset of all the memories, stories, shared experiences, and nuanced feelings that you would call a relationship.

For the business of managing humans, it's helpful to think of AI in the same way people thought of computing 65 years ago, about the time IBM mainframes became affordable for large businesses: AI is a tool that enhances logical human processes to an almost infinite degree, but it is not a replica of a human mind. Like any tool, it replaces or amplifies human effort, and thus it frees the human to turn his or her attention to higher tasks.

That's why the future of work is human.

CONSIDER THIS

Look around your work area and choose one item that has significance to you. Then think how that came to be. It can be as simple as a book that influenced you, an uplifting statement on a card, a project that is completed. Now think of all the people whose work came together to make that thing happen. Even if you choose something you created—say, a presentation—contemplate the computer you used to create that presentation. Imagine the hundreds of thousands of people who contributed to the evolution of that device, from the original designers of computer chips 60 years ago to their successors. Think of the software engineers, the usability designers, the ergonomic scientists, the robotics engineers and data analysts and miners and metallurgists and ship designers and logistics specialists and delivery drivers that got that computer to you. All their work came together in this device that makes you much more productive than you otherwise would be. Now write a note to those people collectively, acknowledging that their contribution made a big difference in your work life. Be specific and mention the difference in detail, for example: "Designer, by making it easy for me to locate documents, you have saved me hundreds of hours of searching through files, like I used to do." Or "Ergonomic scientists, because you spent years of your life perfecting this keyboard, you have saved me from pain in my hands and arms."

How does expressing gratitude in this way feel?

2 | The Future of Work Is Human

Moving from Data Collection to Human Connection

HUMAN MOMENTS

"At Cisco, our People Deal is an agreement about what we can expect from Cisco and what Cisco expects of us. This Connected Recognition program is just one part of that, and the program's DNA is timeless Cisco: recognizing and celebrating good results. The platform, tool and funding for this is, I must say, is pretty cool.

"I received recognition awards from Procurement colleagues for collaborating with them on projects and from other departments when I helped them with business challenges. I saved up several rewards in Connected Recognition to help me fund a seven-day stay at Swissotel's Kamala Beach resort in Thailand.

"Of course, I was touting my awesome #LoveWhereYouWork experience on social media, and when my friends read my posts, they all started asking me how to get a job at Cisco!

"Mostly, I think it's awesome to work at a company that values its people like this. I think Cisco hits the sweet spot in balance between results and caring about people. It's one of many small and big things that make this a great company to work for."

—David Faik, Procurement Manager, Cisco

The World Economic Forum and Boston Consulting Group recently studied the interaction of three factors—technological change, learning evolution, and talent mobility across borders. They came up with no fewer than eight potential future work scenarios, from ever-increasing talent shortages that lead to "hoarding" talent to widespread adaptability in a hyperconnected world.[1] The report emphasizes the key point—technology does not determine the future as much as human interaction with technology and reaction to technological change.

Many of the best jobs of the future, and the fastest-growing jobs today, combine technical "hard" skills and relational "soft" skills. Familiar examples include physicians, nurses, lawyers, and managers. Examples you might not expect include accountants and auditors, financial managers, and computer systems analysts.[2] People who succeed in those jobs in the future will possess not only the math skills to determine real-world needs but also the ability to communicate their analysis to partners like investors and product managers or customers like risk managers and estate attorneys. They will relate the data to the daily lives and aspirations of clients. Communication enables connection. Such skilled communication requires the ability to listen fully, read body language, imagine different outcomes, understand others' creative process, establish trust, and sort through a wide range of needs. Math skills make doing the job possible; communication skills make doing the job well possible.

We are not passive observers of these changes. If you are a leader today, you are right in the middle of it, making change and adapting to change within your own domains. Building a more effective workplace means creating cultures that best express our values as much as our value propositions. The future of work will be determined by the choices we make about how humans live alongside their technological creations, and also how humans choose to interact in the new environment. That means using AI, robotics, and networks as tools to further each organization's mission and beliefs.

• • •

Journalist Tom Friedman says, "I think the companies that are doing best are creating what I call STEMpathy jobs—jobs that combine science, technology, engineering, and math with human empathy, the ability to connect with another human being."[3] Discussing twenty-first century careers, Josh Bersin says, "While the core need for technical skills remains strong, another theme has entered the job market: the need for people with skills in communication, interpretation, design, and synthetic thinking. In a way, we can think of these as the arts, hence the evolution of education from STEM to STEAM [adding Arts]. . . . The jobs of the future, driven by the increasing use of technology taking over rote tasks, require social skills complementing more technical abilities."[4]

THANK **TALK** CELEBRATE

"In a world where competitive advantage comes from empathy and creativity rather than technical prowess and execution, the best leaders are those who lead with relationships at the center of their work."
—Sesil Pir, International Leadership Expert

Work Is the New Community

The workplace is becoming a driving force for progress and change around the world. Even in traditional workplace cultures, the need to hire and retain talented and adaptable people is eroding old barriers.

The downside of disruption has become more evident and pressing around the world. We see political polarization, social disconnection, and tribalism everywhere. As the world's top talent follows opportunities, global urban supereconomies grow, and less attractive economies decline.*

Once, most people looked outside of business to answer big problems—to government, church, or national culture. Now the power of businesses to make change has increased relative to other institutions because businesses have to adapt faster than government or other institutions. Whether inspired by social pressure or self-interest, leading companies are adopting a moral case for their role in the betterment of society. They have listened to the arguments, often made by employees, that their responsibilities go beyond the bottom line. When employees form grassroots coalitions about an issue like environmental sustainability, they do it from a position of power and knowledge. They know what the company can do. They organize to influence leadership's understanding of an urgent social need and connect it to the mission and purpose of the company.[5] Their confidence in companies' ability to make a difference is growing: Between 2018 and 2019 employees' belief that a company can take specific actions that both increase profits and improve the economic and social conditions in the communities where they operate jumped 9 points, to a solid 73 percent.[6]

In today's interconnected world, companies can bring their global power to bear on social needs. Sometimes they are inspired by both principle and self-interest. For example, it was business that first extended benefits beyond marriage to include domestic partners, including same-sex relationships, long before marriage equality was affirmed by the Supreme Court. Businesses were responding to employee demands for equality, and they also understood that extending benefits could be a competitive advantage. Today companies, for example, Cisco, are leading the way in areas such as bereavement leave and medical coverage for genetic testing, which were hardly on the radar just a few years ago.[7]

Examples: Advances in hydraulic fracturing—fracking—of natural gas accelerated the losses of Appalachian coal mining employment. Ride-hailing applications like Uber and Lyft caused the value of taxi licenses to plummet. American manufacturing declined in the 2000s due largely to global competition.

The world's experience with COVID-19 affirmed the importance of work as the new community in so many ways. When millions of employees pivoted from gathering at the office to working at home, we had the universal shared experience of feeling both together and isolated. Everyone felt some sense of disconnection, especially as the novelty wore off—work still got done but small, spontaneous moments of support, gratitude, and friendship became much harder. Speaking at Workhuman Livestream in May 2020, organizational expert and bestselling author Simon Sinek said, "This whole experience has underscored the importance and value of human contact."

Sinek also pointed out, "In a weak culture, people will hunker down and take care of themselves. In a strong culture, people will rise up and take care of each other."

The Cost of Social Isolation

"After years of happiness research, one thing has proved fundamental—the importance of our connections with other people. Yet modern societies are built as if the opposite was [sic] true. We are surrounded by people, yet we feel genuinely connected to almost none of them. The effects are devastating. Social isolation is as potent a cause of early death as smoking; and the epidemic of loneliness is twice as deadly as obesity. We could change this in a day if we all reached out and made at least one positive connection."

—International Day of Happiness

Former US surgeon general Vivek Murthy painted an even starker picture of loneliness in society: "Loneliness and weak social connections are associated with a reduction in lifespan similar to that caused by smoking 15 cigarettes a day and even greater than that associated with obesity. But we haven't focused nearly as much effort on strengthening connections between people as we have on curbing tobacco use or obesity. Loneliness is also associated with a greater risk of cardiovascular disease, dementia, depression, and anxiety."

He added a note of special importance to business: "At work, loneliness reduces task performance, limits creativity, and impairs other aspects of executive function such as reasoning and decision making. For our health and our work, it is imperative that we address the loneliness epidemic quickly." Murthy's recommendations for organizations to fight the loneliness epidemic include strengthening social connections, encouraging coworkers to help others and to accept help when it's offered, and creating opportunities for employees to learn about their colleagues' personal lives.[8]

Loneliness at work is one symptom of the fraying social fabric. Shawn Achor is an expert on the science of happiness, the author of *Big Potential,* and a perennial favorite at Workhuman Live, our annual conference. Writing in *Harvard Business Review* in 2018, Achor and his research partners noted the detrimental effects of loneliness at work: "Lonelier workers reported lower job satisfaction, fewer promotions, more frequent job switching, and a higher likelihood of quitting their current job in the next six months. Feeling a lack of workplace social support was associated with similar negative business outcomes. The economic impact of loneliness is indeed staggering."[9]

It doesn't have to be this way. Our workplaces can nurture a new sense of community, connectedness, and common purpose. This is because companies need to be united in purpose yet also diverse in outlook and background to compete in today's globalized innovation economy. If we want talent and knowledge to flow freely, societal cohesion must become a conscious part of organizational culture. Cultures of support, inclusion, transparency, and trustworthiness attract talent longing for psychological safety and belonging.

THANK TALK CELEBRATE

Achieving a true sense of belonging at work is the end goal of most inclusion efforts. Yet belonging is a feeling. And feelings are hard to influence. A recent international survey we conducted with fully employed workers showed that when employees are able to recognize and thank each other, a sense of belonging goes up 21 percent.

The younger generations in the workplace are noticing. A wide-ranging Deloitte survey of millennial workers found that many look to their place of employment for a sense of purpose, which makes for a more engaged workforce. The authors concluded, "Millennials are, on the whole, working in environments where they feel generally in control and empowered—something that contrasts, perhaps, with the less stable world that exists outside the workplace."[10]

Full-time employees spend a quarter to half their waking hours at work, whether they are 40-hour-a-week office employees or "always-on" remote workers. What if those hours promoted community in the flow of work? What if most interactions helped strengthen ties of trust and interdependence among team members as they drive toward a common goal? What if people found meaning, acceptance, and encouragement to be their best and most complete selves in the workplace?

In that scenario, you'd have a productive, engaged, and learning workforce. Belonging would replace alienation. Unity of purpose would overcome tribalism. Competition and backbiting among employees would be overwhelmed by a larger sense of cooperation and positivity, as each person strived to achieve the best possible performance.

In today's organization of interdependent teams, cooperation and support are more effective than division. Sharing information and ideas is more powerful than hoarding them. Interacting with a variety of people with trust and positivity creates energy.

Architects are studying these trends carefully as they develop new workplace designs, which balance the need for focused, private work with the open seating and huddle rooms that encourage the fast sharing of ideas. They study how remote and on-site employees talk, share information, and make eye contact through conferencing systems. People move among work areas; design accommodates individuals from physical needs to privacy and job needs from open innovation sessions to confidential negotiations. Design for openness only works, however, if a culture of belonging and trust prevails.

Susan Cain, author of *Quiet: The Power of Introverts in a World That Can't Stop Talking*, notes that even as leaders change their management practices to encourage innovation, they must honor the distinct differences among individuals. She says, "Once we start seeing people as individuals, we're less likely to put them in workspaces or workplace routines that don't work for them. We need to build psychological safety, defined as a culture where it's OK to speak your mind, to make a mistake, to make a comment that turns out to be wrong but still be valued. True psychological safety would be the freedom to be yourself fully, with all the light and dark of you there all at once."[11]

Long ago, when distance and communication made for huge barriers among people, communities thrived when they had common purpose, culture, and identity. In the modern networked workplace, distance and communication barriers are slight; yet humans still seek common purpose. In a world of disaffection and dismissal, the new community can be the place where people feel loyalty and unity despite their differences.

THANK TALK **CELEBRATE**

Our surveys show that celebration is one of the most appreciated ways to create community in a workforce. While we've mentioned celebration in various contexts—a diversity of holidays, for example—broadly speaking, three popular milestones call for public celebration.

1. *Workplace anniversaries* are traditional celebrations as people reach 1, 5, and 10 years or more with a company. Workhuman research shows that employees most enjoy shared memories and congratulations from coworkers. Their next favorite forms of commemoration are public and private messages from managers on these anniversaries. Interestingly, the traditional celebration that makes someone the guest of honor at an event is the *least* popular option; only 10 percent of respondents said that would be their preference. The most popular options include shared memories and congratulations from co-workers and managers, and private congratulations from their manager(s).[12]

2. *Celebrating life events* like getting married, having a baby/ adopting a child, buying a house, having a birthday, and retiring are strongly associated (87 percent) with feelings of belonging to an organization. Celebrating just one life event correlates to a 23 percent increase in respondents saying their company has a human work culture. This positive result notwithstanding, 30 percent of employees surveyed say their company had no life event celebrations—zero—in the last year.[13]

3. *Celebrating team success* is distinct from recognizing individual achievement—not a substitute for individual congratulations but a public recognition of the importance of shared accomplishments. Companies we know are quite comfortable with these milestones, which might carry individual awards for team members. We recommend that awards be evenly distributed, sending the message that everyone is important to the group milestone, and that the commemoration be broadcast far and wide around the organization, which gives employees out of the immediate network a chance to chime in with congratulations.

The Personal Is Primary

Social media has grown to be an enormous influence in society and work. For better or worse, Facebook, Twitter, WeChat, Snapchat, Instagram, TikTok, and all the rest condition and shape the media habits of billions, especially people under 30 today who grew up with social media. Its multiple effects include expectations that people share their lives with a community that might be close friends or complete strangers. Social media can bring people together or drive them apart; its influence is an undeniable factor in daily life.

Embedded in all social media is the primacy of the individual— "Here are my pictures, my comments, my links, my tastes, my cares and concerns and prejudices and opinions." Everyone's Facebook account reflects *his or her* story. Everyone on social media—pretty much everyone in the workforce—is powerfully conditioned to position his or her individual story at the heart of a community. This conditioning can become a fundamental tool for building community at work—for making the shared values and goals a new community.

A company that is united in purpose and shared values doesn't need conformity. It contains a universe of experiences. In the past, "the organization man" might bury his (or her) individuality for the sake of corporate unity. Today, an enlightened company culture recognizes that everyone's story is unique and integrates that fact into its culture. All employees are at the center of their individual journeys with the company, telling their own story and writing their own professional narrative.

In a purely factual sense, this has always been so. We see the workplace through the lens of our feelings, beliefs, and experiences. But until now this narrative was only vaguely visible to an organization, in an annual performance review, a résumé, or a years-of-service plaque on a shelf. Immediate teammates or best friends at work might celebrate the arrival of a child, a gold-star performance review, or a promotion, but few organizations had a culture that honored the individual story.

The new community of work broadens that celebration. Organizations that become more attuned to individual experience have the potential for a deeper relationship with employees. The value proposition between employer and employee moves from "You work, and we pay you" to creating an environment where employees eagerly give their best, rather than managing employees as assets or resources to be used up.

Over time, celebrations and peer-to-peer messages create a narrative of the life of an organization. What would it mean to have a record of the good we have done through years in a job? Therapists and philosophers have urged people for centuries to make an accounting of what they have done in their lives, saying, "The unexamined life is not worth living." Yet our transactional bureaucracies discourage us from building a personal record of appreciation given and received. "What have you done for me lately?" is a mordant footnote to accomplishment. It's part and parcel of the short-term thinking that drives so many cultures into hypocrisy, promising to be more human just as soon as the quarterly growth numbers are achieved . . . until the next quarter.

Growth is good; profit is reward and fuel for future growth. But in our pursuit of short-term results, we deplete our emotional portfolio—feelings of purpose, meaning, and gratitude. This has implications that go beyond loyalty. For example, companies can tap into the full creativity of people who happen to be parents by having an environment where they are not worried about taking a day off because a child is sick. It goes beyond acceptance and creates psychological safety. They will feel included and safe in ways they wouldn't feel in other companies.

Mobile technology and 24/7 availability break down the old walls between work and life, and that can result in an intrusive relationship ("I can never get away from my job!") or a more integrated one ("I'm sharing my life with a community of colleagues"). What makes the difference between the extremes is whether the organization authentically cares about individuals and acts accordingly.

New technologies are enabling HR processes and functions to be centered on each individual employee. These personalized apps can create an experience that focuses on an employee's own cycles, projects, and milestones/service anniversaries with the company. This brings an employee's uniqueness and needs to the forefront, using technology to create a better human connection and relevance to the employee experience.[14]

Personalization has evolved from a convenience for daily activities like communicating or shopping into an expectation that the most important activities, including work, can be adjusted to fit a person's individual needs. Organizations with the imagination to personalize life at work offer a compelling experience to the people they recruit. It represents a logical extension of proven benefits like flexible schedules or relaxed dress codes. Note that personalization does not mean compromising on performance; in fact, the purpose of maximizing every employee's experience is to enable people to choose their own best path to productivity.

The new community of work also works *because* of people's differences, a cultural change that reflects the globalized outlook of today's employee. Diversity, inclusion, and belonging (Chapter 10) align organizational culture with the need to hire and retain the best talent. They broaden the pool of available talent. They make companies attractive to more people. They also conform to the way in which work gets done. A team composed of diverse people brings a wider set of knowledge and experience to a problem. They understand a larger group of customers. They bring more ideas to innovation efforts. If a culture stresses open communication, the employees also educate each other in their individual expertise, lifting the performance of all.

"Have You Ever *Not* Belonged?"

Pat Wadors, CHRO of ServiceNow, believes humans are deeply wired to crave belonging. "Even introverts like me," she adds. She likes to get people thinking deeply about their feelings of belonging with this activity at dinner parties (or team meetings):

"I ask a group, 'Have you ever *not* belonged? When did you feel like the other, that you weren't automatically on the team?' The first one to tell a story is tentative. The second goes a little deeper. By the third or fourth story, we're getting into the real stuff.

"A friend of mine was a single parent of color moving into an all-white neighborhood in Texas, with tremendous anxiety about her kids not fitting in. She had positioned them and her in her own mind as 'the other.' She tried to prepare her kids about not having friends, maybe feeling a bit lost. And as she's unpacking, the door knocks, and she opens it. And it's a neighbor bringing not only food but their children and said, 'We are so excited to have you in the neighborhood. We saw you unpacking. We thought we'd lend a hand and share some snacks while we help you unpack if you don't mind.' She was blown away.

"And these kids went in and started playing with her kids without issue. And then the door knocked again and again. She said four neighbors came to her home in a matter of two hours, spent eight hours with her and bought pizza. And by the time her kids went to school, they had over 15 friends."

If you think belonging is a luxury, think about a time you didn't belong.

Continuous Improvement Is a Way of Life

Amazon is arguably the most disruptive company in history: books, video, groceries, payments, electronic home devices. It completely changed supply chain management, and even its warehouse business keeps "disrupting itself" as Amazon makes use of artificial intelligence and automation to streamline delivery of every imaginable good. To the outsider, it might appear Amazon is ready to replace thousands of humans with robots, eliminating jobs for many of its 300,000 US employees.

That outsider would be half right—and half wrong. In July 2019, Amazon announced it would spend $700 million to retrain a third of its workers by 2025. In a tight job market, Amazon has no intention of losing employees to automation; it intends to turn warehouse workers into skilled high-tech employees. At the time of the announcement, Amazon had 20,000 open positions in the United States (and many more overseas). Rather than assume a stable shortage of skills in the marketplace, Amazon determined its best course of action is the "upskilling" of people already drawing an Amazon paycheck. Early in the COVID-19 pandemic, Amazon hired 175,000 additional people. Having invested untold time and money to get talent on board, even in lesser-skilled jobs, the company is disrupting the traditional talent pipeline for tech workers.[15]

The term *continuous improvement* was coined years ago to express nonstop improvements in processes, products, profits, and other business outcomes that could be measured, commonly called *key performance indicators* (KPIs). The Japanese word for improvement, *kaizen*, was a popular term to describe a strategy of continuous, incremental progress by everyone.[16]

Today's technology makes it possible for HR to make continuous improvement a goal for people as well. Employees can understand and track their performance on tasks and even values with instant, crowd-sourced feedback from everyone they come in contact with, from team members to customers. Continuous performance management records the degrees to which employees are growing and improving in their lives at work, adding new data points to older KPIs and using data analysis to establish causality. Broad-based feedback, recognition, continuous conversations, and check-ins can humanize the way we motivate and develop our people.

This change is overdue. In 2013, Eric proposed a complete overhaul of performance management in *The Crowdsourced Performance Review*. Leading companies like Adobe, Accenture, Dell Technologies, and Cigna have since ditched traditional annual reviews in favor of continuous feedback, coaching, development, and conversation. Organizations are accelerating their feedback by using social recognition applications and merging their data into a stream of steady improvement (see Chapter 9).

EXPERT INSIGHT

"The way new businesses are today, individuals have a chance to grow within an organization that never existed before. . . . We are seeing CEOs climbing to the top who never finished university, who literally started off in the mail room. But they're bright, they're energetic, they have taken courses, they've done everything right, and they have proceeded up the ladder. That always wasn't the case, and we're seeing that now in hiring people. We're seeing people being hired not for their skill sets but for their potential, because so many people can contribute to the success of an individual in today's marketplace."

—Rhonda Taylor, Director of Partnership
Success, Fuel50

Pay Is Personalized, Flexible, and Variable

The social recognition technologies that empower managers and HR to see deeply into performance also enable managers to connect compensation and performance with great precision. This is incredibly exciting news for those who seek a fairer, more equitable, and more productive organization.

Up to now, compensation decisions have been more subjective than most leaders would like to admit. Many external factors affect the most well-considered compensation plans, including supply and demand for talent, location of work, cost of living, and innumerable performance-based formulas from stock grants to profit sharing. Yet the defects in compensation are glaringly obvious in decades of studies proving, for example, that women are paid less than men for doing the same job and achieving the same goals. The defects are obvious in the inability of so many managers to fully quantify reasoning for giving one employee 2 percent more than another at the end of the year. And they are obvious as compensation lags other processes, its traditions long grounded in archaic practices that are no longer aligned to a company's structure and productive centers.

Based on new ways of understanding and documenting performance, HR is heading toward rearchitecting pay. The future of pay is going to be more personalized and thus more variable among employees. Human resources has the opportunity to make the variability fair if it is solidly based on transparent criteria and data. Artificial intelligence algorithms can be created that deliberately drive hidden and subtle biases out of the system. How an employee performs can also be judged by widely subjective observers who document the large and small ways someone is contributing to success.

Social recognition applications make this possible. They can measure, for example, the number of times that individuals go out of their way to help others outside their immediate team. They collect critical but hard-to-recognize moments of inspiration, communication, and insight. With centralized, documented social recognition connected to some portion of a person's pay, the "intangible" contributions can finally receive the reward they are due.

Some types of pay have greater potential for positive psychological impact than others. When a company dedicates at least 1 percent of payroll to be awarded by peers to peers, it declares its trust in employee fairness and judgment. That 1 percent threshold is a great milestone for recognition programs—the place where pay feels more democratic and, candidly, more fairly distributed. This kind of program is more agile, too, because everyone's peers are making tangible decisions about each other's pay. People become more accountable to each other.

We've seen another outsize effect of dedicating 1 or 2 percent of payroll to a recognition program—that small percentage is actually a large percentage of disposable income for the critical middle range of compensation.

Here's why: Even in an economy with low general inflation, costs have risen asymmetrically for lower and middle economic groups as a percentage of total income. After people have paid monthly rent or mortgages, student loans, car payments, insurance, taxes, and other fixed costs, their remaining discretionary income is relatively small. The variable rewards of 1 or 2 percent from a social recognition program are thus a much larger percentage of discretionary income to use as one pleases. It might represent 10 or 20 percent of spending on the things or experiences that make life more enjoyable, meaningful, and fun. That one's peers are providing these luxuries, from a vacation to something "I typically wouldn't spend that money on myself," frames this pay in an entirely different way.

We'll have more to say about this in Chapter 11.

Human Resources Must Lead the Way

In the past, HR and managers could make some correlation between behaviors and performance. Archaic software built to "manage" people in the sense of command-and-control was developed with the goal of corporate governance. It does not enhance or illuminate the working relationships, connections, or performance of the workforce. The next phase of HR software will revolve around the human layer—human applications—that lives on top of the administrative layer and makes the most of uniquely human qualities that make human moments that matter. Human applications will include garnering crowdsourced performance feedback; making connections between actions and outcomes, which discover hidden best practices; providing insights to engagement, disengagement, and flight risk; uncovering unconscious bias and confirmation bias; identifying triggers for training and learning; and establishing systems that provide "hints and nudges" that improve performance in small, incremental ways that minimize interruption.[17]

The new technologies signal an evolution from data collection to human connection—using data to strengthen ties among employees, customers, and anyone else involved with the life of the company. They recognize that what's good for the human is good for business.

All these trends reshaping business and management require a positive, resilient, and adaptable culture. While leadership and every employee need to act in ways that promote culture, it is up to HR to be the facilitator, coach, and preserver of the culture.

To make this happen, HR will have to increase its domains of expertise, and the new technologies of the human enterprise make this possible. Human resources must come to embody the ways in which technology advances the cause of making an organization more human by applying its "people skills" to the business and technical skills shaping the new ways of working. Combining those domains looks like this:

- *Strategy.* Hiring, onboarding, management, and retention
- *Intelligence.* Data gathering, taking the pulse of the workforce
- *Analytics.* Interpreting intelligence in terms of strategy
- *Operations.* How it all gets done (includes budgeting)
- *Communications.* Internal and external messaging
- *Learning.* Training managers and executives in the new ways work is done

"HR used to be low-level administrative compliance," says Mary Ellen Slayter, CEO of content marketing firm Rep Cap. "And then they became a centralized shared service. Now, when jobs and teams are assembled and disassembled on the fly, that model doesn't work anymore. So HR has a choice: does it just get demoted back down to compliance? Or will they become integral to facilitating that decentralized shift?"

Slayter continues: "Think about workforce planning. At an enterprise level, we can't make detailed five-year plans because who knows what the teams will look like in five years? Now, we have to think about the next 18 months, and how the workforce will remain agile and able to change quickly. Human Resources is going to have to become agile themselves."

Progress is only possible with a new mindset: To lead with empathy, not fear. To move ahead and allow employees to explore new, game-changing ideas. Crowdsourced recognition provides employees with the right level of ongoing positive feedback and reward to drive a new culture of innovation.

Human Resources has a historic opportunity to measure and enrich workplaces with a more positive employee experience. The workplace has never been more diverse or dependent on making the most of every person. The need to build a positive, inclusive, and more human workplace where people feel a sense of belonging has never been more important. By empowering and recognizing the richness of people's backgrounds and diversity of thought, companies can benefit from their individual strengths. A person who brings his or her whole self to work will feel more respected, empowered, and inspired. And that, in turn, will drive companies to new heights.[18]

CONSIDER THIS

Think about a time when your workplace, past or present, took on the qualities of a community, for example:

- When people rallied to support a fellow employee facing difficulties
- When colleagues celebrated a common achievement
- When friendships made in one workplace continued even as you or others moved on
- When someone demonstrated the courage and trust to be his or her authentic self rather than engage in image management

Finally, write down three actions you can take to build a trusting community at work.

3 | The Employee Experience

Create Connections to Restore Humanity
in the Workplace

HUMAN MOMENTS

Steve Pemberton grew up in foster homes in New Bedford, Massachusetts. The child of a single mother and a father lost to gun violence, he was one of those lost in an overwhelmed system, subject to abuse and neglect he was too young to understand. When he was 1½ years old, a babysitter wrote, "Dropped Steve off at the latest family his mother is boarding him out to . . . he cried his heart out . . . this little boy doesn't have a chance in the world."

But one day, another neighbor named Mrs. Levin noticed the young African American boy reading a tattered paperback. The following week she brought him a box of books, and his mental and emotional liberation began. He discovered he loved to read, loved to study, and could ask other grown-ups for help. And others did help, eventually giving him a permanent home. He went on to college and a career in business, and he wrote the bestselling memoir *A Chance in the World*.

Today Steve Pemberton is the chief human resources officer of Workhuman. He speaks around the country about his story and about the stories of all children who need a chance—and the power of one person, in one moment, to make a difference in another's life.

"You have an enormous unrealized asset in your organization," says Nataly Kogan, author of *Happier Now*. "And that enormous unrealized asset is the emotional health and happiness of your leaders and your employees. We cannot squeeze out more productivity, more efficiency. We're all working nonstop. But research has shown that when we feel good, when we cultivate true emotional health, we operate at the highest level of our potential across every single metric. If you want better performance, if you want greater resilience, if you want higher company profits, revenues, there is one place to go."

Nataly presented her findings at Workhuman Live 2019. In her exhaustive research on happiness, she's learned that it is not a passing state but a skill—with big implications for the experience employees have at work. "Focusing on the most positive moments of everyday life . . . makes people less stressed and more productive. The key is to capture these moments."

A positive employee experience is what attracts and retains the best employees. In the words of LinkedIn's Nina McQueen, "Culture reigns supreme." Conversely, 70 percent of professionals in the United States would not work at a leading company if it meant they had to tolerate a bad workplace culture.[1]

IBM/Workhuman data shows that more positive employee experiences are also linked to better performance, extra effort at work, and lower turnover (including "turnover intentions," i.e., considering leaving—a key attitudinal factor in low-unemployment economies). Organizations that rank in the top 25 percent of employee experience, for example, see returns on their assets that are triple those that score in the bottom 25 percent.[2]

We've seen that the human enterprise is evolving from the confluence of many external forces—a view from the outside in. But people experience work and life from the inside out. They each have a unique set of experiences and a unique point of view about their life story. This is what drives their beliefs, their loyalty, and their willingness to put their best efforts into a job—that magic but all-too-rare quality we call engagement.

Just as our mobile devices have eroded the physical barriers between work and life, so also our psychological barriers between them are disappearing. You cannot separate what's going on outside of work from what's going on inside of work. They are inextricably linked in the minds and hearts of employees. While this is obvious when you're checking e-mails at 11 in the evening, we think the division between work and life has always been a bit of a fictional concept. "I had a bad/great day at work" is the opening line of a million stories. We come home to our partner and ask, "How was your day?" We know that a happy, healthy life outside of work helps people be more productive, while problems at home tend to erode someone's productivity.

Since work and life are inextricably linked, why do so many still view professional life as separate from personal life in terms of our values and behavior? The social habits of organizations, created in the last century, deferred to power at the top of the organization, and because most people sought security in a lifelong job, they deferred to power and prestige as embodied in their managers and company executives. Face-saving, loyalty, and office politics were valuable because they helped provide job security.

Through centuries of regulated, inflexible, and efficient organizational models, people were conditioned to think that the best organization is hierarchical. The organizational model built to facilitate efficiency—strict hierarchy, top-down decision making, strategic planning and execution, staffing plans—turns out to be poorly suited to the world it created. Since few organizations were concerned about "meaning" and operated only to create customers and make profits, it was assumed that humans have to be bribed or cajoled or bullied into conformity.

"For centuries, we organized businesses in a way that went against the grain of human nature," says bestselling business author Daniel Pink. He adds:

> And we did that because it was more efficient. We had mechanisms that were very controlling. Mechanisms that treated people like cogs in a machine or replacement parts. But I don't think that's the human condition. I don't think the human condition is to be controlled or to be interchangeable with other human beings. But there was an efficiency in organizing companies that treated people that way.
>
> Now, because the nature of the economy has changed, I think that it is more effective, not to mention more humanistic, to organize companies in ways that go with the grain of human nature. To treat people like autonomous, self-directed individuals. To give people a chance to make a difference, to make a contribution, or to allow them to experience occasional moments of practical joy.[3]

As technology and business culture distributed power more widely around the organization, bureaucracies collapsed under their own weight. More nimble competitors passed them by. The war for talent, now well into its third decade,* empowered the best employees to choose their workplace based on more subjective criteria than money or security. Even in the throes of recession, the change in attitude among employees prevailed—people expect work to see them as whole persons, not just task-performing assets, and they have the power to choose organizations that satisfy those expectations.

---

* "The War for Talent" was a prominent McKinsey study published in 1997. It was expanded into a book in 2001 and is still in print.

Pink continues:

Once, most of the abilities that people needed to deploy on the job, whether they had a blue collar or white collar, were routine. That is, people were following scripts, following a recipe, doing repetitive tasks. And they could be doing it with their brain or their body, processing paper at an insurance company, or they could be turning the same screw the same way on an assembly line. But no matter which domain that they were in, the work was routine. It was algorithmic. People were just following procedures. Now that all the routine work is going to machines, to robots, to algorithms, to software, we actually need people to be their full self. We need to have a three-dimensional view of who human beings are. And therefore, going with the grain of human nature is not only kinder, but savvier for business.

Management visionary Gary Hamel captures this dynamic when he urges, "We need to move from a world of bureaucracy where the goal was maximizing control to a world of humanocracy where the goal is maximizing contribution."[4]

This is the trend, but progress is slow worldwide, says Hamel. At a Workhuman conference in 2019 he asked:

How is it OK that less than 20 percent of employees around the world are regularly consulted about goals, and the way their own work is done? What about setting your own goals? What about making your own decisions? What about picking your own colleagues?

How is it OK that the average first-level employee in a large company is buried under eight levels of management? No wonder they feel trapped, no wonder they feel powerless, no wonder they feel they don't have a voice. How is it OK . . . that 68 percent of people think that new ideas are greeted with skepticism or hostility [and] they feel there are few rewards for taking a personal risk?

When a company is in this sorry state, the best talent—those with a choice—will find that out quickly and either stay away or depart, leaving the less talented behind.

And they *will* find out. We live in an age of radical transparency, where prospective employees rely on crowdsourced ratings and comments about companies from websites like Glassdoor and LinkedIn and surveys like the annual *Fortune* magazine "Best Companies to Work For" reports. Company ratings are just as trusted as consumer ratings of restaurants, airlines, and hotels. The employee experience is now public—part of a much larger public demand for transparency.

The story of Uber shows the promise and perils of transparency. At the beginning of 2017, the ride-hailing service was held up as the disruption story of the decade. An easy-to-use app had turned the tightly held taxi business upside down. Using the power of transparency that alerted drivers and riders where they could find each other, Uber broke down the barriers to driving or hailing a cab for tens of thousands of people, then millions. A key feature of Uber's app was the ability of drivers and riders to rate each other based on their experiences. Five-star drivers made more money because riders could see they offered a great ride. It was all there in the app, for anyone to see. Just a few years after its founding, Uber was valued at $70 billion. Its brash, hard-driving CEO, Travis Kalanick, was hailed as a Silicon Valley visionary.

Then, on February 19, 2017, a former employee named Susan Fowler posted a 3,000-word essay on her personal blog, detailing the toxic sexism and power plays of Uber's top managers. She wrote of sexual harassment and threats of retaliation from "high performers." She exposed the HR department's unwillingness to take action.

Her post went viral. Others came forward with more stories. A #deleteuber movement spread online, harnessing the same power of networks to magnify a message that had grown Uber's business. Within four months, Kalanick and 22 others were forced out. Transparency brought Kalanick to the top and then brought him down.

That's the power of transparency.

When Workhuman released its own voice of the employee (VoE) solution, called Moodtracker, we found that employees loved to give feedback—and often. This pulse feedback has helped companies diagnose organizational issues or concerns. The VoE solution provides leaders with recommendations on what actions to take to impact positive change, based on survey results.

People love to talk about workplaces they like, on social media and in conversation. They talk about their workplaces in recruiting videos and blog posts. Most importantly, they talk about their workplaces with each other, a simple way in which team cohesion and belonging grow in the human enterprise. Transparency isn't just about sharing business information but about sharing the bonds that unite a diverse workforce.

Double Standards Can Be . . . Really Weird

"I was at my new job at a tech startup for a month, and I get invited to the board meeting. I was the only woman in the room. As the meeting went on, I noticed that 9 of the 14 men had beards. And I couldn't help seeing this: they sat there in the whole meeting touching their beards, curling their beards, smoothing their mustaches. And I thought, 'These are men of power. If a woman sat in this meeting and played with her hair, she would immediately be tossed aside as someone that didn't have the polish or refinement or couldn't carry herself.' It was one of those moments in life when you think, 'Oh, my God, this is so weird.'"

—Renee Kaspar, Chief People Officer,
Octane Lending

Organizations, Reorganizing

An organization needs basic systems and structures to get things done, but it also requires a culture that affirms and lifts up human nature instead of working against it. Employee engagement and enthusiasm create the esprit de corps that energizes today's successful organizations.

Four changes in organizational structure—from centralized command-and-control to decentralized innovate-and-learn—magnify the importance of the individual. They have to do with human networks, hybrid job arrangements, and learning.

Strict, Permanent Hierarchies Have Been Replaced by Networks of Teams

People no longer occupy the same place in an unchanging organization. Today's companies are a series of teams. That's where the strongest employee connections are built. Employees join teams focused on specific opportunities or problems, create solutions, and eventually redeploy in different configurations. Team engagement is a critical component of the employee experience, more significant to overall satisfaction than general company engagement. Product development and service improvements happen faster when decision making is done at the team level. People form a wider circle of connections as teams come together, work, and disband. Knowledge and initiative spread more widely as people learn how and where the best work gets done. Team leaders learn where to focus their attention.[5] Even where common skill sets cluster in departments—HR, marketing, product, finance—work often involves cross-functional projects. This means people must form trusted relationships quickly and communicate well across disciplines.

Hybrid Organizations Contain Different Job Arrangements and Career Paths

Today's organizations are likely to include full-time, part-time, contract, remote, and gig workers who share responsibilities based on a fluid, project-based team structure. It's also common to have three generations of employees, with widely different needs and life experiences, working together. That means the company culture should make extra efforts to make all the generations feel they belong. But even in companies with a lot of long-tenured workers, hybrid teams don't confer the same automatic identity as the old "silo" structures. Team success depends on trust and mutual respect, and leaders must build cultures that enable trust and respect to flourish through genuine moments of appreciation, communication, and shared accomplishment. Timeliness and frequency of these moments of appreciation matter, too. When recognized within the last month, 86 percent of employees say they trust one another, 86 percent say they trust the boss, and 82 percent say they trust senior leaders.[6]

The Response to Disruption Is Nonstop Learning

Amy Edmondson, Novartis professor of leadership at Harvard, is a leading expert on how organizations innovate. She says, "If you stop to recognize the uncertainty out there, then it's far more important to make sure people have good strategies for learning and experimenting, so that they can learn in real time and communicate and coordinate with each other on the job."[7]

Disruption and change demand that employees become not just lifelong learners but flexible, fast learners, able to adjust quickly to new technologies, methods, roles, and business models. In addition to training in class or online environments, this is becoming part of every job—what employment expert Josh Bersin calls "learning in the flow of work." Employees who integrate continuous learning into their jobs make the workplace more dynamic and accelerate change with creativity and innovation.

Positivity Versus Burnout

Change is stressful, and the acceleration of change is only making this worse. It's a major factor in burnout.

In 2019, the World Health Organization called burnout an occupational phenomenon caused by "chronic workplace stress that has not been successfully managed." WHO will update the description of burnout in the next edition of the *International Classification of Diseases*, noting it is characterized by "increased mental distance from one's job, or feelings of negativism or cynicism related to one's job; and reduced professional efficacy."[8]

In the face of continuous disruption, how can we weave resilience into our daily work lives? Organizations need to fill a reservoir of positivity and trust that empowers people to survive the inevitable challenges of business and lean on each other.

To win in this new environment, businesses must harness our messy idiosyncrasies and emotions to free people to connect with each other as human beings and restore humanity in the workplace. That creates the psychological safety needed to build successful teams.

On one level this is simple: It's about asking questions, providing safety and connection, growing learning, and keeping harmony with the environment, while taking into consideration the far-reaching consequences of business decisions for suppliers, partners, the next generation, and the environment. Those who can do all this, as well as learn and adapt quickly, will create a business ecosystem that can enable growth and even radical innovation in their industry.[9]

But even if it seems simple, that doesn't make it easy to accomplish. Organizational inertia is a powerful force, and bureaucracy's greatest strength is maintaining the status quo. Fortunately, people have the power to create a great workplace in any industry, no matter how traditional it might seem to an outside observer.

Management professor Christine Porath of Georgetown University has found that "organizations reap many benefits from creating more human workplaces, including better employee performance, improved safety and health, and greater worker satisfaction and commitment. This finding is true across industries and applies to blue- and white- collar employees and to small and large organizations. Evidence shows that employees thrive in caring workplaces. Thriving employees are not only satisfied and productive but are also actively engaged in shaping their own and the organization's future."[10]

For example, in the mid-2000s, low-margin retailers like Costco, Wegmans, and Trader Joe's outperformed their competition by offering employees slightly better pay and benefits than their competitors.[11]

But they didn't stop there: They all promoted cultures of respect, internal mobility, and caring that made them perennial members of the great workplace surveys.

The lesson from these companies? The employee experience determines whether you'll have sustainable advantage or steady decline. Rapid innovation and change cycles put a premium on adaptability and trust, which require healthy human relationships and shared purpose. The relentless need to grow employee skills requires that employees be engaged and resilient and be lifelong learners. Employees only achieve in a culture that puts a premium on their shared humanity.

Money, prestige, and demands for loyalty won't sustain advantage— only a human-centered workplace can do that. And you have to do it across the board. Put another way, if you're going to make your workplace human for the right reasons, you have to go all in.

EXECUTIVE INSIGHT

"When our executive team is reluctant to do something a little progressive, or innovative, I tell them, 'There is a collective and growing distrust in business in this country and all around the world, because businesses have followed an old way of behaving and thinking. The customer is demanding a new way of businesses showing up, and the employees are as well. If you don't do that, your competition will.'"

—Kat Cole, COO and President,
North America at FOCUS Brands

Leaders who commit to building trust will find that employees are willing to offer it. The 2019 Edelman Trust Barometer found that globally, 75 percent of people trust their own employer (compared with trust ratings of 56 percent for business in general).

Millennials and generation Z, the present and future leaders, are true believers that business has a responsibility to values as well as profits, and they express this belief as consumers and employees. For example, a majority of millennials give serious consideration to the gender, ethnicity, age, and range of backgrounds of an employer's workforce when considering whether to work there.[12] They feel accountable to protect the environment, promote social equality, and behave ethically. As they join the ranks of management and fill the ranks of the most valuable employees, the younger cohorts say work is the place where they feel their power to put their principles in action.

If an organization can meet its criteria *and* its employees publicly promote its culture, the transparency of social media and the power of peers will convince potential employees and others that it's a human enterprise, aligned with their values and taking its place as a responsible and positive part of society.

CONSIDER THIS

If you are a manager, choose an employee on your staff who recently did an outstanding job or went the extra mile for the team. Write the employee a four-part note:

1. Saying exactly what the person did
2. Explaining the impact the person's action had on you, the team, and the company
3. Telling how the person's actions embody the organization's highest purpose
4. Expressing thanks

Before you send this message, write a short description, for yourself, of how you would feel receiving it. If it feels good, send that note to the employee.

4 | What Do Employees Want?

People Bound by Trust and Goodwill Accomplish More Together Than Alone

HUMAN MOMENTS

"Eighteen months after LinkedIn launched its Bravo! program, I joined them for an in-depth analysis of social recognition in the company. The data showed not only the ripple effect that occurs in terms of performance (54 percent of employees who received 3-plus awards showed a year-over-year increase on their performance rating) but the actual creation of praise recipients into praise providers. People are becoming happier and more engaged, and they're part of the process of making other people more positive and engaged. What I love about this research is it shows the repetition of praise within the program is what matters—the continual bringing it back to the forefront. This means we need to activate champions at every level of our organization to be those praise providers."

—Shawn Achor, author of *Big Potential*

A surprising and threatening dynamic at the most basic level of communication exists between employees and their managers. Everyone receives instructions and directives from managers, but 58 percent of employees *never* hear thanks from their boss, and 37 percent of leaders say they avoid giving positive feedback.[1]

What's going on is an old-fashioned mix of power and vulnerability. Aided by hoary clichés like, "Why should I thank someone who's getting paid?" and "I don't need to baby my people," leaders have learned a habit of silence as part of an outdated notion of what it means to hold power. Leaders (especially men) sometimes avoid displays of appreciation because it doesn't suit their image of how a leader behaves. It's ironic that this notion has been handed down as part of the outdated command-and-control mindset.

Again, research points out that this model has outlived its usefulness in the modern company. Gallup found that "businesses that orient performance management systems around basic human needs for psychological engagement, such as positive workplace relationships, frequent recognition, ongoing performance conversations, and opportunities for personal development, get the most out of their employees." And yet Gallup's global engagement analytics find that in cultures with a strong historical tradition of hierarchical leadership, managers find it hard to adopt a "coaching" mindset that focuses on helping employees reach their potential. Gallup cites the work cultures of East Asia as an example and notes that just 6 percent of employees there are engaged at work.[2]

Brené Brown, speaking at Workhuman Live in 2019, described the typical consequences of incomplete communications and cold relationships at work. She said, "In the absence of data, we make up stories. The stories we make up inflate our fears, our shame triggers, and our greatest insecurities, because that's the best way for the brain to keep us safe." Noting how powerfully this habit takes over in a stressful situation, she asked, "How many of you have ever led a team through change where you spent 90 percent of your time whack-a-mole-ing stories that people were making up?"

Without positive feedback, humans fall back on protecting themselves with variations on this internal dialogue, which accelerates into a whole set of negative assumptions. "My boss never says thank you" becomes "My boss hates me" or "My boss thinks I'm doing a lousy job" or "Something's very wrong in the department." And this negative spiral goes on and on until it becomes fear, resentment, and disengagement.

Flourishing

"People spend over half their waking hours at work. That's an enormous amount of their lives, and so you have to ask: What role does work play in their lives beyond a paycheck? How do you create the conditions in which human beings flourish? And by flourishing, I mean in the broadest sense: How do people become happy? How do they become satisfied? How do they become contributors? How do they become the best versions of themselves?"

—Daniel Pink, bestselling author of *When: The Scientific Secrets of Perfect Timing*

Individuals have to become aware of their own negative storytelling, as Brown teaches. How much easier that would be if a workplace encouraged employees to assume the best? The most powerful way to reprogram negative habits is to substitute more positive behaviors in our routines.[3]

People are storytelling, meaning making, purpose-driven, relationship seeking, and individualistic. They respond best to values and feedback that they can relate to personally. They crave authenticity and acceptance of their values. They want to take off the masks that once protected them but now hinder their best work. They want to feel safe, energized, and valued by the mini-society that is work, and they reward a culture that embraces those qualities with higher performance.

Storytelling is foundational to every culture. It's through stories that we turn abstract ideas into tangible reality. Storytelling evolved to help us survive, argues author Jonathan Gottschall, because they guide us through complex social situations "just as flight simulators prepare pilots for difficult situations."[4] Stories illuminate every aspect of our lives—adventure, moral conflict, ambition, destiny, love, and work. At work, we tell stories to show how things are done, to make relationships vivid, to show behavior we approve. Really good public speakers illustrate their most important ideas with stories because stories are more memorable than concepts, facts, and data. The data we extract to help manage an organization ultimately becomes relevant because we ask, "How does this confirm or change how we behave?"—thus turning data into narrative.

People tell stories; let's harness that innate need. Let's enable them to share positive stories about their work, stories of overcoming problems and seizing opportunities and creating innovative solutions, and they will build a narrative more accurate and powerful than any employee handbook.

Meaning making is part of storytelling. Most stories not only tell what happened but encourage people to think about what it means. Consider the difference between these statements:

"Sonia answered the phone."
"Everybody—here's a big shout-out to Sonia, who didn't let a little
thing like closing time last Friday keep her from helping a worried
customer!"

The first is a statement of fact. The second tells a story that gives meaning to the behavior, shows appreciation, and recognizes how Sonia's actions deserve appreciation. A story thanking someone or a job well done is infinitely more memorable than a slogan like "The customer comes first."

Speaking at Workhuman Live in 2018, human rights lawyer Amal Clooney pointed out that stories affect people more powerfully than dry facts. In her work, she finds that people can sometimes lack empathy when those suffering are described in large numbers, but their individual stories can affect others more deeply, driving them to action. Recent social movements like #MeToo and the March for Our Lives have grown in power by personalizing statistics. Stories embed meaning in abstractions, and Clooney asked attendees to "make a difference in a way that's most meaningful to you."

Culture Versus Money

All of the stats tell us that right now we have more jobs available than skilled workers to fill them. That puts a premium on those skilled workers who might be persuaded by an offer of more money to move. You can't necessarily fight that dollar for dollar, but if you create a superior experience for them, right down at the peer level, many of them will reason, "This other company wants to pay me 10 percent more, but this is a terrific place to work. I am recognized for the work that I do. I've been given opportunities to showcase it. I've been able to teach others. My performance has been managed in a way that improves and enhances my skills. This organization is committed to me, and increasing my value. Is 10 percent a reason for me to walk out the door?"

Compensation is a factor, but it's not necessarily the deciding factor. Recognition, appreciation, gratitude, a culture of learning, and a culture of investment are much more important.

—John Baldino, President, Humareso

Entering the Cognitive Era

The history of business measurement is the story of learning to correlate actions to outcomes and to understand their interaction. In the industrial era, "scientific management" focused on task-oriented laborers whose primary output came from their hands. Productivity was measured in how many widgets could be produced in an hour or a year by the workforce. People manipulated machines. Standardization made scale possible, and as production grew and costs fell, profits grew as well. Tools and technology from steel mills to tractors increased physical productivity, enabling people to produce more product with less effort.

Starting around the 1950s, knowledge and expertise became the defining feature of work in the world's developed economies. Productivity grew as knowledge and skills increased. One financial analyst working with a calculator, and then a basic computer spreadsheet program, could do the work of many bookkeepers working with leather-bound ledgers. In this period, successive management models like management by objectives and "reengineering the corporation" made complex processes more efficient. "Mental productivity" increased, and profits followed.

Now we are entering the cognitive era, a time when terms like *productivity* acquire additional meaning. In this new era, machines are able to learn and interact with humans in ways that feel more natural. When our devices appear to listen and understand what we say, the boundaries between people and technology blur. When our work technology magnifies our cognitive processes, software and data are like extensions of our minds.

Efficiency isn't just a matter of making things or processes faster or cheaper. In the cognitive era, qualities like imagination, insight, collaboration, and communication are at a premium. In the words of Columbia Business School professor Rita Gunther McGrath, "Many are looking to organizations to create complete and meaningful experiences." McGrath argues that management is entering a new era of *empathy*.[5]

Rather than diminishing the role of people, in the cognitive era people are at the forefront of working with and realizing the benefits from new technologies to achieve more than we could even imagine in the industrial or knowledge eras.

The cognitive era requires a different relationship between people and their tools. It's no longer enough to maximize output in tangible objects or efficient processes, trusting that profits will follow. Now the key to growth is each individual's engagement with work, because that's what drives imagination, problem solving, and innovation. To express the cognitive in terms of agile management, the work plan is only a starting point, and once a project or idea is begun, the willingness to change, alter, adapt, and imagine new solutions is paramount.

The challenge for leadership in the cognitive era is to create the conditions where humans are fully engaged in their work, because mental and emotional engagement is directly tied to productivity. Engagement cannot be commanded from the top down or outside in, any more than human feelings like loyalty or trust. It is completely voluntary and completely individual. People decide to be engaged because the organization inspires their commitment.

We know that, globally, engagement figures are low—Gallup's surveys consistently find that about one-third of employees are actively engaged in their work. The 65 percent of employees who are not engaged represent an amazing opportunity to increase productivity. How much more profitable would a fully engaged workforce make an organization? How many more customers might an organization acquire? How many more patients might it serve? How many more patents might it win?

Recognizing that the battle for the hearts and minds of employees is played out daily through their workplace experiences,[6] organizations are now reexamining their employees' experience at work as a path to improved job performance and sustained competitive advantage.

Measuring the Employee Experience

To understand the ideal employee experience, the IBM Smarter Workforce Institute and Workhuman conducted a global research study in 2017. We began by conceptualizing an employee experience as a positive and powerful—and ultimately human—experience, in which employees are able to invest more of their whole selves into the workplace.

We analyzed 20 years of data from global recognition programs used by our customers, which include more than 50 million moments of gratitude expressed among 5 million employees, their peers, and managers. The data contains tremendous insights into the world of modern work and provides a background for interpreting and understanding the survey and other research.

The study explored three questions:

- What is the ideal employee experience in today's workplace?
- What impact could a positive employee experience have on key outcomes?
- How can organizations drive more positive and human employee experiences?

The answers to these questions resulted in the development of the Employee Experience Index, which quantifies the employee experience by addressing:

- *The environment.* Including a strong sense of organizational trust and enabling supportive coworker relationships
- *The work.* Emphasizing the meaningfulness of the work and providing continuous feedback, recognition, and growth
- *The person.* Acknowledging the importance of empowerment and voice, as well as opportunities to disconnect from work and recharge[7]

Basing our work on what the index discovered, we developed a framework of six human workplace practices that measurably improve the employee experience.* They are:

- Organizational trust
- Coworker relationships
- Meaningful work
- Recognition, feedback, and growth
- Empowerment and voice
- Work-life balance

---

*This list also appears in Chapter 1.

When leadership and management put these practices into action, the result is positive employee experiences along five dimensions:

- *Belonging.* A feeling of being part of a team, group, or organization
- *Purpose.* An understanding of why one's work matters
- *Achievement.* A sense of accomplishment in the work that is done
- *Happiness.* The pleasant feeling arising in and around work
- *Vigor.* The presence of energy, enthusiasm, and excitement at work

Visualizing the findings as an actionable path to improving the employee experience (Figure 4.1), we see that improving human workplace practices results in better business outcomes. The research found that organizations that score in the top 25 percent on employee experience report nearly three times the return on assets and double the return on sales compared with organizations in the bottom quartile.[8]

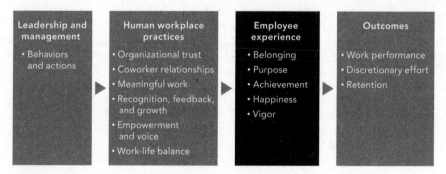

Figure 4.1 Leaders to People to Outcomes
Research shows how human-centric leadership produces improved business results.

Engaged employees have pride in and are satisfied with their organization as a place to work, and they advocate for and intend to remain with their organization. However, employee engagement doesn't tell the whole story. Alongside engagement, our study mapped employee experience and how engagement and experience interact. As Figure 4.2 shows, different levels of engagement and experience result in different individual mindsets.

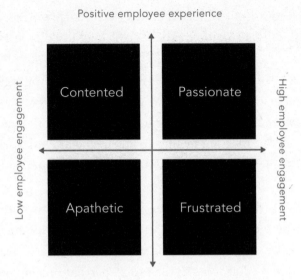

Positive employee experience

Contented   Passionate

Low employee engagement   High employee engagement

Apathetic   Frustrated

Negative employee experience

Figure 4.2 Different Feelings of Engagement and Employee Experience Create Different Mindsets and Behaviors
Clockwise from top left: When employees report a good experience but exhibit low engagement, they feel *contented* but don't perform to their potential. That represents an opportunity to improve productivity at very low cost, if you can move those employees to performing closer to their potential. When employees are positive about their experience at work and high in engagement, they feel *passionate* about their work and organization. When employees are engaged with their work but have a poor work experience, they tend to be *frustrated*, and just as those in the "contented" quadrant, they represent a lost opportunity for growth. When employees are negative about their experience and low in engagement, they appear *apathetic*, which is the worst combination from both the personal and organizational point of view. Where is your workplace on this chart?

These mindsets have broad implications for performance because employee experience and engagement act in a continuous cycle. One reinforces the other, and conversely, the absence of one dilutes the effectiveness of the other.

Employees with more positive experiences at work are much more likely to report significantly higher levels of discretionary effort. In fact, we found discretionary effort is almost twice as likely to be reported when employee experience is positive rather than negative (95 percent compared with 55 percent).

Employees with low Employee Experience Index scores are more than twice as likely to say they want to leave compared with those with more positive experiences. The difference is more than 20 percentage points (44 percent versus 21 percent) and means that employees with positive experiences are 52 percent less likely to intend to leave their organizations.

Comparing companies with high versus low Employee Experience Index scores reveals some straightforward insights about employees at the higher-scoring companies:

- *They work harder.* Discretionary effort is nearly two times higher in positive work experiences.
- *They perform better.* Workers with positive experiences are more likely to report high levels of performance (23 percentage points higher).
- *They stay longer.* Workers with high Employee Experience Index scores are 52 percent less likely to leave.

The Employee Experience Index is an ongoing study. In Chapter 5 we'll show how it informs some of the workplace practices that help people enhance and improve their day-to-day experience of an organization.

Building Community

Professor Jeffrey Pfeffer of Stanford University, an expert on organizational behavior, writes, "Almost anything that brings people into contact in a pleasant and meaningful context—from holidays to community service to events that celebrate employee tenure or shared successes such as product launches—helps build a sense of common identity and strengthens social bonds." One of Pfeffer's top suggestions to promote well-being in the workplace is simply to encourage people to care for one another.[9]

It sounds obvious, but if well-being (and its related benefits) were foremost in the minds of leaders, most companies would be cathedrals of caring. Most companies haven't made that cultural journey yet, either because they have misplaced views about the cost of building community or because their leaders perpetuate the old command-and-control mindset that says everything that happens in a company is ultimately the product of executive strategy.

We've found that, given just a little encouragement, people will create community in their workgroups, departments, and companies anywhere in the world. They instinctively know that people bound by trust and goodwill can accomplish more together than they could alone.

Speaking at Workhuman Live 2018, Simon Sinek described this trusting culture. The author of *Start with Why* and *The Infinite Game* said, "You have to have a trusting, vulnerable team. That requires an environment in which people feel that they can raise their hand and say, 'I made a mistake. I'm stuck.' Or they can say, 'You've promoted me to a position, and I don't know how to do the job.' Or even, 'I'm having trouble at home, and it's affecting my work. I'm scared. I need help.'

"When people can say that without fear of humiliation or retribution, without putting themselves at risk when the next round of layoffs comes . . . that's a trusting and vulnerable team."[10]

EXECUTIVE INSIGHT

We are big believers in the power of celebration to build community. There is a feature of Workhuman® Cloud called Life Events® that's our favorite for the effect it has on employees. Life Events is an online community celebration of the human moments that matter most in our lives, not only as employees but as people. Employees celebrate new parenthood, weddings, and other milestones by posting congratulations in text or video or pictures to each other's timelines. It's almost impossible to describe the difference between seeing a milestone notice using stock photography and prewritten messages and receiving heartfelt, individual messages from friends and colleagues one after another. The authenticity has a power that's hard to describe. And because it's open to all, everyone can see the jokes or funny photos or sincere advice and recollections. We don't habitually allow ourselves to be so supportive and relaxed in a business setting.

Big life events become part of your identity all day long, not just outside of work. So why not celebrate them? Whether someone is graduating from night school or retiring or taking a foster child into their home, the outpouring of support and even love binds the community together in a way that can never be duplicated by "official" means.

—Eric Mosley, Co-founder & CEO, Workhuman
and Derek Irvine, Senior Vice President,
Client Strategy & Consulting, Workhuman

What This Means for Leaders

Employees want belonging, purpose, achievement, happiness, and vigor. They want meaningful work, personal and professional growth, empowerment, and a feeling of contributing to the life of a supportive community. Employees put their greatest trust in peers, and storytelling is central to both growing professionally and building community. Organizations in the human decade thrive when they really live these values and provide these opportunities, but traditional management wasn't founded on those principles. The question facing leaders now is, What do leaders themselves need to change?

Any business can have a great employee experience, as long as its commitment to the well-being and growth of each individual shows up in the words and behavior of leadership at all levels, day after day, in times of easy success and in times of difficult setbacks. We have found great employee experiences in all different industries and a variety of cultures. We find them in management consultancies, supermarket chains, and tech giants.

Leaders in the organizations we've studied see themselves as mentors, coaches, and conveners of many talents. They are not the command-and-control leaders of the past because they have come to understand that in an organization of any size, those people were never really in control—they just had the illusion of control because they had the ability to hire and fire. Now, when the competitive edge of companies is measured in unique human abilities like innovative thinking and creative inspiration, effective leaders balance analytical skill with human values. They are data-driven and also story-driven, and while they insist on evidence-based decision making, they are not dogmatic about methods. They set goals and empower employees to achieve their highest accomplishments. These leaders achieve those goals by supporting and inspiring employees to stretch themselves, knowing they might fail but learning in the process.

Leaders in the human decade are ethical. They break down walls of mistrust that have built up through generations of us-versus-them thinking among executives, managers, and line employees. In recent years they have come to see diversity and inclusion, privacy (including data privacy), and psychological safety (typified by the #MeToo and antibullying movements) as profound cultural issues, worthy of strategic investment.

Leaders have faith in the intelligence and adaptability of employees today. They hire people for those qualities because agility and all it implies is the way to survive in a disrupted world.

At Workhuman Live 2019, Cisco's Ashley Goodall made the case that the only practical definition of a leader is someone whom other people are willing to follow. Referring to a host of great leaders, he pointed out that not all were personally ethical (Steve Jobs) or great planners (Winston Churchill) or compassionate (General George Patton) or even successful in their lifetimes (Susan B. Anthony). But people followed them because they were clear in their goals and in the meaning of their work. And it turns out that second factor, a sense of meaning, is incredibly motivating.

People invest more of themselves in a job that gives them a sense of meaning. It's that simple and that profound. A leader must build the organization's culture around its mission and be willing to evolve any part of the business continuously toward fulfilling that mission. Profits fuel the journey toward that mission; people achieve it. And they achieve it best when they spend part of every workday on the most human of activities: connecting with others, giving and receiving thanks, and celebrating the milestones that we all find meaningful.

What's needed is a combination of leadership, culture, and technology to make those things happen across organizations large and small. We call them human applications, which promote and facilitate human moments that matter, and they have the power to both reveal and reinforce the best qualities of the human enterprise. Before we detail how human applications work, however, we need to explore why they work by understanding three profound, human qualities that ignite performance, qualities we address in the next chapter.

CONSIDER THIS

Think of someone in your workplace with a significant life event approaching:

- A work anniversary
- A wedding or union
- The birth or adoption of a child
- Earning an academic degree or completing a program
- A significant personal milestone such as running his or her first charity half-marathon
- An honor or award or distinction from an outside organization (e.g., SHRM accreditation)
- A positive mention in the media
- An internal award, such as being honored for outstanding performance
- Return to work after a significant illness or injury

Write 100 words to the person offering your congratulations, gratitude, or good wishes. Then read what you have written aloud. How does this make you feel about yourself, the person, and the workplace where you can express these wishes?

5 | Purpose, Meaning, and Gratitude

Purpose Belongs to All. Meaning Is Unique to the Individual. Gratitude Builds Lasting Connections Between People.

HUMAN MOMENTS

"As I was recovering from a recent car accident, I went for a walk in the woods with my daughter and our dog. We decided to push on a bit farther than usual and saw rows of bright colors through the trees ahead. With my dog barking at the flapping noises, we saw something beautiful. Someone had run lines of string between many trees, creating a zig-zag pattern like a huge cat's cradle. On the strings hung hundreds of colorful pieces of cloth with expressions of gratitude written on them, all joyfully waving in the wind. We walked through the web reading:

'I am grateful for my family.'
'I am grateful for these woods.'
'I feel so lucky and grateful for my best friend.'
'My work in a hospital makes me feel grateful that I am healthy.'

"My daughter explained this had started as a short-term school project a few years ago. Would strangers take a moment to write a message of gratitude and leave it for others to experience? The response was overwhelming. The network of lines and banners continued to grow and grow. Ultimately, the school decided to leave the experiment in place to continue to expand organically.

"My daughter and I each reached for a piece of cloth and marker. I wrote how grateful I was for my family and friends helping me each day to recover. My daughter simply expressed gratitude in the goodness of others.

"The surprising success of this school experiment reminded me of my job at Workhuman. I thought this is exactly what makes social recognition programs work as well—when given the opportunity, the innate human desire to express gratitude emerges, thereby creating a permanent, never-ending web of human connectedness."

—Grant Beckett, Vice President, Product Strategy at Workhuman

If we asked five randomly selected employees at your company what its purpose is, would we get the same answer each time? We think so, because everyone should know and support a company's unifying purpose. It is the very heart of a company's existence—its reason for being.

If we then asked five randomly selected employees in your organization what their work means to them, would we get five different answers? We hope so, because people come to work with a unique set of experiences, temperaments, skills, hopes, dreams, and all the rest that make each of us unique. Meaning is a person's interpretation of how the company's purpose is relevant to their individual life. It guides and justifies decisions at work.

Finally, if we asked these five what they are grateful for today, we'd probably get a long pause and then a simple answer like, "I'm grateful for my family." But would any of those five say they are grateful for something or someone at work? If we also asked, "Did you express gratitude to someone at work today?" how many could honestly answer yes?

The more we learn about purpose, meaning, and gratitude, the more we realize that they are the heart of the employee experience. Purpose belongs to all. Meaning is unique to the individual. Gratitude builds lasting connections between people. Each is distinct, and when all three are present, a company thrives, because these are what connects us to work.

THANK TALK CELEBRATE

These deep emotions are the foundation of THANK, TALK, CELEBRATE.

THANK is gratitude turned into action.
TALK is how we share our sense of meaning between organization and individuals.
CELEBRATE is how we share our humanity and our common purpose.

Connecting Work and Purpose

"Companies with a strong sense of WHY are able to inspire their employees," writes Simon Sinek, author of *Start With Why*. "Those employees are more productive and innovative, and the feeling they bring to work attracts other people eager to work there as well."[1]

Purpose is an organization's role in society—its fundamental, irreducible reason for being. Every company or enterprise has a purpose, and it understands at a gut level what that purpose is. When all employees from top to bottom are aligned with a stated purpose, we can say it's the authentic expression of that company's values.* Sometimes purpose is expressed as a mission statement, and effective ones capture the essence of a brand both inside and outside the company. You can't fake purpose. Here are four examples, including ours:

---

*And if the stated purpose is not authentic—if leadership isn't walking the talk—people know that too.

JetBlue. "To inspire humanity—both in the air and on the ground."

Merck. "To discover, develop and provide innovative products and services that save and improve lives around the world."

Google. "To organize the world's information and make it universally accessible and useful."

Workhuman. "To lead a movement that celebrates the power of humanity in the workplace to energize cultures, unlock human potential, and unite workforces around a shared purpose."

Unfortunately, mission statements are hard to keep simple, and they often fall victim to classic bureaucratic control. They end up being a lengthy chain of platitudes that don't resonate with employees' lived experience. Gallup recently found that only 39 percent of employees in large organizations clearly see the connection between the job they do and their organization's purpose. Gallup researcher Maria Semykoz analyzed how that level of disconnection weakens performance: "It is critical that every project, every task your organization pursues is directed toward your company's purpose. Otherwise you'll spin your wheels [which is] incredibly costly in an environment where your competitors are multiplying and developing exponentially." In short, without a clearly articulated and simple purpose, a company will be overcome by purpose-driven competitors who are inherently more efficient.[2]

Without a shared purpose, employees see their relationship with a company as transactional—working for pay and whatever psychological reward comes with doing a job. That's the source of mordant sayings like, "They pretend to pay us, and we pretend to work." So much for engagement.

Without shared purpose, things get even worse on the management side: Managers and executives also treat employment as transactional, getting the most work for the least cost in the name of efficiency. This classic oppositional setup is all too familiar; it's the antihuman organization.

In contrast, people in a purpose-driven organization transcend the transactional because they see their daily efforts building something bigger than themselves. Managers make decisions by relating how work on a project or a program ties to the shared purpose. Executives clarify strategy with an authentic vision of how a long-term initiative advances the shared purpose.

> Employees in a purpose-driven organization transcend the transactional. They see their daily efforts building something bigger than themselves.

Shared purpose is democratic. It belongs to everyone and can't be quantified like pay or ranked in an organization chart. The entry-level employee can be just as invested in an organization's purpose as the CEO.

Being invested in a purpose means knowing why you're here and what you're doing is of value. It means you are part of a shared journey. It means understanding how your personal purpose connects with the corporate purpose—your work magnifies your life.

Having a higher purpose means attracting the most valuable and hard-to-get employees. Seventy percent of tech employees, some of the most difficult to hire and retain, say it's important to work for a company with a greater purpose. Twenty-eight percent say they would not even work for a company that doesn't offer them a job with meaningful social impact.[3]

Purpose shows in bottom-line results. A Harvard Business School study determined, for example, that companies that lead with purpose are more likely to grow. The study found that 58 percent of companies with a clearly articulated and understood purpose experienced growth of more than 10 percent, whereas only 42 percent of companies not prioritizing purpose showed similar results.[4]

Purpose is reinforced by strong peer relationships. Successful nonprofit organizations like churches and service clubs know that people initially come because they are interested in the mission or the message, but they stay when they form strong relationships. That's why one of the most effective practices in corporate onboarding of new employees is assigning them a peer guide or mentor, to ensure they have a strong sense of belonging from the outset. Those mentors can relate daily actions—"Why are we doing this?"—to the company's higher purpose.

As our work lives become more a matter of moving from team to team and project to project, it becomes more important to reinforce ties among peers, face-to-face and long distance. Shared purpose is the emotional core of those ties.

Corporations have gotten the message and are thinking more about their true purpose than they might have in previous decades. Today, there's a significant business advantage in being a purpose-driven organization because people want to buy from companies that are ethical; they want to buy from companies that are making a positive difference. They just don't want only to buy from companies that make efficient products and have great profits. People know that a company needs to make profits to survive, but more and more consumers want to know that the companies they support are doing important things in the world.

According to the 2019 Edelman Trust Barometer, the top five communications topics that are most effective in increasing employer trust are an organization's contributions for the betterment of society, its values, its vision for the future, its mission and purpose, and its operational decisions. The report found that 67 percent of employees expect an organization to have a greater purpose and expect their jobs to have a meaningful social impact. Furthermore, 74 percent of employees expect a job to provide a sense of personal empowerment and expect to know what's going on, to have a voice in planning and key decisions, and to work in a culture that is values-driven and inclusive. The report establishes that meeting such employee expectations is one of the strongest ways to build trust.[5]

Purpose is such an important part of being human that if an organization can tap into people's purpose—knowing why you're here, knowing that what you do is valued, being part of a shared journey—then people will feel attachment far greater than the ordinary. When people have visibility into how their personal purpose connects to that of their peers and the corporate purpose, and an understanding that the corporate purpose is larger than generating profits, they develop a powerful sense of belonging. They give themselves to the organization because in a tangible way their work and lives flow into the larger stream of something greater than themselves.

What Is Your Purpose?

To consider your own purpose and attitudes at work, ask yourself:

- Why are you here?
- Is what you do valued by others?
- Are you part of a shared journey?

Now flip the script. How do you help others? Do you:

- Understand why they are here?
- Appreciate why they and their contributions are valued?
- Recognize how they are part of a shared journey with you and others?

Thanking more, talking more, celebrating more—together—helps answer all six questions for you and those in your work circle.

___

Corporations have begun to see themselves as purpose-driven organizations for two reasons. The first is simply that certain things, like protecting the environment or championing human health, are just the right thing to do. The second is that as society changes, there's a significant business advantage in being a purpose-driven organization because so many people want to do business with companies that are ethical and making a positive difference in the world. This is a worldwide, generational culture shift in markets where customers have a choice to make purchases that reflect their larger values. Consumers believe that how a company treats its employees is one of the best indicators of its level of trustworthiness.[6]

Companies also see the competitive advantage of having purpose-oriented employees. Although a minority of employees are primarily purpose-oriented (as opposed to achievement- or money-oriented), they are more likely to be leaders, self-starters, and growth-oriented, both personally and professionally.[7] This is exactly the profile of employees that suits the new agile model of how work gets done.

The Value of Meaningful Work

Meaning is different from purpose. Purpose is shared; meaning is personal. Employees can share the same purpose but feel differently about their roles. For example, a hospital's purpose could be stated as, "To provide compassionate care to our community." An emergency room nurse there might find his greatest sense of meaning by making quick decisions in acutely stressful situations. A patient advocate might find her greatest meaning in helping a family afford care. A recruiter's great pride could be finding community-oriented employees.

Employees want to believe their work is meaningful, and this is particularly true of the upcoming generation of employees. Millennials and gen Z employees say meaningful work is important to their choice of a job and an employer. Trust is a factor in that choice, however, because if employees suspect a company's stated values are self-serving or inauthentic, motivation stalls and can even drop.[8] In other words, you can't fake meaning—people feel it or they don't.

Workhuman's Employee Experience Index found that meaningful work is the largest contributor to a positive employee experience, according to our research. When we weigh which of the six workplace factors make a positive experience, we find that the top three factors account for more than half the difference between a positive or negative experience. (See Figure 5.1.)[9]

Building upon a foundation of meaningful work (which contributes 27 percent to employee experience), we found that a more positive employee experience can be inspired by combining and integrating the five other human workplace practices seen in Figure 5.1. The first four in terms of the next highest percentages include enabling empowerment and voice (contributes 17 percent to employee experience), fostering a culture of recognition, feedback, and growth (contributes 16 percent to employee experience), supporting coworker relationships (contributes 16

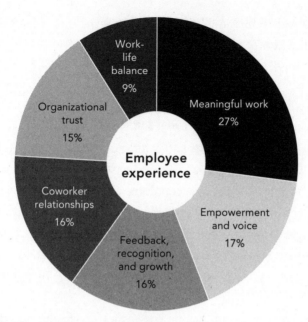

Figure 5.1 Meaning Leads to Positivity

Meaningful work is the largest contributor to a positive employee experience.

percent to employee experience), and building organizational trust (contributes 15 percent to employee experience). The final driver of a more human workplace is work-life balance and opportunities to recharge and disconnect, which contributes 9 percent to employee experience.[10]

When asked in a 2017 Workhuman survey, "What makes you stay at your company?" the top answer for 32 percent of respondents was, "My job—I find the work meaningful." Among those who had been recognized within the last six months, 93 percent agreed with the statement, "The work we do at my organization has meaning and purpose for me."[11]

Purpose: Reaching Outside the Workplace

Sometimes a sense of purpose grows in a company because employees form bonds in volunteer work. Talia Edmundson of RevZilla, a Philadelphia-based online retailer of motorcycle gear, notes that philanthropic activities give employees a chance to form bonds outside of their regular workday and in the process share facets of their whole selves that might otherwise not be shared. RevZilla has a volunteering program called ZLAnthropy, which periodically surveys employees, most of whom live in Philadelphia, about their concerns. Edmundson cites examples from employees: "They might think about folks who can't afford a good meal. They might be concerned with animal welfare or a broken education system." RevZilla supports and celebrates employees' involvement outside of work with programs like New Leash on Life USA, a recidivism reduction program that pairs rescue dogs with prison inmates who are approved for a 12-week job readiness program. Some employees help with the dogs; some volunteer to teach job-readiness skills to inmates. And when the CEO hosts RevZilla's weekly all-hands meeting, employees share stories of what they're doing together to make Philadelphia a better place.

Edmundson points out that the connection inside and outside of work isn't so distant: "Motorcycling is very community-based, and we are a community as well—when people feel happy and fulfilled outside of work, that's when they give the most at work. We want to be part of a healthy outlet for people's passions."

The culture shift isn't universal or complete, but the trend is clear, and the addition of purpose as a brand attribute is nowhere felt more strongly than in employment. Again, millennials and generation Z want businesses to meet societal needs. These employees are global in their outlook, and they look to employers to be good global citizens, which means balancing profit with protecting the planet; embracing diversity, inclusion, and social mobility; promoting learning as part of daily work; leading the way in protecting privacy and preventing digital threats; and acting ethically in their business practices.[12] Businesses that fulfill these promises attract and retain the best and brightest talent. According to consulting firm Mercer, thriving employees are three times more likely to work for a company with a strong sense of purpose.[13] Human resources leaders get the message—concerns around corporate responsibility to address societal issues doubled among them from 2018 to 2019.[14] As they seek to improve the employee experience, leaders need to understand that meaning is a critical component. As Deloitte researchers put it in their comprehensive HR Trends report of 2019, "We see an opportunity for employers to refresh and expand the concept of 'employee experience' to address the 'human experience' at work—building on an understanding of worker aspirations to connect work back to the impact it has on not only the organization, but society as a whole."[15]

People seek to belong. When you consider the role of relationship and community in the human enterprise, says Shawn Achor, you understand that work can contribute to basic happiness. Achor observed at Workhuman Live that the original *Star Wars* catchphrase was "May the force *of others* be with you" (emphasis added). He stressed the importance of putting the force of others back in the formula of finding happiness and meaningful life. As people become more positive, more connections are made. "If we're trying to achieve happiness and success by ourselves, we can't get there," he said. "We can go further together and enjoy the experience."

While it's true that unhappy employees often quit because they suffer a difficult relationship with their manager, the opposite is also well documented (e.g., people with strong relationships to managers stay longer and are more productive and more engaged). Good managers understand intrinsic motivation, and their individualized approach to building relationships results in higher productivity.[16]

Good managers also remember that every employee is an individual in all the senses I've discussed. People experience their own story, seek their own meaning, determine their own purpose, and make relationships according to all their life experiences, temperaments, desires, life stages, and beliefs. Good managers in the human enterprise empower everyone to act on this fundamental truth because it is the most powerful way to create engagement and belonging, which drive corporate goals like growth, profitability, and longevity.

As we noted in Chapter 4, people are storytelling, meaning making, purpose-driven, relationship seeking, and individualistic. Organizations are managed by principles and measurable results. So the next question for the human enterprise is, How do you measure the employee experience?

Gratitude—the Great Connector

Great leaders instinctively know that the more gratitude in a company, the better it performs. Our data confirms this, over and over again.

Through social recognition, more than 5 million humans worldwide are experiencing the rewards of aligning a culture of gratitude to shared purpose. We at Workhuman have observed millions upon millions of positive interactions between people in the workplace, all based upon the giving and receiving of recognition—managers and peers recognizing each other for work well done and shared values demonstrated. We have developed progressively more detailed insights into how these moments of giving and receiving gratitude connect to business results. And recently, with the addition of deep data analysis, we've been able to show what that data reveals for critical issues like performance management, compensation, and diversity.

Gratitude is gaining traction as a subject of serious study for organizational research, and it should. As we pointed out in Chapter 1, when the competitive advantages of nonhuman attributes in a company diminish, the human attributes become more valuable. You see hundreds of serious studies in business journals on topics like belonging, mindfulness, grit, vulnerability, loyalty, and attachment because we are finally able to measure these qualities. Gratitude magnifies all these positive attributes.

We were inspired by the outpouring of gratitude we saw worldwide during the early days of the COVID-19 pandemic. When we looked at the language of recognition moments in our database, words like compassion, hope, reliance, and contribution became more common when people thanked each other. That spring, Workhuman created a website where people could thank healthcare workers (www.thankhealthcare.com) and it grew exponentially with words of gratitude from around the world.

People approach the word *gratitude* with different concepts of what it means. We're all familiar with the idea of counting your blessings or feeling grateful for an unexpected stroke of luck. As researchers like Shawn Achor, Nataly Kogan, and Brené Brown have shown, actively practicing that form of gratitude is a significant step toward personal happiness.

Kogan points out the biological basis for bringing more gratitude into our lives. She says:

Feeling good is not the first desire of our brain. Its primary function is to protect us from danger. That's why we're much more sensitive to negative stimuli because they are typically signs of danger, and our brain is trying to notice those to protect us.

Gratitude is the most powerful antidote because it quite literally asks the brain to come off its auto-pilot of looking for what's wrong and register even the small positive moments in a day. When you share gratitude with someone, you remind yourself that you have people in your life who you appreciate, who you want to be kind to . . . and 11,000-plus studies connect gratitude to greater well-being and productivity.[17]

At Workhuman we study the ways in which gratitude changes behavior and feelings in the context of an organization, and we pair the word with verbs: to *express* gratitude, to *receive* gratitude, to *experience* gratitude, to *be* grateful, to *spread* gratitude. We have learned to look at gratitude from both sides—from the receiver of gratitude and also the giver.

Gratitude Changes the Person Who Receives It

An employee turns in a bit of great performance, and a manager or peer says, "Thank you" or "Great job!" The receiver feels amazing about that kind of appreciation and goes on to repeat that positive behavior in some way. The employee's performance goes up. The employee's morale goes up. The employee's energy and engagement go up. Positive reinforcement has the power to do that to anyone.

EXPERT INSIGHT

Embodying and practicing gratitude changes everything. It is not a personal construct; it's a human construct—a unifying part of our existence—and it's the antidote to foreboding joy, plain and simple.
—Brené Brown, "Dare to Lead"

There's a lot of science backing up the benefits of gratitude to individuals and organizations. Greater Good Science Center at UC Berkeley produced a white paper assessing dozens of academic studies that explored gratitude's effects. Among its findings were:

- Grateful employees are especially good performers when they are involved in creating new ideas or managing relationships.
- Employees who feel gratitude tend to bring more effort to work at their organizations (such as volunteering for additional tasks).
- More grateful people are less likely to suffer from burnout or depression and are more resilient following traumatic events.[18]

The white paper also shares a keen insight from a 2017 study suggesting we think about gratitude in organizations at three levels: episodic gratitude (based on a particular experience), persistent gratitude (feeling generally grateful in a particular context, e.g., a workplace), and collective gratitude (persistent gratitude that is shared by members of an organization). The model suggests that "gratitude at the organizational level can be facilitated by frequently cultivating episodic gratitude in individual employees."[19]

Robert A. Emmons, author of *Gratitude Works!*, shared some remarkable findings about the breadth of gratitude's benefits on Workhuman® Radio:

In 20 years of research I've learned that gratitude brings benefits in all spheres of life—relational, physical, and psychological. Gratitude has the power to heal, energize, and change lives.

It's not surprising that research proves gratitude makes us feel better psychologically—for centuries people observed that the royal road to happiness is counting your blessings. Now, science is discovering that gratitude works literally under the skin, that is, physiologically. People recover more quickly from illness when they practice gratitude. You can gradually lower blood pressure and improve immune system function. Gratitude can facilitate better sleep. And now some of the most recent research is looking at hard measures—what we call clinical biomarkers for things like inflammation for heart disease, stress hormones, and even something as complex as biomarkers on chromosomes. When people practice gratitude, they're more likely to take care of their health—eat a healthy diet, not smoke and abuse alcohol, in general exhibit overall better health-protective behaviors and less risky behaviors. Gratitude is good medicine.

Gratitude creates bonds between people that satisfy deeply ingrained needs for attachment and belonging. When people receive a recognition award, there is always some gratification in the material or monetary value of the award, but the deeper and more lasting effect on them is the bond that their gratitude toward another person creates.

When managers do something to breach that wall of authority and let a bit of their own humanity show—when, as Brené Brown says, they have the courage to be vulnerable—they show confidence in people and gain trust. And gratitude feeds that positive cycle.

Gratitude Changes the Giver

We're used to thinking about gratitude from the receiver's perspective; we are just now beginning to understand the significance of gratitude from the perspective of the giver.

Contemplate that moment of appreciation through the lens of the giver. The act of giving thanks and appreciation at work (as in life) can be even more profound than the act of receiving. When you give an award, when you write a special message describing how it impacted you, you expose yourself a little more. You are just a bit vulnerable at that moment. You're authentic. There's really no room in your head for cynicism at that moment when you write that special message describing how impressed you were with that piece of performance.

Speaking at Workhuman Live 2019, Brené Brown made the connection among bravery, vulnerability, and gratitude, saying, "Everyone who's brave risks heartbreak and disappointment and failure. That's the nature of courage . . . [but] the people who can fully lean into joy despite their vulnerability have just one thing in common: gratitude."

Giving recognition is a moment of gratitude. It affects how we think, almost for the rest of that day. It's a deeper reaction than just saying thank you. Recognition acknowledges an interdependency when someone says, "I couldn't do this without you" or "We are better off because of what you did." It creates a symbiotic relationship between employees and stronger ties among everyone who witnesses that moment of authentic gratitude. It breaks down cynicism.

Why is that? Gratitude is bigger than just saying thank you. It's a personal reflection. When you give gratitude, you have to take a step back. You have to think about how that activity, or that performance, affected you, and that puts you in a different mindset. You take time out of your day. Giving gratitude for someone's extra effort is itself extra effort. You are inspired to take time out to give that thanks. We often tell people, start by saying the words "I am grateful for" when you give recognition, because it puts you in a different mindset. It raises the stakes in the relationship in a good way.

Giving gratitude creates a connection. You create a solidarity and often a healthy emotional interdependency between the giver and the receiver. They become bound together. The receiver gets this amazing lift, but the person giving is saying, "The thing that you did, I was affected. It affected me." That is just a profound message to give to another human being.

When you give gratitude in a social recognition program, over and over again, it changes you. Each time you give gratitude, you feel a little better. That positivity seeps into your outlook. Then over time, it literally changes you forever, because in those moments you are not cynical. You are not bitter. You are not negative. You are purely positive. You're authentic, and you're a little bit vulnerable. Gratitude changes the giver.

How Much Gratitude Is Optimal?

Gratitude itself is becoming a movement spilling over into the world of work. Look at all the books urging people to be actively grateful, from Oprah's gratitude journal to Brené Brown's soulful books about courage and vulnerability at work. They are fulfilling a need for more connection to what matters most in life, even if finding that means adopting new habits. At presentations, we like to quote Maya Angelou, who said, "Let gratitude be the pillow upon which you say your nightly prayer," and afterward people always come up and remark how important that advice seems today.

How much gratitude-based recognition is optimal? The answer is . . . more. There isn't a limit on the amount of authentic recognition that should be given to maximize performance. Think for a moment about yourself: How often would you like to be recognized in a year? Experience shows that most people believe they do something worthy of recognition about two to three times per quarter. Some clients have a pace of recognition that is much higher, and as you'd expect, they experience higher positive outcomes overall. But organizations have to start somewhere, so let's say you want recognition for almost all employees (giving or receiving) about once a month; that's a tipping point we have found to unleash gratitude's power. Investing at least 1 percent of payroll for peers to give and receive messages and tangible rewards based on authentic expressions of gratitude can be the trigger for success.

The commitment of 1 percent of payroll shows up in our research as the threshold at which the positive effects sustain themselves. (In Chapters 8 and 11 we'll expand on the business case for the 1 percent figure.) That amount of recognition is enough to create a base of positive giving and receiving thanks. It's transformative for the culture, and it's also transformative for individuals because exercising that active gratitude puts employees in a different mindset that brings all the benefits mentioned earlier.

The fundamental mistake most companies make is that they tiptoe into programs that give a little recognition here, a little there. They wait for big events like annual bonuses or retirements to make any mention of gratitude, and as a result the flywheel effect of many small moments doesn't ever get under way. To borrow an engineering term, there isn't enough throughput if you express gratitude once or twice a year.

Purpose, meaning, and gratitude go further than any pay scale or benefits package to create feelings of attachment among employees. It's hard to predict how jobs, technology, business models, or working conditions will look a few years from now. People will nevertheless be motivated to achieve their highest potential at work when they feel purpose, meaning, and gratitude. As long as you put people at the center of your corporate lens, their performance will be your organization's greatest source of survival, competitive advantage, and longevity.

CONSIDER THIS

This exercise is about sharpening your perspective on the most important idea or purpose of your organization. If it's captured in a mission statement, write that down. Or work with a trusted work partner or team. Ask each other, "What is the one thing that we must do best to achieve our purpose?" Then look at your to-do list and decide which of those tasks really contribute to the purpose.

6 | Human Moments That Matter

Administrative Applications Focus on Process, Human Applications Focus on People

HUMAN MOMENTS

"I was given a recognition award after working on a big acquisition that required me to work some weekends and a lot of late nights. At that point in time, my children were 7 and 10, so they definitely noticed when I wasn't around.

"The award that I got included 'Disney bucks,' which are like gift certificates for Disneyland. So of course, I took my kids there. And while we were having a great time there, I told them that this was something I had gotten as a reward for my good work. And they said, 'Wow, this is so cool! Mom got to go to Disneyland because of work!' They were too young to understand why something like mergers and acquisitions means you have to get on a conference call on Saturday night. But they *definitely*

understood why someone would say 'thank you' and give you a present, and how that ended up with them being by a pool at a Disneyland hotel!"
—Christina Hall, CHRO, LinkedIn

"Data is foundational," says Gabrielle Thompson, SVP of Acquisitions and Total Rewards at Cisco. "It's no longer the case that one powerful person in a company owns data. It's accessible to all, connecting all sorts of information in a huge variety of ways."

Thompson suggests this ocean of data changes the jobs of HR and leadership. "The key value someone provides now is to tell an accurate story with the data. If you look at any one piece alone, you might get a different story than when you put many pieces together. Is it trending toward something that helps you predict future events? What actions might you want to take in a given situation? The capability to analyze all that information to tell a story that others can understand and take action—that's the power data can give to the many rather than the few."

Leaders like Thompson have a new take on the old saying, "If you can measure it, you can manage it." Rather than rely on top-down goal setting and "managing to the goal," they are looking at how the massive data-generating capabilities across an organization, from applications to financial results, can create insights into *how* work is getting done. This brings a whole new dimension to management and leadership. We no longer have to wait until the year-end or quarterly numbers give a big-picture view of how the organization is doing. Data in the human enterprise allows anyone to understand the story of what's really going on. We might say that we build our organization's *qualitative* story through *quantitative* tools.

People analytics is still a young science, but its promise is so great that more than 70 percent of companies say they consider it a high priority. Successful experiments like Google's Project Oxygen have managed to identify the practices of top-performing individuals and teach them to others. The next generation of people analytics is going beyond individual performance to understand how the interplay among people across an enterprise drives performance.[1]

A constant refrain among the human resources professionals and corporate executives who attend the Workhuman Live conferences is, "Why do you study all the details of human behavior in the workplace to determine the employee experience, when most of this is common sense?"

Adam Grant, the bestselling author of *Originals*, answers that question in three ways. Grant is a social scientist and a professor of organizational behavior at Wharton, and he has an unquenchable thirst for data. He says:

> First, very often research does not confirm our intuition. It challenges or complicates common sense, and that's an opportunity to learn something new.
>
> Second, even when research does confirm intuition, there are lots of practices that people might recognize as effective but underestimate how powerful they are. For example, I wanted to test whether meeting a client or customer or end user of your product or service would increase your motivation and your productivity. I told colleagues about testing this in a call center and they said, "Of course, meeting customers would motivate you because it would show you how what you do is valued and appreciated." That was common sense.
>
> However, we were all unprepared for our finding that meeting a single person who benefited from your work for five minutes could lead to a 142 percent increase in your weekly effort and 171 percent increase in your weekly revenue. We realized that we had anticipated the direction of an effect (like appreciation) but not the strength of it.
>
> Third, when a community comes together, they come together because there are meaningful relationships to be built and meaningful ideas to be shared. And I think that normally happens

through people's individual experience. There's additional value in doing research at the level of the community. You can bring multiple companies together and test the effect of a business practice across multiple companies, multiple industries, and multiple countries. Rather than rely on intuition based on the experience or intuition of an individual, there is a chance to accumulate knowledge and generalize it in a way that doesn't always happen.

We live in a data-obsessed business environment. Google and Amazon popularized the idea that every important business question should be settled with data, an idea that has become embedded in today's strategic decision making. At leading companies, you'd better bring your data to the meeting if you want to be heard. And thanks to ever-increasing power to gather and analyze data, it's theoretically possible for people in any department to get data to prove (or disprove) their ideas.

Human resources overall has been resistant to this change until recently. The classic HR director from the past was a master of soft skills and left data management to the IT and finance teams. That's changing with widespread acceptance of HR software in areas like benefits administration and recruiting that automate long-established practices. That's the administrative layer of software, which helps checkbox functions like corporate governance, legal compliance, and process management.

Those checkboxes are necessary, but they can quickly squeeze the energy out of a workforce. Administrative software has a way of categorizing everyone according to just a few criteria, and it monitors big, impersonal data like costs, with the inevitable result that the software becomes focused on making sure you don't spend too much on your biggest cost, people.

Administrative applications make old routines more efficient, but they don't change the way people interact, collaborate, innovate, and create in the new agile way of working. Instead, these applications make sure people are conforming to the way the applications are set up. In many places, they become tools of bureaucracy, the sworn enemy of innovation, creativity, and individuality.

Process is necessary but not sufficient. Kat Cole, COO and president, North America at FOCUS Brands, puts process in perspective when she says, "Sometimes companies get so comfortable with their processes, in their systems, in their positions, and in their structure, that if those things go away, so too does the connection to people. And it shouldn't be the case. Those processes and technologies allow visibility and metrics and benchmarking, and they're incredibly helpful. But being good to people and letting them bring their whole selves to work isn't dependent on technology. The best of leaders have always done it."

People are your biggest investment, not your biggest cost. You invest a fortune trying to find them, train them, increase their skills, and make sure they know the right thing to do in both clear or ambiguous situations. They need tools that enable them to carry on the most human and valuable activities, such as innovation and collaboration. And HR needs tools to understand how to get the best people, or not leave a whole group of people behind because someone somewhere set up an administrative tool that reflected a limited view of a department or a skill set or a job title. You have to be able to gather data that sees the whole picture of work—what people are doing day to day, how they're doing it, and what results they get. And you have to do this in a way that still respects the privacy and dignity of the individual. Because that data will reveal the truth of what's going on, in a positive sense. Leaders can see a snapshot of work activity in real time, without waiting for a milestone to confirm that the right things are happening.

For example, how can you foresee innovation? How do you learn after the fact what series of actions led to breakthrough ideas? Until recently, managers depended on the "postmortem" meeting in which the members of a team review the work that brought them to a certain point. But memories are notoriously unreliable, and such analysis not only is inherently subjective but suffers from unconscious human bias. It's natural to celebrate success and take or share credit for it. It's painful to admit responsibility for failure and not dilute one's part in it. And innovation, like creative problem solving, is all but impossible to plan (otherwise it wouldn't be innovative or creative). You can only set the stage for innovation to take place, support the right conditions through time, notice when it happens, and raise everyone's understanding that innovation is a good thing. You reward it with celebration, recognition, and reward. And in terms of understanding how an innovation really happened, you can use this system of record of human moments to track those elusive human connections that led to a breakthrough. Recognition and gratitude for innovative thinking and ideas can be the lens that brings reality into focus. When you know how it really happened, you can fine-tune work routines and skills to make the next innovative moment more likely.

Taming the River of Data

Tech visionary Kevin Kelly wrote, "Every company these days is basically in the data business and they're going to need AI to civilize and digest big data and make sense out of it—big data without AI is a big headache."[2]

Every day, billions of devices—from smartphones to the most advanced computers, from highway crossing cams to heating systems to the 60 to 100 sensors in your car—are recording and transmitting data along the internet. It's impossible to imagine the amount of data; comparisons like "If every data point were a molecule of water, we'd fill the Mississippi" are colorful but beyond human comprehension. Data is the river that runs through everything, but without intelligent and purposeful analysis, it might as well be a raging flood sweeping away everything in its path.

Data scientists search for ways to use that data to accomplish something worthwhile, whether that's finding a cure or improving an employee's experience of work. That takes (1) designing a method to gather the right information in the first place and (2) analyzing data with advanced tools like AI, machine learning, and natural language processing. It's impossible to overstate the importance of building, collecting, and understanding data in any business, and advances since the growth of cloud computing (which makes big data processing available to almost anyone) are mind-boggling.

Consider traffic apps: You ask your smartphone, "What's the best route to work?" In seconds, natural language processing analyzes and translates your question into relevant queries to big data applications distributed in massive data centers, maybe thousands of miles away. They process local street maps, dynamic location information from thousands of other smart devices in cars (what direction, how fast they're moving, how many are in a given mile of road), alerts from public utilities, and other data to suggest the best route and tell you when you will arrive. And that's just getting directions, a focused and relatively simple bit of data processing.

Now imagine all the interactions among hundreds or thousands of people communicating with one another through a workday and getting tasks done. If you gathered every action and every word of every moment, you'd have an unimaginable amount of data.* You would be able to identify which actions result in positive outcomes, from the number of sales someone closes to the number of $100 million patents a company generates.

Qualitative data analysis, including natural language processing, can tell people a lot about what people are thinking as well as doing. This has the potential to show managers how to adjust their work to make the most of positive behaviors and productive skills and check unproductive or negative patterns that might otherwise remain obscure.

Tools like that would gather a ridiculous amount of data, because they would measure what's going on person-to-person across every layer of the organization, not just top-down items like hours worked or pay scales. An earlier book, *The Crowdsourced Performance Review* (written by Eric), discusses "lifelogging" the organization through this data, which would create a narrative of how all accomplishments, failures, false starts,

---

*You'd also have a serious responsibility to protect privacy, which we'll address in the next chapter.

and big inspirations happen. Since the publication of that book in 2013, the capability of data tools to capture that narrative has grown exponentially. When that data is modeled on a narrative that is positive, based on trust and goodwill among peers, the record becomes a rich story: It tells not only *what* happened but *why* and *how* it happened.

The most recent generation of enterprise software points to the power of making and analyzing connections among people. Slack is one of the more successful tech companies in recent years because it harnesses the power of collaboration, connecting people to each other in a much more efficient way than the systems that most companies have put in place. Microsoft Teams, Cisco Webex, and other Slack competitors have different features, but all revolve around the central idea of easy collaboration across multiple platforms from networked desktops to smartphones on the road.

Management expert Gary Hamel recalled a thought experiment that provoked laughter at Workhuman Live 2019 and perfectly captured the power of transparent communication in an organization. He said, "Why do we have all these bureaucratic hurdles around business travel? In many companies, if you want to travel, they will tell you which airline, which hotel, how much you can spend. You have to get somebody's permission in advance as if you were a kid. But what if we blew that all up for 30 days? OK, anybody can travel anytime on business. If you want to fly Emirates first class, go ahead. No worries. Knock yourself out. But when you come back, we're going to take all of your travel expenses, and they're going to be posted online so that everybody can see them."

Gary concluded, "Bureaucracy zero, Freedom one!" and he's right. His thought experiment makes the point that the need for bureaucratic processes can be blown away by transparency, individual accountability, and mutual trust. Peer pressure and shared values take the place of top-down control. And if people want to spend tens of thousands more on travel than their peers do, let them be fully accountable to their peers.

The power of open, transparent facts makes much of the bureaucratic sclerosis unnecessary by removing the secrecy and privilege that pervades an old-fashioned enterprise. This is why "sharing" applications are also subversive in the best sense—instead of hoarding information and data, they open it up for everyone to share the same facts and the same truth.

There are drawbacks to all this openness, not least of which is the temptation at work and home to overcommunicate, to overwhelm important information with trivial commentary—or as data scientists like to say, to lose the signal in all the noise. That problem is answered by the development of software that helps people sort through the vast trove of data and knowledge moving around a company. Some of it is powered by artificial intelligence, some by individual preferences, and some by clever add-ons that customize the tools.

THANK TALK **CELEBRATE**

Transparency has the power to break through some of the unconscious walls we put up around ourselves in the workplace. Personal life events like a marriage or a work anniversary are opportunities for people to join in celebrating the feelings we typically don't share in a formal setting. When you do this on a social media platform in a workplace, it broadens each employee's picture of his or her colleagues. Like gratitude, good wishes are beneficial to both the receiver and the giver. We (Derek and Eric) have worked together for 20 years—you'd think we would know each other pretty well. But it's one thing to know that Derek is the father of two sets of twins, and it's quite another to see a continual happy stream of congratulations from all over Workhuman when he posts pictures of the first day at school in his Life Events feed. Eric gets to know Derek through others' experience of him, and through fellow employees Eric gets to know his old business partner (who lives thousands of miles from Eric's office) a little better.

All these are legitimate needs: We need to know what's going on in detail without getting overwhelmed. We need to promote openness while protecting privacy. We need to comply with employment laws and organizational values while cutting out bureaucratic waste. We need to promote positivity and a great employee experience while respecting privacy and individual needs. Developing applications that can do all this is an enormous and energizing challenge.

The next layer of useful applications sits on top of the administrative layer. It will enable and enhance human interactions in the workplace while creating a knowledge base and a narrative of how work gets done. All the facets of the employee experience described in Chapter 2 can be measured in detail, and the analysis of that data can lead to incredible insights into what's really going on in a company, beyond the slogans and, as Adam Grant suggests, even beyond what intuition or "common sense" says is going on.

We call this next layer *human applications*.

Human Applications

Administrative applications focus on process. Human applications focus on people and promote and facilitate human moments that matter.

Human applications are designed to build and support relationships among people, increasing alignment among employees in terms of shared values, shared goals, and shared culture. These applications work to instill a feeling of inclusion and belonging among diverse individuals, whose common ground is the "village" of their workplace. These applications bring people together through feedback and support, recognizing effort and celebrating achievement. Above all, they promote connectivity, engagement, and well-being in each employee in a way that is natural, because they are built on informal, moment-by-moment communication. They give employees, managers, and leaders the ability to express their thoughts and ideas, to support one another, and to bring people together as they pursue goals and get results.

That's the front end—the part that connects people and gathers user-generated data. Social recognition is the user-friendly face of human applications, a system of record for human moments. On the back end, software applications process the information and connections people have created to paint an incredibly wide and deep picture of what is going on in the company. Through advanced data analysis, human applications reveal hidden patterns and data points that might otherwise go unnoticed. They reduce risk by identifying problem areas before those problems become crises. Because they can map the interactions among people, applications like these can discover subtle features of an organization: Who is influential, what amount of communication between cross-functional teams is optimal, how does innovation happen, who is contributing outside the immediate circle, and many more.

Workhuman's core business since the beginning has been recognition technology, and so we've paid a lot of attention to the data gathered in the act of individuals recognizing each other for the work they've done. We've logged more than 50 million recognition moments among people over 20 years, and our view of human applications is informed by diving deep into that data for guidance in learning what this software can do for people and organizations.

We have come to appreciate what a treasure trove that store of data is, as the capabilities of data analysis grow. Before describing how recognition helps to drive the human enterprise forward, it's helpful to share the principles that we mean when we say human moments that matter.

By design, every human application has the following components:

- It is employee-driven, collaborative, and social.
- It is deeply relationship- and connection-focused.
- It is equally inclusive, open, and accessible to all.
- It includes crowdsourced content and employee voices.
- It actively supports diversity and individuality.
- It is engaging and encourages continuous feedback.

Human applications must also be technically advanced, including:

- An engaging, accessible user experience that makes people want to use it
- Easy-to-understand analysis and data visualization

- Integration and adaptability with other HR technologies
- The ability to share data, analytics, and reporting with other HR technologies
- AI capabilities that enable the applications to become more useful over time
- Scalability and security, which today means cloud-based

Human applications—a source of truth for human moments—thus designed can bring value to the most important employee-centric principles of the human enterprise:

- *Engagement.* So much time and thought are given to improving employee engagement that one obvious point can be overlooked: Give employees a way to engage with each other near and far through positive interactions and communications.
- *Alignment and belonging.* Because human moments that matter build and support good relationships at the grass roots, they help people feel they belong. They solidify bonds of trust and goodwill. By reinforcing and reiterating common goals, they build alignment. Alignment is one of the most underappreciated qualities of employee development, and one that human apps can significantly influence. Too often, development and alignment efforts end at onboarding, and company values and vision are mere words in a handbook.
- *Diversity and inclusion.* Human applications are natural tools for supporting diversity and inclusion in so many ways that we've provided a separate chapter (Chapter 10) laying out the case for their centrality in any D&I effort.
- *Retention and employer brand.* When you use human apps, you create an emotional bond between colleagues, from employee to manager, and from employee to organization, and that bond raises the emotional stakes of leaving the "village." Employees who feel an organization really cares about them are less likely to leave. Conversely,

according to a 2018 Paychex[3] report, 53 percent of departing employees felt their employers didn't care about them as an individual contributor.

- *Performance management.* This topic is so important to understanding the value of human applications that we've addressed it in a separate chapter (Chapter 9). For this principle, intuition is correct: People who feel more connected and encouraged at work tend to be more productive. According to Gallup,[4] however, only 27 percent of workers strongly agree that the feedback they currently receive helps them do their work better. Clearly, managers need to learn ways to make feedback better.

- *Vision, goals, and values.* According to a recent study,[5] perceived organizational support, supportive leader behavior, and employee alignment together explain 56 percent of the variance in work engagement, and of the three, the biggest contributor is alignment. Human apps like recognition and feedback bring employees into daily proximity to company values and goals and help align employees regularly with company vision.

- *Trust in leadership.* According to Deloitte,[6] only 27 percent of employees who intend to leave trust their leadership, compared with 62 percent of those who plan to stay. Human apps increase trust by increasing transparency across the organization and bringing leadership into more consistent and direct contact with employees on a regular basis.

Designing Connections

"I went out one night to a sports bar in Chicago to watch the Duke basketball game. At the bar, this guy came up to me and started chatting. Turns out he went to high school with one of the assistant coaches at Duke, a former player. Then suddenly he says, 'I know you didn't have to come out tonight. I know you had a lot of choices. I just really appreciate that you chose to come here.' I watched while he said the same to every guest.

Well, of course he turned out to be the owner, but I don't think I've ever felt that appreciated for going out and drinking a couple of beers and having a meal than I did that night.

"In customer experience design, there are certain moments that have disproportionately high impact on how you feel about the experience. Successful businesses don't leave those moments to chance. The best businesses in the world design moments that have the greatest impact.

"Now, overlay that idea right on top of work. That's the opportunity we have in the workplace—to design the kinds of connection that people make. You can have these moments of truth all day long, every day. In fact, they're happening anyway, for better or worse. The question is, are you intentional about it or are you leaving those to chance, because if you're leaving those to chance, then you're probably losing in the long run. But if you design the workplace so positive experiences are happening, good things follow."

—Jason Lauritsen, author of *Unlocking High Performance*

Human applications make these insights possible because, again, they draw narrative out of data. They correlate behavior with outcomes. Adam Grant suggests that some contributions people make can be overlooked because the right questions aren't being asked. For example, who are the effective mentors in an organization? Common sense suggests that they're the leaders who give time and attention to less experienced employees, and that is true, but with human applications we now have data to validate some of our commonsense assumptions. We can measure the promotion rates and advancement of the people certain managers mentor, and we can see how in particular that mentoring works. We can measure how often managers praise or instruct employees and analyze the language they use through natural language processing. We can measure the types of impact the people they mentor have on the organization. For example, do they contribute an outsized share of revenue or innovative ideas? Do they become mentors themselves?

Kate Hastings, VP of Sales Productivity at LinkedIn, says:

Finding the human in the data is absolutely critical, and when you have it, you make it relevant by layering anecdote on top of data. I had an attrition problem in our Dublin office, and I dug around and discovered someone at another company was poaching people on my team. The local manager said, "We lose people all the time." I looked at the data and said, "The woman they just poached is responsible for the last three citations LinkedIn had in The Financial Times." As soon as people could link a statistic like attrition rate to a story that expressed someone's value in a personal way, they sat up and took notice.

Her colleague Holly Lignelli, director of LTS Solutions–Global Accounts and Connected Enterprise at LinkedIn, also believes that using human applications to discern a story helps a company wade into the ocean of data effectively. She explains:

A lot of times, people get caught up in all the data available internally. You can't answer every question in the universe, but you can start by benchmarking. What are your urgent challenges compared to other organizations? If you're thinking about the gender breakdown of your software engineers and discover you have 30 percent women, you might think you really have to get to parity between women and men. But if the benchmarks say the average is 15 percent women in software you can think about what you're doing right, what you're doing more effectively than others. That will lead you to redouble those efforts rather than changing course, which you might do without comparative data. . . . The most important thing you can do is go into data with a hypothesis and discover the data points that will prove or disprove your hypothesis. That's when the conversation really starts to get interesting.

Working in the Cloud

The next chapters will show how enterprise-level human applications combine thousands of data points with deep analytics to reveal what's really going on in an organization. Workhuman is a social recognition company designed for human connection. We know that social recognition is the key that unlocks all this rich data. We call the marriage of recognition, data, software, and analytics the Workhuman Cloud.

Until recently, it was especially difficult for data and narrative to work together, but the capabilities inherent in cloud computing have changed that as completely as it changed our earlier example of getting directions on your smartphone. Cloud computing takes the big data processing chores out of the device in your hand and enables them to happen in vast networked data centers.

Now it's possible to create a deep store of data points and analytics that measure the most urgent questions enterprises face. Analytics make what's hidden clear. They create insight. They set a platform of undeniable data that cuts through wishful thinking or frustrated confusion.

The second half of this book explains how such analytics are created through peer-to-peer recognition and how THANK, TALK, CELEBRATE applies to performance management, diversity and inclusion, compensation, and leadership.

CONSIDER THIS

List all the systems your company or team uses to enable how work gets done. Now separate this list into two groups: systems that support or enable process and systems that support or enable people. Which group delivers more value in the end?

PART II

BUILDING A HUMAN ENTERPRISE

7 Recognition: The Heart of Working Human

Community Flourishes When People Recognize Others with Whom They Work and Spend Their Time

HUMAN MOMENTS

"Merck has always been a company that has put our patients and people first. When you think of that caring kind of environment, recognition fits in really well. We are also a big company, with about 70,000 people around the globe, so we want them to be able to say, 'Thank you,' in as many different languages as possible.

"Two of my favorite moments: We were at a Digital Innovation Summit soon after we launched Merck's Inspire recognition program. An employee stopped by the Inspire booth to let us know how she was able to go to Lowe's and completely redo her bathroom with all of the points she received from her recognition, which she was so thrilled about. I know another colleague in one of our Asian markets, who was so excited about being able to go online and shop for luggage before going on vacation.

"If you're a social person and you use Inspire even to say, 'Thank you,' it's more than just you and the person who receives that thanks. Other people see it and say, 'Hey, Sally, great job. You are always so helpful.' And then they build on that. People love to receive a personal note of thanks, and to express gratitude. It's a win-win either way."

—Michaela Leo, Director of Compensation
Programs and Analytics, Merck

Social recognition is the means by which human applications, which promote and facilitate human moments, both serve human needs and accelerate an organization's performance. We all want to feel valued and appreciated by others. We all want to feel a sense of belonging and connection. Applications that tap into these human needs can help employees feel attached and engaged with the organization. THANK, TALK, CELEBRATE is the heart of working human through the practice of social recognition.

Social recognition is the practice of people recognizing and rewarding each other's efforts, using positive feedback to unlock human potential. It's the foundation for creating a more human workplace because it reinforces shared *purpose* and gives individual *meaning* through *gratitude*. A consistent stream of gratitude and acknowledgment improves performance, deepens relationships, drives engagement, ties together geographically dispersed teams, inspires better work, and builds trust in your brand.

We live in an increasingly social world, where our connections to others have become essential to our own growth and success. As we've seen, effective work is becoming less dependent on hierarchy and more dependent on networks of relationships. The way we share information at work now depends on inclusion—of peers, direct reports, and others across all areas of the organization.

When we say recognition is social, we don't mean that it is frivolous or chatty or filled with cat videos. We mean leveraging technology to amplify exemplary work performance and broadcast it all around your

company, so that everyone can see the company values in action, participate in congratulating and reinforcing that behavior, and be inspired to
emulate it.

When a manager or a peer expresses thanks to someone, we call that
a recognition moment, or a moment of gratitude. For the purpose of
improving the workplace, we're talking about more than common cour-
tesy, like thanking someone for holding a door open. When we talk about
recognition, we mean recognizing the everyday moments of special effort
that people do in their jobs. Recognition calls out employee performance
and makes a permanent record of the effort and the thanks.

That permanent record, capturing the moment, is the raw material
of human applications. Workhuman has captured 50 million of these
moments in its social recognition database. That's 50 million moments
of gratitude shared among 5 million employees in 160 countries, and
it contains an amazing amount of information about how people can
interact positively.

• • •

There are three essential reasons to create moments of gratitude. The
first is the gratitude itself, with all the derivative benefits we've described
for both the giver and receiver. That positive energy echoes out into the
culture, as more and more people describe good performance and extra
effort, saying "Thank you" within their teams and departments and locations. Eventually, it spreads everywhere, creating an organization-wide
network of goodwill.

The second reason to have gratitude moments recorded in a social
recognition system is to create teachable moments, when you can highlight positive behavior and positive results for all to see. You provide
raw material for understanding subtle organizational dynamics like the
power of hidden influencers—employees whose positive effect is far
larger than their public persona (introverts, for example, who avoid the
spotlight but promote learning and critical thinking more effectively
than flashier colleagues).

The third reason to have a social platform driven by gratitude is to expand and enrich a database of human-to-human interactions, all in a positive light, and thus find evidence-based pathways to better performance. Data analysis can identify which interactions produce which benefits. It can produce "aha moments" for HR and other leaders. For example, analysis can identify times when one behavior or management technique is effective in one location or culture but neutral or even negative in another. It maps how teams work together across borders and time zones. This is particularly interesting for multinational companies because the data goes right down to the individual team, manager, or employee performance.

On a macro level, gathering all this data and making it anonymous (to preserve privacy and company confidentiality) enables users to continually understand how the networks in and among organizations operate, wisdom that can improve management's effectiveness in a human enterprise.

THANK TALK CELEBRATE

Wharton Professor Adam Grant recalls the power of giving gratitude when he and colleagues tested it in a stressful work environment. He recently recalled, "We knew gratitude boosts satisfaction, but our question was whether it also increased motivation or performance. We randomly assigned one group of employees in a call center to keep gratitude journals and write about things they appreciated. We also randomly assigned another group to keep contribution journals about things they had done that other people were grateful for. We found that the latter group worked harder and made more calls over the next few weeks compared to the employees who were focused on their own feelings of gratitude. They were in an active mindset—they felt, 'I made a difference today. I have something to offer.'"

An Ideal Social Recognition Scenario

Before we go into the details of social recognition's benefits, it's helpful to imagine what an ideal recognition scenario would look like:

> *People at every level of the organization are noticing good work in peers, managers, and staff. There's a cadence to the recognition—it's not everyone, every day, but a steady drumbeat of messages with clear structure and guidelines. Recognition always comes with a personal written record of what someone did and why it matters. It always connects the recipient's behavior to the company's purpose and values, which everyone knows by heart because the social recognition system continually reinforces them. Recognition always comes with a tangible award of real value, typically points or gift vouchers that the recipient can redeem for an object or experience that is valuable to him or her. The value of the award is commensurate with what is being recognized.*

Digging into that ideal description, we see that social recognition promotes benefits beyond momentary gratification. Let's expand on that scenario point by point:

People at Every Level of the Organization Are Noticing Good Work in Peers, Managers, and Staff

Recognition heightens awareness of what good work looks like. Because everyone can participate, it promotes a sense of belonging and cohesion. It is democratic in the best sense—the people's decisions set the course of the culture.

A Steady Habit with Clear Structure and Guidelines

When everyone shares a habit, it's woven into the company culture. It's bounded by structure like any other business practice; therefore, recognition can be measured and connected to outcomes.

Recognition Always Comes with a Personal Written Record of What Someone Did and Why It Matters

There's a tremendous difference between a perfunctory "Nice job" and a personal message. People might appreciate the former for a moment, but they connect emotionally with the latter. When someone doing the recognition makes a bit of effort and adds something personal to the recognition moment, the give-and-take of gratitude brings that relationship a little closer.

It Always Connects the Recipient's Behavior to the Company's Purpose and Values

Purpose and values are not just words that we repeat—in great organizations they are a living presence that guides behavior moment by moment. A recognition program that is not linked to core values is like a ship with no navigation—aimless and off course. Workhuman research in partnership with the Society for Human Resource Management (SHRM) found that 70 percent of companies using recognition tie it to values. Connecting recognition to values benefits HR goals such as building a positive employee brand, reinforcing strategic business goals, boosting employee engagement, increasing productivity, and delivering a strong return on investment.[1]

Recognition Always Comes with a Tangible Award of Real Value

We're often asked, "Why not a simple thank you?" The answer is that while a thank you is great any time, recognition with a reward is qualitatively different from thanks alone. It's a business practice (albeit grounded in our most human needs), and giving a tangible reward produces a bigger, longer-lasting impact. Real value proves the company is invested in the employees' well-being. It reminds the recipient later of the behavior that inspired the recognition, over and over again. The reward empowers peers to make a material difference in the lives of their colleagues. When people choose their own award, it is the ultimate customized experience, honoring their individuality. It's a practice with an incredible return on investment (as we'll document later). And in our most recent study, in

2019, 74 percent of employees told us they found e-thanks alone to be either disappointing or less fulfilling than a message with a reward.[2]

The Value of the Award Is Commensurate with What Is Being Recognized

Different behaviors have different degrees of benefit, and this ideal recognition is flexible in its rewards to acknowledge that reality—just like compensation does. (Chapter 8 offers guidelines for determining the level of award.)

The ideal recognition scenario reaches every part of organizational life with a sense of shared positivity. It's a virtuous cycle, in which more recognition creates more good feeling. More gratitude. More optimism. More energy. More visibility into what good looks like. And more recognition of behaviors that are aligned to the company's values. And that creates quantifiable results.

Recognition and Results

According to an annual survey Workhuman conducts in collaboration with the SHRM, HR practitioners say their employee recognition program helps with organizational culture (85 percent), employee engagement (84 percent), employee experience (89 percent), employee relationships (86 percent), and organizational values (83 percent).[3]

Regular, ongoing recognition breaks feedback down into small, individual moments. It's easier because you're noticing and appreciating great work in real time and in manageable bites. By embedding such feedback in the day-to-day, it becomes part of your regular routine, and giving consistent, ongoing feedback helps you positively affect behavior and reinforce values for your team.

Gallup's 2017 State of the American Workplace report found that only 3 in 10 employees had received recognition or praise for doing good work within a seven-day period. "By moving that ratio to 6 in 10 employees," the report reads, "organizations could realize a 24 percent improvement in quality, a 27 percent reduction in absenteeism, and a 10 percent reduction in shrinkage."[4]

Recognition also provides you with information to make the job of managing easier. Each recognition moment adds to a broader picture of strengths and weaknesses. When it comes time to create individual development plans or evaluations, you have a real-time record of that worker's achievements as they were created in the moment—and not recalled months after the fact. Recognition can thus be applied to performance management in several ways (which we'll describe in Chapter 9).

Social recognition is peer to peer, which means it can be given from anyone to anyone. This democratic orientation is a strong countermeasure against the bureaucratic notion that only managers are entitled to judge performance. Peer-to-peer recognition means employees are noticing and applauding their colleagues' performance, creating a rounded, crowdsourced picture of each employee. And when it's clearly tied to organizational values, recognition encourages everyone to reinforce what it means to be part of the organization.

Recognition is a great way to get new employees quickly oriented. By recognizing them during their first weeks and encouraging them to recognize others, managers and peers show the newest hires firsthand what it means to truly practice your values and what behaviors are most beneficial to all.

Social recognition shows a positive impact on key business metrics that impact a company's bottom line. For example, a 2017 poll by TJinsite/TimeJobs.com[5] found that more than 35 percent of employees consider lack of recognition of their work as the biggest hindrance to their productivity.

Professor Christine Porath of Georgetown University, author of *Mastering Civility,* notes the similarity between recognition and civil behavior at work. She writes, "Civility builds relationships that help people accomplish tasks and provide personal support. By being civil, employees boost their "social capital," resources that help them thrive and achieve their goals. Social capital resources include knowledge, advice, contacts, emotional support, and goodwill. All of these resources help employees succeed in job searches, increase promotion potential and pay, and improve organizational influence. *Each small act of kindness and respect contributes to a cycle that fosters greater civility among the people in one's network. Giving works the same way. Giving thanks, acknowledgement, attention and feedback is civility in its finest form"* [emphasis added].[6]

Recognition and Employee Engagement

Employee engagement has been top of mind for HR professionals and strategic-minded leaders for more than a decade, and research keeps confirming its importance. A meta-analysis of 263 research studies found that organizations with the most engaged employees outperformed those with the least engaged employees along many dimensions:

- 22 percent greater profitability
- 21 percent greater productivity
- 65 percent lower turnover
- 10 percent better customer ratings
- 48 percent fewer safety incidents
- 28 percent less theft[7]

According to Gallup, employee engagement has lately been on the rise as a result of greater satisfaction with recognition received for work accomplishments and for relationships with coworkers and with supervisors.[8] The difference is significant: 83 percent of employees who receive recognition of their performance and 80 percent of those receiving feedback report a positive employee experience, compared with 38 percent and 41 percent, respectively, of employees who don't.[9]

Building engagement means participating in its four essential components: *enablement, energy, empowerment,* and *encouragement.* If you want to create a workplace of truly engaged employees, each of these four elements must be alive and thriving in your organization.[10] These human workplace practices ultimately contribute to a positive employee experience and, as this research shows, potentially enhance financial performance.

Enablement means helping people do their jobs, providing the means to accomplish work and also getting rid of impediments. It might mean approving the purchase of a second monitor for a workstation or changing a work schedule so someone with an aging parent can spend every Friday tending to the parent's needs. It might mean confronting a team member whose rudeness is alienating others and teaching the person more positive behaviors. In each example, employees get the message that helping them succeed is a management priority.

Mark Royal, senior director at Korn Ferry and author of *The Enemy of Engagement*, observes, "If organizations want to get the most out of the engagement and motivation that they are working so hard to build, they also need to think about enabling employees, or putting them in a better position to succeed."[11]

Energy might seem an individual quality (as in "He's so energetic"), but it's always responsive to context at work. Tony Schwartz, CEO and founder of The Energy Project, says companies that measure effort in longer work hours are using the wrong metric. It makes more sense to help people manage their energy.

"Time is a finite resource," says Schwartz, "and at some point, people don't have any left to invest. Energy is something you can expand, regularly renew, and use more efficiently."

Schwartz explains that energy, like so many other human qualities, is an interaction among several factors. Unlike machines, human beings require four separate sources of energy to operate.

Schwartz defines those sources as (1) *physical energy*, the quantity of energy available to a person, (2) *emotional energy*, a qualitative state that we can imagine on a scale from negative to positive, (3) *mental energy*, the ability to focus on one thing at a time, and (4) *spiritual energy*, derived from the belief that what we're doing really matters.[12]

Companies that help employees manage physical, emotional, mental, and spiritual energy demonstrate significant improvements in

engagement. They do this by cultivating positivity, good working conditions, common values, and a common purpose.

Empowerment nurtures and sustains engagement over the long run.
Empowerment transfers the power to achieve results from the manager
to the employee. Empowerment is the foundation of accountability.
When people can really make decisions and take action without asking permission every time, they own the results, and they can deliver on
commitments.

The feeling of empowerment is subjective. Employees who work
and connect in ways that best suit them feel a sense of agency and work
more efficiently. A 2017 study by the IBM Smarter Workforce Institute
and Workhuman found that organizations that deliver a positive experience—in part by empowering employees—outperform their cohorts
threefold for return on assets and twofold for return on sales.[13]

Encouragement can mean a simple word of support. It can be given
in an unexpected recognition of a job well done or a gesture of gratitude.
Sometimes people downplay the impact encouragement can make, especially in bureaucratic settings. They think it's only needed in an urgent
or stressful situation. But if you make encouragement a habit, it builds
a foundation of confidence and resilience that will support employees
all the time. It literally means "giving courage" to employees, which is
another way of empowering them.

Engagement is a state of mind unique to each employee, but engagement doesn't happen on its own. People in leadership positions who want
the proven benefits of engagement should ask themselves, "What am I
doing today to build, enable, energize, empower, and encourage everyone
in this organization?"

Peer-to-Peer Interaction Builds Community

The good news for executives trying to build a feeling of community in
their organizations is that most of the work is not up to them. Leaders
can initiate cultural change. They can teach the principles of community like belonging and inclusiveness—and most importantly they can

practice those principles frequently and publicly—but ultimately a community is built from the ground up, in thousands of little interactions. Peer-to-peer interaction is most impactful because peers are significantly more trusted than executives.[14]

"Positive inception [the beginning of positivity] works best when it comes from someone other than the team leader," says Shawn Achor. "In other words, anyone, with any role or title, can create positive inception if he or she appeals to value and meaning."[15]

Achor became well known as an evidence-based researcher on happiness. Today, in addition to writing fine books like *Big Potential,* he trains people at companies and other organizations to understand the "social scripts" of their workplace and change habitual behaviors to create positive cultures. "As a group, people can write the social script and norms once they realize that they are not victims of the culture but co-creators of it," he says.

A key point of the training is that regular employees, not just top managers, can acquire the skills to change the script in multiple situations from negative to positive. And building community is a big part of the change. At a national financial services firm, an underperforming, demoralized team showed a 50 percent rise in revenue and the highest engagement scores in the company after receiving Achor's training.

Community flourishes when people recognize others with whom they work and spend their time. It creates trust and builds a "community story" of how people accomplish common goals by working together. This works best when that recognition connects to shared values and activities.

Peer-to-peer interactions in an organization are where culture really exists, not in words on a mission statement but in the reality of daily life, where expectations of behavior arise. As Charles Duhigg wrote in his bestselling book *The Power of Habit,* "If you ignore the social obligations of your neighborhood, if you shrug off the expected patterns of your community, you risk losing social standing. . . . On the playground, peer pressure is dangerous. In adult life, it's how business gets done and communities self-organize."[16]

The power of values-based recognition to build a sense of community shows up in research we've done at Workhuman, using an independent market research firm. Among organizations where peer-to-peer recognition programs are tied to values:

- 93 percent of employees agree that "the work we do at my organization has meaning and purpose for me."
- 88 percent describe their overall work experience as positive.
- 80 percent say "I love my job."
- 90 percent describe themselves as engaged.
- 84 percent would recommend working at their organization to a friend.[17]

An advantage of peer-to-peer recognition in building community is proximity in time. Immediate feedback is memorable. When someone says "Thank you" or "Good job" shortly after the action recognized, a host of positive associations knit themselves into one of those little stories we as humans tell ourselves. When peers recognize each other quickly and frequently, all the positive effects of a culture of appreciation are magnified. We humans are wired to need frequent reminders of our value in our communities.

Workhuman CHRO Steve Pemberton points out that "the first picture is rarely the full picture," meaning simply that our understanding of each other's contribution and place in the community of work grows and changes over time. Frequent peer-to-peer stories build a full narrative of individual and group identity.

How important is frequency? Derek likes to illustrate the natural power of frequent, small recognition with this joke: "I love my kids. And so on January 1 each year I tell them I love them and they're good kids. If one does something good on June 16, I make a note to thank him next January 1 for being good, and on the next New Year's Day I tell my kids that I love them and I thank them for being good."

How effective is that scenario? And yet organizations act like this all the time by scheduling annual performance reviews. They wait weeks or months to note good news, while the internal PR group gets all the approvals from up and down the chain of command. And as time passes, the power of the message diminishes.

Five Ways Feedback Is a Gift

1. **Feedback helps us connect actions to goals.** *Thoughtful, detailed, and specific feedback* gives employees and peers the tools they need to reach their goals and excel.

2. **Positive feedback encourages people to do their best work.** We often think of feedback as a mechanism for change and improvement, but it can also be a powerful "green light" to encourage employees to keep up the good work they are already doing. *Positive feedback* can be a needed boost to confidence and success for many employees.

3. **Feedback builds trust and belonging.** Giving and receiving feedback fosters trust and vulnerability within organizations, building relationships and employee loyalty. Studies have shown how important *manager relationships* are to our sense of community and happiness at work.

4. **Timely feedback can prevent big failures.** Most of us can think back to professional advice that saved us from going off the rails. If *we wait too long to give feedback*, often by the time we hear it, the damage has long since been done.

5. **Feedback can help direct career growth.** Another direct application of feedback is helping employees *achieve a specific aspiration or goal*. Mentoring and coaching through feedback helps employees with goal setting and tracking progress. This feedback is employee-driven and future-focused.

Recognition and Retention

Turnover cost employers $600 billion in 2018—the highest rate since the recovery began—and research by the Work Institute estimates that will rise to $680 billion in 2020. During times of low unemployment, it's not surprising that people feel more comfortable switching jobs. What's more surprising was the Work Institute's conclusion that "more than three in four employees, 77 percent, who quit could have been retained by employers."[18]

In exit interviews, people said the most important reasons for leaving their jobs were (1) better career development, (2) better work-life balance, (3) poor manager behavior, (4) improved well-being, (5) greater compensation and benefits.

When people quit, it's usually too late to persuade them to stay. People rarely broadcast their unhappiness in a job and almost never confide to a manager that they are looking elsewhere. This situation is exaggerated in a command-and-control bureaucracy, where employees who get the recruiter's call fear retaliation if anyone suspects they're looking around. But even in more relaxed cultures, would any employees want to broadcast the fact that they're open to leaving? At best that would make them appear disloyal or discontent; in the worst cultures it puts a target on their backs.

Social recognition bypasses that dynamic because it acts as a kind of early-warning system that something's not right. Say there's a production supervisor named Andrew. He's recognized by peers for his dedication to quality, and his recognition timeline contains many stories of how Andrew directed his group to be uncompromising about shipping perfect orders every time. In the three years Andrew has worked at the company, Andrew's manager hasn't recognized that kind of performance. Is everyone else right and the manager wrong? Or is something else going on—perhaps the manager isn't judging Andrew by the same values as his peers.

Human organizations are complicated to manage, and the recognition system can't always say what's up, but it can tell HR and upper management early that there's a situation that needs a closer look. Andrew is much more likely to stay with the company if his above-average dedication to quality is recognized by his manager. We know this because it shows up in our data year after year.

Eaton Corporation, a multinational maker of power management systems, found that the probability of employees leaving declined precipitously as their recognition increased. Employees who were recognized four times in a year left Eaton at half the rate of those with no recognition. After one year, recognized new hires left the company at one-third the rate of those who received no recognition.

The power of giving gratitude was also evident in the data, as those who both gave and received recognition/thanks/gratitude have the lowest turnover rate—less than half of those who never gave or received it.

A study of retention at JetBlue published in *Harvard Business Review* revealed that for every 10 percent increase in people reporting being recognized, JetBlue saw a 3 percent increase in retention and a 2 percent increase in engagement. The study noted, "Turnover can be one of the most expensive problems at a company; research [shows] the costs of replacing an employee range from 20% of their salary to 150%, depending on how you calculate it. So, a 3% change in this number can represent tens of millions of dollars depending on the scale of the company." (In addition, the JetBlue data also showed that engaged crew members were three times more likely to "wow" their customers and twice as likely to be in the top 10 percent of net compliments reported by customers. Thus, recognition is not just an issue of employee retention; it has an impact upon customer satisfaction and loyalty as well.)[19]

Another Workhuman study found a remarkable correlation between recognition and retention in the high-burnout profession of nursing. Turnover was cut in half for nurses who received just 3 to 4 moments of recognition per year versus those receiving no recognition. Nurses who were recognized 8 to 12 times a year—every 4 to 6 weeks—showed dramatic differences in probability of leaving (Figure 7.1).[20] And in a longitudinal study with a large healthcare system, Workhuman found that stronger recognition cultures are correlated with higher inpatient satisfaction scores by 2 to 3 percentage points. In such a high-stress profession, feelings of inclusion, belonging, and gratitude among employees naturally lead to positive impacts on patients.[21]

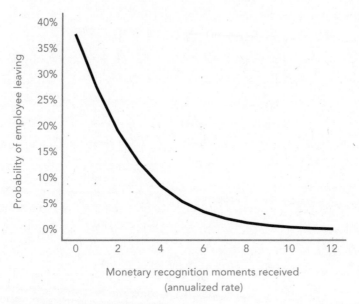

Figure 7.1 Recognition Lowers Turnover
Nursing staff who are recognized show dramatically reduced turnover.

Does being recognized make someone more likely to stay, or are those who are more likely to stay also earning recognition because of their high performance? In our experience, the answer is: both. Again, let's acknowledge that organizations are made up of human beings, with all their individual talents, needs, ambitions, strengths, and shortcomings. We know that both giving gratitude and receiving gratitude create positivity, and that good data analysis is an aid to good management, not an end in itself.

The more salient point is this: Without a culture of goodwill and gratitude, one that ties recognition to performance, a company is depriving itself of both insights about why people leave and the chance to prevent attrition. And a company will end up losing more good people to its competitors.

THANK TALK **CELEBRATE**

We've worked with a woman named Alice for 10 years, so we know her pretty well—but 95 percent of our experience with Alice is at the office. A recognition feature called Life Events recently gave us a delightful new look at her life. When she got married, a timeline in the company's recognition system captured an outpouring of good wishes from our offices all over the world. There were memories of Alice's early days and congratulations to her new husband. We followed them on their honeymoon to Bermuda, and one of our favorite customers, JetBlue, gave them the red-carpet treatment. When they were leaving the plane, the JetBlue associates presented them with a handmade card wishing them happiness.

Sometimes the simplest parts of recognition are the most meaningful. We had a pleasant office relationship for 10 years, but to be exposed to her life outside of work makes it a deeper connection for all of us. It's a shared community. There is no "outside of work." We're all human beings inside and out. There's no line.

Seeing the Unseen

Figure 7.2 is a data visualization of one of our Workhuman Cloud customers and the activity that the company has in its recognition program. You can immediately sense the power of this amount of goodwill being generated for the people and going from person to person all over the company. What you might not see at first glance, however, is how these recognition moments can render a rich array of insights into the organization. Each dot represents a person in the company, and each line represents a message of gratitude, recognition, and notice. Each of those recognition moments contains quantitative data such as which organizational values the recipient exhibited and the relative scale of the person's achievement, e.g., a range of impacts from "solving a tough problem" to "hitting 250 percent of target sales."

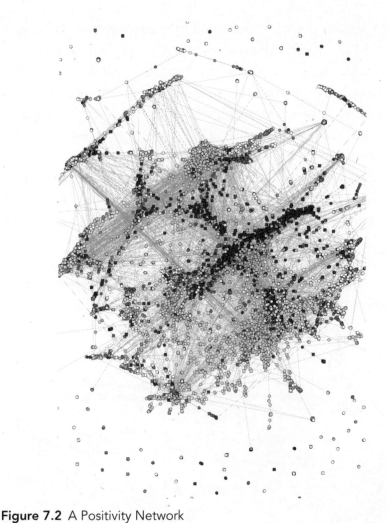

Figure 7.2 A Positivity Network
The dots represent people in the company. The lines represent positive reinforcement from one to another.

Going deeper, each of those recognition moments contains a personal message from the giver to the receiver. When you apply advanced natural language processing to all those messages, you have an incredibly nuanced and detailed narrative of what's going on throughout the network.

Natural language processing, advanced data analysis, and artificial intelligence are game changers for leading and managing organizations. Now we can map recognition activity against many important outcomes for evidence-based understanding of how recognition affects engagement, retention, participation in an employee referral program, or the relative importance of company values. You can see which teams are citing helpful cross-departmental work and who might be isolated.

Figure 7.3 is a detail of the Figure 7.2 network map. The two large clusters represent two teams that work closely together—for example, a tech development team and a product management team. The tightest connections between them are a pair of teams that work especially closely. Let's call them marketing and development. You would expect to see a lot of activity within teams and between closely related teams. But notice that there are a few members of the development team and the marketing team who are in close enough communication that they're recognizing each other, meaning they see each other's work and know how it relates to the overall company goals. They are creating ties between teams that typically don't talk much.

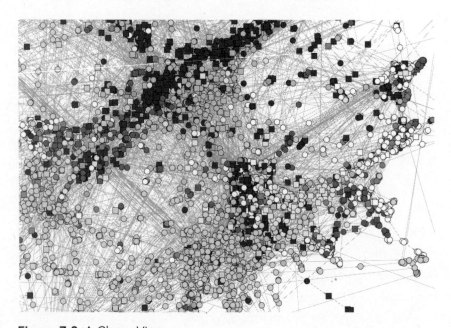

Figure 7.3 A Closer View
Focusing in on part of the positivity network reveals details that show close ties between departments.

Dig deeper: Let's say the marketing team is in Chicago, and the development team is split between northern Virginia and Poland. There's some great communication going on here, and the people giving and receiving gratitude could be excellent liaisons between disciplines, locations, and even countries. Apply natural language processing to the recognition messages, and you can quickly locate and build on positive relationships.

Zooming in even closer on the network map (Figure 7.4), we can see a few people who are "super-connectors." They give and receive recognition far more than average, which probably means that they are high performing and also that they have big networks around the company. These people carry an outsized power to promote values and help others. They are invaluable aids in times of change, because they are trusted and influential out of proportion to others, wherever they land on the organization chart.

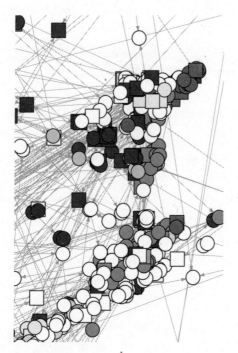

Figure 7.4 Super-Connectors

An even closer examination of the positivity network reveals people who are widely trusted and connected across the company.

These super-connected employees might be almost invisible to top management. They are hidden influencers who, because their recognition activity is by definition positive, are quietly reinforcing the values and purpose of the organization. The breadth of their network activity means they merit consideration for additional roles, for example, as mentors. Hidden influencers are often more interested in the work itself and their personal meaning than they are in power or bureaucratic gamesmanship. Finding them through social recognition is a way to bypass the flaws of typical office politics. (And if they prefer to remain quietly doing their job and recognizing others, the correct response to them is, "Thank you!")

Natural language processing adds an uncanny depth to network analysis. Analyze messages across millions of social recognition awards, and you can profile the temperamental qualities of people who succeed in certain positions. We can confirm common wisdom about some jobs; for example, the data says humility is more valuable in healthcare than in technology. But there are also subtle clues that can help at hiring time. For instance, empathy (the ability to imagine other people's thoughts and feelings in a situation) turns out to be a key to effectiveness in certain technology positions; empathy helps app developers imagine someone's experience using the app.

People receiving recognition containing certain keywords tend to be high performers. Collect the recognition awards of the most accomplished employees, and you find terms like *amazing, priceless, indispensable, inspiring, immensely helpful*. If you then search for these terms in the recognition comments received by employees with few network connections, you have a short list of people who are not necessarily visible but who are potentially high performers and are as yet unnoticed. That's a source to nurture for the next generation of leadership.

A customer in a large industrial sector wanted to raise the profile of its safety initiatives. This is good for morale and profits, and it also tends to positively impact other performance metrics.[22] The client company decided to emphasize safety in recognition awards, and where safety was mentioned in the social recognition system, the client combined it with root cause analysis of safety incidents. The client analyzed both safety awards (who was recognized, why, and at what level) and the language used in awards (*extra effort, successful shutdown, selfless dedication*) to find who promoted safety well and how they did it. The result was a lowering of the industry standard total recordable injury rate (TRIR) by 80 percent.[23]

A Note About Privacy

The issue of data privacy could fill an entire book in itself, and technology moves so fast that the technical details of such a book would be out of date the moment it's in print. Suffice it to say that those who adopt the benefits of social recognition are obligated to adopt principled and transparent privacy standards. Data analysis at a macro level must be done so that individuals aren't compromised. All the employees in the system have a right to know how and when and where their data will be analyzed. Confidential communications between employees remain confidential unless they threaten or infringe on the rights of others.

Stacia Sherman Garr, a human capital researcher and cofounder of RedThread Research, has spent years dealing with privacy. She says having and using such collective data is inseparable from responsibility to individuals: "You always have to think about the ethics component. It's never enough to say, just because we can do it, we should. I always ask myself, 'If the person on whom we're doing this analysis knew exactly what we are doing, would they be comfortable with it?' Is it right to drill down to the individual level on this particular piece of information? Is it right to sort data by this particular factor?"[24]

Natural language processing, advanced data analysis, and artificial intelligence empower HR with strategic capabilities in many of its domains. In later chapters we'll describe their importance in performance management, diversity and inclusion, and compensation. Human resources can lay a foundation for these and other benefits by learning the best practices we've come to understand. That's the subject of the next chapter.

CONSIDER THIS

Think of a recent time someone thanked you. Did you say, "No problem," and forget the moment? Did you say, "You're welcome," and
mean it sincerely? How did that thanks make you feel: self-conscious,
or gratified, or pleased, or happier with the relationship that those
thanks expressed?

8 | Recognition: Basics and Best Practices

What's Good for People Is Good for Business

HUMAN MOMENTS

Several years ago, Baystate Health phased out its antiquated recognition program during a period of fiscal belt-tightening. Jennifer Faulkner, vice president, Team Member Experience & Talent Management, explains, "We had an informal, manual, cash-based program. It was difficult to manage and wasn't delivering the value or impact we needed."

In 2015, Baystate Health partnered with Workhuman to launch its new peer-to-peer social recognition program, Baystate Celebrates! The program includes a public newsfeed of recognition moments where all employees can see and share their congratulations, as well as Service Milestones, a way to celebrate service anniversaries. "Together, these two elements create a powerful community celebration of our employees," says Faulkner.

Everyone in the organization can give and receive recognition through Baystate Celebrates! from a PC or the mobile application, which CEO

Mark A. Keroack, MD, once called his favorite app. "We call Dr. Keroack a recognition rock star," says Faulkner. "He's a super user and was an early champion of the program. You can imagine what it's like for any of our team members to get a recognition from the CEO. And when he recognizes members of management, they experience what that feels like and are often inspired to recognize others."

We like to say that any recognition is better than none, but there's a significant difference between the recognition practices of just 10 years ago and today's evidence-proven best practices. With all the changes taking place in the human enterprise, lagging recognition systems just won't provide the value that modern systems will. In this chapter, we'll prescribe the practices that make the most of a recognition investment, and then we'll model its return on investment. We'll start with a "field manual" of tactical, person-to-person techniques—what to recognize people for, when to recognize, and how to make the greatest impact. Then we'll share the key metrics that tell strategic users they are building an enduring recognition practice into the company culture.

Some Recognition FAQs

First, some quick answers to the most common questions people ask about recognition:

What Keeps Recognition from Being a Popularity Contest?

We have rarely seen this happen, because as a crowdsourced program, recognition tends to be self-regulating. When people tell why they're sending recognition, they pause and ask themselves, "Is this worthy of a public shout-out?" A sound recognition system has scaled levels of reward and approval, just like sound budgeting of any kind. For example, a level-1 recognition moment might be authorized by anyone, while a level-5 recognition event may be approved at a more senior level. The training and communication leading up to a program's launch helps employees understand what actions go beyond the job description.

Does It Always Have to Have a Tangible Reward? What About E-thanks?

E-thanks and a thank you e-mail are OK for modest contributions, but they only represent the individual giver, not the organization. Although words are powerful, employees appreciate when companies "walk the talk." Not only do employees appreciate it when there's more investment in their recognition program, but many positive outcomes, such as employee engagement and retention, directly correlate to tangible rewards; that is, the higher investment in recognition's tangible rewards, the better the numbers.

Does That Mean Awarding Cash?

Recognition programs are best tailored to the organization. In our experience, cash-only awards blur the lines between recognition and such cash rewards as bonuses and sales commissions. Simply put, cash is the currency of compensation. Recognition needs a different currency.

Most successful practitioners stress maximum choice and flexibility, such as a point system, so the recipients can choose a reward most meaningful to them. In addition, the ability to accumulate points from many awards and spend them all at once, for example on a vacation hotel, is a popular and effective option. (We'll go deeper into the relationship of recognition and pay in Chapter 11.)

Why Should Recognition Be Tied to Company Values?

The purpose of social recognition is to reinforce a company's purpose and the significance of everyone's work. That varies from company to company, so naming specific company values bolsters a sense of identity. Great leaders remind employees of their company values over and over; with social recognition, both the giver and receiver of thanks think of the specific value and its importance.

What About Levels of Awards?

Each award conveys to its recipient a certain level of acknowledgment and appreciation, so it's important to get that level right. A low-level award in exchange for months of work on a project might backfire on employees who feel like you are damning them with faint praise. Likewise, giving a large award for a minimal effort cheapens the award itself and makes it seem as if it is easy to achieve with no real effort.

The optimal number of awards typically includes five tiers of reward level to choose from, so people can be sure they are calibrating the degree of reward to the behavior.

EXPERT INSIGHT

"At my previous company, there was a gentleman who worked in one of our distribution centers, a fantastic employee who had been recognized many times by his peers. When his mother's oven broke, he used all of his points in our recognition program to buy her a new oven. They went to the store, and when they picked it out, they took a picture standing together next to the new oven, and then he sent the picture to remind us how grateful he was that recognition had made that moment possible. In that moment, he remembered all the different positive comments he had from his coworkers. And later his mother said how happy she was that he was being recognized for all his good work!"

—Amanda Linard, Director of Compensation, Getinge

Is Recognition Just for Line Workers?

This is a common misconception. In fact, we find that giving recognition affects management staff as much as or more than the people lower on the pay or seniority scale. LinkedIn found that highly compensated employees who received recognition showed a higher retention rate than the company average for their peer group. In fact, it took just one recognition award to cut turnover in half for this group of employees. Receiving four awards cut turnover by 75 percent. LinkedIn CHRO Christina Hall notes, "People ask, 'Why would someone who makes a six-figure salary and a big stock award care about these smaller awards?'

The answer is that we really see that human nature is such that frequent peer-to-peer awards have a great impact."[1]

Hall's comment is one more perspective of a larger point: People see recognition as different from their "contract" with an employer. LinkedIn, where 90 percent of awards come from peers, is a perfect example of that qualitative, emotional difference. In terms of emotional impact, the fact that someone makes a high salary isn't relevant; the relevant fact is that a peer went out of the way to express gratitude.

There are myths of self-sufficiency that attach to high earners, as if they didn't need recognition and gratitude. Even in organizations where executives and managers are charged with giving positive reinforcement down the organization chart, they don't receive a lot themselves. That's another situation where we often see a eureka moment, as leaders internalize the positive effects of receiving and giving gratitude.

Recognition at a Glance

Recognition encompasses many different practices that all share certain qualities. If your recognition satisfies these at-a-glance principles, you're on the right track.

Recognition is always:

- Positive
- Appreciative
- Specific
- Consistent and fair
- Merit-driven
- Unexpected
- Frequent
- Global

Recognition:

- Is social (seen by others in the organization or team)
- Celebrates effort, contribution, and achievement

- Happens as close as possible to the event
- Resonates with values, goals, and purpose
- Comes from anywhere—manager, peer, subordinate, another department or location
- Has appropriate substance and weight
- Recognizes an individual's uniqueness
- Is authentic and sincere

What to Recognize

Anyone should be able to give awards to anyone else in an ideal recognition setup, so it's important that everyone know what is worthy of recognition. Daily activities at work come in such a variety that the reasons for awards will vary in both qualitative and quantitative impact. The common denominator is *behavior*—something that can be described and qualified and adopted by people who see the award.

You might recognize something that was relatively easy to do but had a phenomenal impact on the organization, or by contrast, something that failed but took a huge effort and resulted in a lot of learning. Both are valuable. You can recognize creative solutions to everyday challenges or behavior that shows persistence in pursuit of a worthy goal like delighting a customer.

Whether peer or manager, you can recognize:

- Something that people should do more. This is a quick and powerful form of positive feedback.
- Something others should be doing, such as when someone breaks out of routine and makes a positive difference.
- Behavior that embodies company values. For example, if "accountability" is a value, recognize someone who takes ownership of a big problem when he or she could have legitimately stepped aside.
- Extra, discretionary effort is a good sign that recognition is appropriate. *Examples:* Someone stays through a weekend to ensure

success on a late project, or a manager goes hands-on with a task "beneath a manager's status" because an employee was sick.

- Did a customer, vendor, or business partner notice extra effort on someone's part? Call it out to everyone with recognition.

- Showing humanity without thought of reward should occasionally be rewarded. Someone just takes it on to clear out the ancient files clogging that unused office, getting them shredded and shipped out. Someone offers to take a job candidate to lunch when the interviewers ran late. A person organizes meals to be delivered to a sick colleague. Thank them. Your humans will notice.

- *Managers:* Did an employee make your life easier? The employee might have given you small favors of time or attention or taken over a routine task when you were extra busy. A small consideration like this deserves a small award. Volunteering to give you a big hand with a project deserves a more substantial shout-out.

When to Recognize

Recognition should be available for everyone, from anyone. Because peer-to-peer recognition is so memorable, all employees should keep their eyes and ears open for moments that deserve recognition. Managers should make a habit of asking themselves, "Has anyone here done something worthy of notice and gratitude?"

Recognition should come as close to the event inspiring it as possible, when the memory of a moment's action and the result are fresh. This inspires others on a team to understand how certain actions are exceptional and reinforces the message of gratitude. Don't wait for an annual performance review or quarterly check-in; the recognition system will make a record of the behavior you can refer to at those times.

Unexpected recognition magnifies its impact. By focusing on company values and employee effort rather than waiting on long-term deliverables and deadlines, the person giving recognition makes it part of the human-to-human connection. Deliverables are in the job description;

recognition is often, but not always, for behavior beyond required results. And the surprise nature of spontaneous thanks breaks recognition away from the organizational routine, which makes it memorable. (Mobile recognition apps make on-the-spot recognition easy.)

How to Make the Greatest Impact

In Chapter 4 ("What Do Employees Want?"), we suggested that specific expressions of gratitude have a lot more impact than simple thanks. How you recognize—your words, timing, and specificity—makes an enormous difference in the impact of a recognition moment. This can be a test for people who are unsure about their writing ability, but taking the time to write a careful recognition message magnifies all the good that recognition awards confer.

The first rule is, Give details. Be as precise and explicit as you can about what someone did that was worthy of recognition. One simple technique is to use the PAR (problem-action-result) template: "Bill heard an unusual ticking sound in the polishing unit and decided it was a potential safety hazard. He shut down the unit, notified his team down the line, and got maintenance to replace a defective bearing that might have resulted in a bigger problem soon. As a result, Bill helped our team maintain its perfect safety record for 2020." Telling a short story like this makes the incident memorable for the recipient and anyone else seeing the award.

Consider that everyone should be comfortable and clear reading your message. The tech team in Belarus is not going to understand the compliment, "Mary is the perfect utility infielder!" (For that matter, many metaphors having to do with sports, gambling, drugs, alcohol, military jargon, or favorite television shows risk falling flat. Also, sexist and other potentially offensive language has no place in recognition.)

When you've taken the time to craft a specific recognition message, encourage others who might see the award to congratulate the recipient, which builds community feeling and amplifies the message.

Use the person's name, and if the message will be read by people who don't know the recipient, add a mention of where they work and what they do. Say something unique about the recipient and describe the person's impact in the context of shared goals. For example:

> ### Your role in our success
>
> I have seldom seen anyone as tenacious as you were, Nina, on the rollout of our latest update—from the evenings you spent building support materials, to the countless meetings you spent building consensus. Our customers noticed, too, and Bill called today to tell me they just got approval on the job. Our success is due in no small part to your perseverance and energy. You truly embody our company value of determination. Thank you for your passion and commitment to excellence. Everyone, please join me in congratulating Nina!

THANK **TALK** CELEBRATE

Jenessa Disler, Bell Flight's manager of Culture and People Development, is structuring performance management around wide-ranging conversations. She says: "As we try to humanize the organization, we talk a lot about the simplicity of continuous conversation, ongoing conversation. In terms of performance management, we have the opportunity to create a system that allows for people to have those honest, vulnerable, authentic and powerful conversations. We're trying to not create a process that managers and employees have to subscribe to, but rather a process that accommodates what people are already doing. How can we encourage authentic, development-focused, meaningful, learning-focused conversations? And what environment will make people feel safe enough to unleash those conversations around the organization?"

Everybody Gives and Receives

Research company Gartner has studied recognition for years, and its analysis offers some subtle advice for practitioners. In a 2018 report the company wrote:

> *While well-intended, purely using recognition and rewards on an infrequent, exclusive and set schedule (e.g., annual) will have limited sustained impact. Key problems include:*
>
> - *Recognition and reward for employment tenure by definition is limited to the population of the employee base reaching the set time thresholds with no additional effort required of the employee.*
> - *Recognizing a winner and runners-up for innovation or outstanding contribution/service only impacts a small group of "winners," and is sometimes only contested and won by the same small group of individuals.*
> - *Many organizations are no longer one-size-fits-all in terms of employment contract type. Even historical categories such as full-time employee and part-time employee are no longer strictly the norm, given the popularity of organizations of also using contingent labor. Moreover, what is meaningful as recognition and reward will be different depending on the individual.[2]*

The report concluded that some of the business practices most positively affected by recognition include engagement, performance management, learning and development, and onboarding. Peer-to-peer recognition helps all these.

Because peer-to-peer recognition is so meaningful to giver and receiver, everyone in the organization should be encouraged to recognize. That's why we think of peer recognition more as everyone-to-everyone programs. Widespread participation magnifies the benefits, and leaders can ensure greater participation in the following ways.

Communicate! Social recognition will be a new practice for most, so to make recognition effective, any rollout of a recognition program should be accompanied by frequent communication about what it's for and how to use it. Be candid about how data will be used and how privacy will be respected. Encourage everyone to practice—like any other work skill, recognition takes a bit of practice.

Share a summary of best practices listed in the "Recognition at a Glance" section above (p. 125). Encourage people to notice one another doing recognition-worthy work. Require managers to adopt frequent recognition habits early, and regularly update everyone on participation rates. Make it clear that everyone is expected to participate, and answer anyone who has questions. This is how any new practice, from cost containment to recycling, gets woven into the daily life of an organization.

Managers and executives with responsibility to approve awards should do so in a *timely way.* This sends the message that recognition is a key part of work, not a nice-to-have.

Identify and address inequity. It's up to leaders to monitor things like award levels and messages and to help prevent mistakes or misuse of the system (we have seen little of the latter, but it can happen). A social recognition system can be set up with alerts to catch innocent mistakes. For example, if two managers each designate a recognition to the same person for the same behavior, one recognition can be modified into congratulations or highlighting an award.

Long after a program is in place, *newcomers can use it to get onboard quickly.* Recognition is a fantastic way for getting new employees quickly oriented to a culture, and it's a surefire way to help employees internalize your company values and understand what it means to live them. Nominate new employees soon after they begin to resonate with your values and goals, and then invite them to notice and recognize their peers for doing excellent work. This helps them understand how their work and their efforts align to company values and contribute to company goals.

The Facts About Frequency

One fact about recognition that surprises first-time practitioners is that it is more effective to spread the same value of awards over a year than to give it all at once.

Psychologists have learned that the frequency of positive reinforcement is more important to human happiness than its intensity.[3] We can illustrate this finding with a calendar.

Many companies give individuals an annual bonus. Let's say it's $2,000, paid at the start of the year. If you map the relationship of a 625-person company from the point of view of a person receiving a bonus, it looks like Figure 8.1.

There's the relationship—"the company" gives individual bonuses. Let's say in this case the company has given Amy an annual bonus of $2,000.

We know from research that the psychological "glow" of good feeling, engagement, energy, and attachment to the company from that award lasts about three or four weeks. After that, Amy's emotional attachment to the organization returns to a set point—a kind of equilibrium. Figure 8.2 maps that surge in positivity.

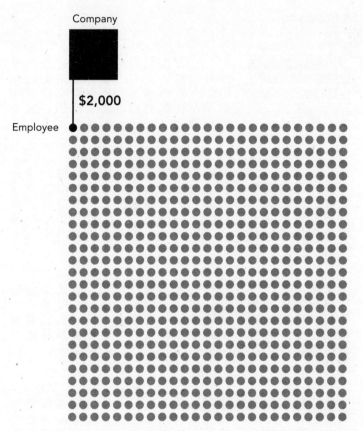

Figure 8.1 The bonus awarded once a year by a traditional company.

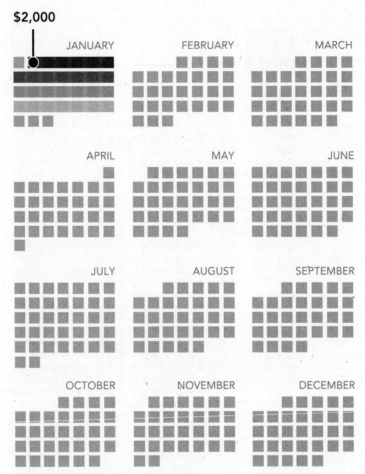

Figure 8.2 The traditional bonus creates a surge of positive feelings for three or four weeks.

There are two big problems with this. The first is that when that $2,000 is spent, there's no fuel left to boost Amy's engagement anytime in the following 48 weeks. The second is that the award came from one place, "the company" or the manager, and we've lost the advantages of peers adding value and boosting the energy and engagement mutually. There's no connection built between Amy and her colleagues. There's no network effect or strengthening of remote ties. It's fine as far as it goes, but this scenario misses a lot of opportunities to improve overall performance and engagement.

As an alternative, let's see what happens when that same $2,000 is spread out in smaller increments of $50 or $100 or $250 throughout the year, empowering managers, peers, colleagues, and other people all over to recognize Amy's contributions and work. Amy receives frequent messages in a great variety, from all over, reinforcing how much her colleagues value her and how valuable her contributions are to others. Amy's calendar of positive surges would look like Figure 8.3.

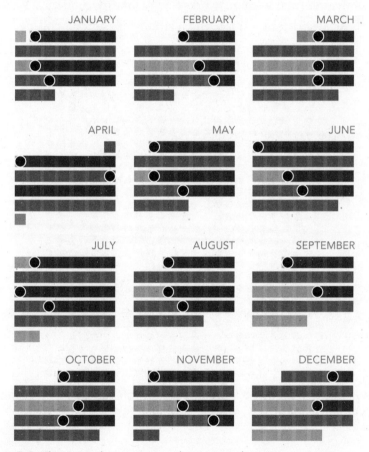

Figure 8.3 The same bonus, spread out over the year, maintains a steady surge of positivity and good feelings about the company.

These awards are not all coming from the big, faceless company. They're coming from colleagues showing gratitude—a steady stream of goodwill. They're coming from different departments and levels of seniority, and maybe one comes from the CEO. Each one of those awards, each one of those thank you moments, will give Amy a three- or four-week lift, and they will all overlap. You'll have stimulus right through the year. For the same investment, the positive effect on Amy is spread out over the entire year.

But it's not just about Amy! There's another advantage to frequent recognition in an everyone-to-everyone program. It provides a richer view of the informal social networks that help work get done. When you map those awards, you can see the relationships among colleagues and peers. (See Figure 8.4.)

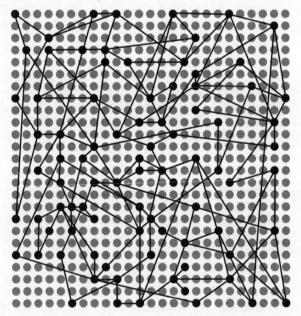

Figure 8.4 Crowdsourced, peer-to-peer recognition creates a map of the company's "positivity network," giving insights to performance and relationships.

Every one of those lines in Figure 8.4 represents a moment of gratitude given and received. Every connection means that a positive action and attitude have been documented. Every connection means that the results of that action and the values it embodied were recorded. Among humans, the swell of positivity becomes a tidal force. And for the company, the record of recognition maps who is doing good work, how good work is done, and where recognition-worthy behavior is happening. Dive into the data that this network represents, and you'll find out:

- Where innovation is thriving and where it needs improvement
- Where safety is top of mind
- Where customer services rise to the level of obsession
- Where a group is lagging or needs help understanding how to put a company value into practice

All this activity, captured and analyzed, is literally the story of the organization—all positive and all creating greater community.

Cisco analyzed data from nearly 60,000 employees who received awards in their program, called Connected Recognition. The analysis showed a strong positive correlation between engagement and more frequent, smaller awards received throughout the year. In fact, the most engaged Cisco employees received an award every 30 to 40 days and from at least 10 unique nominators throughout the year—an effect symbolically appropriate for the leader in networking technology.[4]

Lessons from a Handbag

"My chief of staff lives in Dublin, and she earns recognition awards from people for the work that she's done because she is just outstanding. The other day she was visiting in the office and the strap on her old handbag broke. I joked with her, 'Oh, I guess we haven't paid you enough—you need to replace that bag.'

"She said, 'No—I bought this handbag using my Bravo! points from lots of recognition awards, and I just love it because it reminds me of this person and that person and all the people whose awards enabled me to have this beautiful bag.'

"That everyday symbolism is one of the things about our Bravo! program that I love. In 2019, we had 58,000 moments of recognition globally, and 90% of those were peer-to-peer."

—Christina Hall, CHRO, LinkedIn

Calculating the ROI of Recognition

"Recognition is an investment in people," says Gabrielle Thompson of Cisco. "It's going to retain talent. If you've got the right talent, you're going to drive revenue growth. It's an initial investment with a future payoff."

Recognition more than pays for itself, and like every other strategic business practice, it needs to be assessed on the results it delivers. Even the intangible benefits of social recognition, such as a feeling of belonging and goodwill, lead to quantifiable, dollars-and-cents returns.

One of the clearest calculations on which to judge recognition is its effect on voluntary turnover. Let's run some math on a sample company with an 11 percent voluntary turnover rate, which is below the US 2018 average (Figure 8.5).[5]

As the figure shows, the bottom-line turnover costs are $41.3 million. Assuming frequent recognition decreases that $41.3 million by half, the cost of turnover would come to $20.65 million.* Even if the company's recognition program reduced turnover by just 20 percent, the savings would more than compensate for the 1 percent of payroll benchmark number (at a $400 million total payroll cost).

Again, smaller and more frequent awards are more effective in reducing the probability of leaving than larger, less frequent awards. In a typical case study, we found a drop in turnover probability relates to scales of frequency and size of award (Figure 8.6).

---

* We've noted (in Chapter 7) that industrial company Eaton found that those who received just three to five recognition awards had a 50 percent lower rate of quitting. LinkedIn showed similar results.

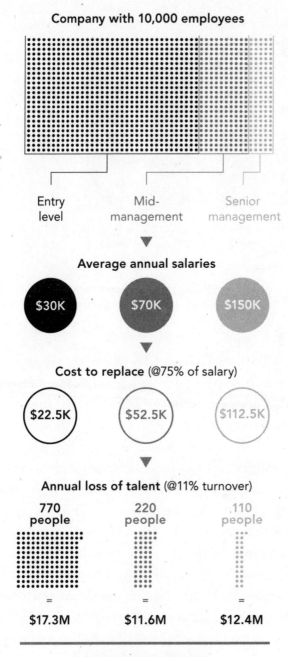

Figure 8.5 Calculating turnover cost in a 10,000-person company.

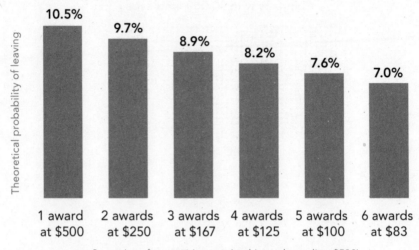

Figure 8.6 Frequent Small Awards Decrease Turnover
Smaller, more frequent awards are more effective than larger, less frequent awards.

Industrial firms, which have a lower average per capita salary, can double the decrease in their turnover when they invest 80 percent more in a recognition program. Technology firms, which tend to have higher compensation, achieve the same effect when they increase investment by 50 percent.

Relative comparisons also make the case for an investment in recognition. For example, we saw earlier that social recognition increases employee engagement. Abundant research from organizations like Gallup shows that organizations that are the best in engaging their employees achieve earnings-per-share growth that is more than four times that of their competitors. Business units in the top quartile of engagement achieve 21 percent higher profitability and better employee health.[6] Unless your organization is in that top quartile, the 1 percent investment is easy to estimate based on improving engagement.

A more detailed way to understand recognition's return on investment is to view its net effect as the sum of improving three large categories of performance indicators, as seen in Figure 8.7.

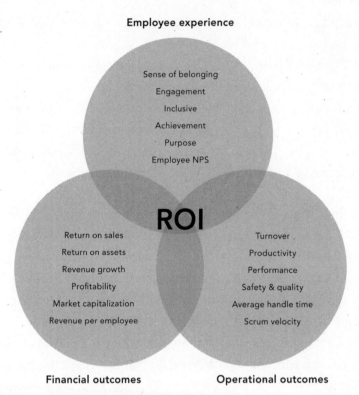

Figure 8.7 Where Recognition ROI Is Found
Full ROI combines improvements in three overarching domains of business.

Workhuman has a formula called the Workhuman Recognition Index, combining operational factors of a recognition program: reach + frequency + value + connectivity.

Let's look at productivity as an example. Research published by Workhuman and a business consultancy found that the firm's consultants exceeded their target billable hours by as much as 3.6 percent when they were more frequently recognized. In 2018 the Human Capital Management Institute performed an analysis of its member companies and found that Workhuman customers showed average increases in employee productivity of $1,737 per employee versus companies that were not Workhuman customers. For a 15,000-person organization, that would produce an annual benefit of $26 million compared with industry peers.[7]

As Figure 8.7 indicates, the ROI of recognition is multifaceted, and isolating one factor doesn't show the comprehensive argument to add social recognition to a company's culture. As a matter of business practice, it's good to calculate the validity of investing in any program. As a matter of making a workplace more human, more cohesive, and more engaging, social recognition pays for itself in tangible and intangible benefits.

It's good business to judge human-centric practices in business terms like ROI, but in the final analysis, the intangible benefits have enormous value that grows over time. And so the choice is not either being good to the business or being good to the people. It's not *either-or*; it's *both-and*. Both profits *and* people. Both leading in numbers *and* leading in the employee experience. Both growth *and* gratitude.

We'll let Kat Cole, COO and president, North America at FOCUS Brands and a favorite speaker at Workhuman Live, have the last word in this chapter:

Often, choosing the work human value side of things has a super solid business case. Sometimes it doesn't. As someone who runs a business, I would be failing you if I didn't allow for that. [But] I really struggle to think about positive people practices that don't have a financial ROI. In our company, we're constantly working on improving the employee experience, whether it's paternal leave policies or vacation or flexible work . . . all of that costs money. But losing talent costs a ton. We have to remember that people build the overall value of the business. And if we don't do these things, we will diminish the value we're getting out of the people.

What Recognition Is Not

Recognition is not vague. "Thanks for all you do" is not recognition. It is a platitude. And your employees recognize it as one. To be impactful, recognition must be specific and call out exactly what was so remarkable.

Recognition is not an entitlement. Recognition should never be applied evenly to everyone regardless of merit. This reduces appreciation to a meaningless perk and robs it of all meaning and power. If someone hasn't been recognized in a while, it might be tempting to give a token award . . . but not if the person hasn't earned recognition.

Recognition is not focused on the company or manager. One critical mistake some managers make is to assume that employees will enjoy what they themselves enjoy. Great recognition is focused solely on the employee's contribution and empowers the recipient to choose a tangible award.

Recognition is not a popularity contest. Good recognition is thoughtful and transparent and must be given always on the basis of merit and never on the basis of popularity.

Recognition is not an incentive. Incentives are expected and come as a result of meeting a set goal. Recognition comes spontaneously based on performance. Incentives have their place, but they are not recognition and will not elicit the same results.

Recognition is not one-size-fits-all. Different people respond to different motivations. Recognition awards should be respectful of that uniqueness, particularly when you are connecting recognition with a tangible reward to make it more lasting. Ensure that recognition and reward also incorporate individual choice.

Recognition is not trinkets and trash. Don't make the mistake of letting a pin or trophy stand as a surrogate for a heartfelt message of thanks and a meaningful reward. Years ago, these items were the currency of recognition, but most of them are gathering dust in the back of closets.

Recognition is not an annual event. Don't save it up for the annual performance conversation. If recognition for good work isn't timely, employees may not put forth the same amount of discretionary effort or even understand what the most valuable behaviors are and when you want them (and others) repeated.

CONSIDER THIS

Set a timer for five minutes. Think of someone who helped you in your work. Compose a message of gratitude to the person. Tell the person what he or she did and the impact it had on you. Don't stop writing for five minutes. When you are finished, pause a moment, and then describe the effect that expressing gratitude has on you.

For managers with budgetary authority: Calculate the cash value of 1 percent of your payroll. If you were to build out this 1 percent without expanding the total expenditure of your budget, how much would you have to deduct from other line items such as:

- Training
- Travel and entertainment
- Outside vendors and services
- Bonuses, merit pay increases, and other direct payments

9 | Performance Management

The Ultimate Learning Technology Is Conversation

HUMAN MOMENTS

The Leadership & Organizational Development team of CAE (a global leader in training for the civil aviation, defense and security, and healthcare markets) was given the task of completely overhauling its performance management process. Manager Lisa Stedel-Smith describes the process of reinvigorating the review:

"It came out loud and clear in our employee surveys that our performance management process was not contributing to a positive employee experience. Our CEO said, 'We need to blow this up,' and gave us full support."

CAE employees worked hard all year, but the once-a-year performance evaluation was focused on a five-point rating scale, not the rich feedback and development piece of the conversation. Ratings weren't adding value; they were detracting from what the conversation needed to be about.

Stedel-Smith says, "CAE instituted a new system called CAE+me focused on ongoing, frequent one-to-one conversations, multisource feedback, and agile goal setting. We make it an open conversation that they may have a number of times throughout the year, and user experience and value is at the center of this approach. It's opening up the dialogue and people are having more authentic conversations. . . . It was a whole mindset shift from performance management to performance development, and it's about growing, developing people, transparency, and the user experience."

Marine Messin, CAE's director of Leadership & Organizational Development, adds: "The rating system just gives management a false sense of security. This is more transparent and creates a richer conversation and understanding. And yes, it requires more courage from leaders."

Eric wrote *The Crowdsourced Performance Review* in 2013, just as leading companies were taking a hard look at their performance management systems. What we believed in 2013—that the traditional performance management system was broken and new models of continuous performance improvement would take hold—has become common wisdom today.

For example, researchers at the management consultancy Deloitte found that performance management procedures consumed close to *2 million hours a year*, much of that spent behind closed doors discussing outcomes of the process. The finding led them to a radical redesign of Deloitte's performance management system.[1] Large firms like Accenture, Cigna, Adobe, and GE also overhauled their performance management systems and philosophy.

Traditional performance management systems relied on a regular cycle of goal setting and review. Employees were given goals at the beginning of the year, and at the end of the year they would review their results with a manager in the formal performance review conversation that business writer Daniel Pink called a form of kabuki theater—a highly stylized ritual. Then new annual goals were decided, and the process lapsed for the next 52 weeks. (Compensation systems were similarly engineered to "plan forward, review backward.") Despite those kinds of efforts in many companies, only 2 in 10 American employees said their performance was managed in a way that motivates them to do outstanding work.[2]

The business environment no longer tolerates this ponderous pace. Conditions change too quickly, and performance management has to become as responsive to change as the rest of the organization. Setting annual targets and reviewing them later is giving way to continuous conversation and assessment of where the employee, team, and business are going right now.

The focus on organizational agility has accelerated the use of continuous feedback. At GE, for example, performance conversations return to two basic questions: "What am I doing that I should keep doing? And what am I doing that I should change?" The answers might change depending on the competitive environment, financial needs, or innovative ideas.

Since 2013, we've seen that crowdsourcing performance management with peer-to-peer feedback is indeed more effective and more equitable than the old ranking systems. In addition, we've seen the growth of several trends that show great results in a human enterprise:

- The performance conversation focuses more on positive than negative feedback.
- The conversation is becoming more focused on learning and growth.
- Greater emphasis is placed on small, incremental, concrete check-ins throughout the year.
- The manager's role evolves from command-and-control to coaching.

- There is much more sophisticated use of data analysis and more subtle insights into performance factors, such as hidden influence and invisible micro-biases.
- Apps similar to social media and project-sharing software provide new ways of using conversation to manage performance.

The folks in the HR community have led these trends because they understand the flaws in traditional performance management. Today, only about half of HR professionals think their current performance appraisal process is accurate. And they are doing something about it.

EXPERT INSIGHT

"The biggest limitation of annual reviews . . . is this: With their heavy emphasis on financial rewards and punishments and their end-of-year structure, they hold people accountable for past behavior at the expense of improving current performance and grooming talent for the future, both of which are critical for organizations' long-term survival. In contrast, regular conversations about performance and development change the focus to building the workforce your organization needs to be competitive both today and years from now.[3]

—Peter Cappelli and Anna Tavis, writing in
Harvard Business Review

Flip the Focus

When you move away from command-and-control environments, the entire person becomes the center of business strategy. As the team at CAE discovered, an annual ranking system is an encumbrance rather than a facilitator of performance. Periodically assigning a number to people based on the performance of the past year is essentially dehumanizing—as if you could contain all the experiences and work of a year into a single digit. If we did that to companies or the national economy, we might briefly understand where we are in a given moment, but we'd never understand how we got there or where we intend to go. We use detailed financial and economic analysis to understand those; why should people be different?

Almost no employees look forward to a traditional annual appraisal. They approach it with at best a nervous expectation that they will find approval and at worst anxiety. If they have prepared for the review, they try to remember times in the past 52 weeks when they were proficient. Perhaps they remember getting a bit of recognition or praise six months earlier. Even when they approach the review with confidence, there's a sense of being judged—because they *are* being judged.

When do employees look forward to an annual appraisal? When it's done with a manager who they genuinely feel has an authentic interest in their development. When they know the manager will be fair and impartial (although most appraisals are subjective by nature). When they have a clear picture of how they have done throughout the year because they can review it in detail—week by week or month by month.

Even in that positive case, when you step back and view the annual appraisal, the greatest flaw is its structural focus on past performance, driven by a bureaucratic need to divide up rewards in terms of bonuses, merit pay increases, and potential career tracks. Gary Hamel observes, "One of the great flaws of all traditional organizations is that people compete for a scarce resource called promotion, and it is a zero-sum game."[4]

The classic old-school review was focused about 80 percent on the past ("... and that's why we're giving you a 3 percent raise") and 20 percent on the future ("Here are your goals ...").

The key is to flip the focus from past performance to future development. Employees and the organization are better served when we reverse that ratio. Make the discussion 20 percent about the past and 80 percent about the future. And since "the future" becomes an ever-changing present, the best performance management is designed to help employees deal with that degree of change right at the time it happens.

Large organizations are getting the message: About 70 percent of multinational companies have been moving toward a future-focused model of performance assessment. They face headwinds in the form of bureaucratic inertia and competing models of how to focus forward most effectively, but the movement is well under way.[5]

Performance management in the human enterprise resembles the rest of work: It's not a frozen moment in time but a continuous process of incremental change and adjustment. One end of the continuum is positive feedback, and the other end of the continuum is developmental feedback.

Positive Versus Negative Feedback

According to Dr. David Rock, cofounder and executive director of the NeuroLeadership Institute, the current state of feedback is broken. He noted, "Feedback either does nothing, or makes things worse, more often than it makes things better." The misconceptions are that we hate feedback, that it's best to focus on errors, and that feedback must be giver-driven.[6]

EXPERT INSIGHT

"What we want, the common denominator that I found in every single interview, is we want to be validated. We want to be understood. I have done over 35,000 interviews in my career and as soon as that camera shuts off everyone always turns to me and inevitably in their own way asks this question "Was that OK?" I heard it from President Bush, I heard it from President Obama. I've heard it from heroes and from housewives. I've heard it from victims and perpetrators of crimes. I even heard it from Beyoncé and all of her Beyoncéness. She finishes performing, hands me the microphone, and says, 'Was that OK?' Friends and family, yours, enemies, strangers in every argument in every encounter, every exchange I will tell you, they all want to know one thing: Was that OK? Did you hear me? Do you see me?"[7]

—Oprah Winfrey

In fact, humans crave feedback because that's how we learn everything from the moment we're born. Positive feedback reinforces behavior with positive feelings such as pride or a sense of accomplishment. Unfortunately, traditional feedback styles often feel negative. They affirm the bureaucratic power imbalance between manager and employee; i.e., one is allowed to criticize and direct, the other to accept criticism and be directed. Feedback that focuses on errors is helpful in the context of learning to do better. Studies show that we benefit from, and even crave, critical feedback, but that it should always be given in a committed, thoughtful, and fair way for maximum effect. While it may be tempting to avoid giving critical feedback, it's important not to dodge it, especially when it is requested by someone who wants to improve.

This might seem obvious, but peoples' fear of criticism can only be overcome when developing and growing the individual becomes more important than preserving and growing the structures of control. People who think critical feedback is given and received without fear in their organization should ask themselves how freely they criticize their boss.

"Developmental feedback" sounds like a euphemism for criticism, but there are key differences between them. Developmental feedback centers on the person, not the organization. It is about growth—acquiring skills and experience, taking initiative, learning new information, or broadening one's point of view. Developmental feedback analyzes failures and mistakes in detail, in a spirit of accountability but not punishment. The difference is critical, because accepting failure and admitting mistakes fuel greater trust and risk taking.

Developmental feedback is not about being nice but about empowering people. Steve Jobs was famous for his verbal assaults on employees whose work he found disappointing. Less widely known was his ability to detach his judgment from personal animosity or prejudice. "If you had a flaming fight with him one day, the next day it would most likely be business as usual," writes Apple marketing executive Ken Segall. "The hard reset ensured that every situation would be dealt with on its merits."[8] Setting Jobs's temperament aside, his purpose was to continually push people to do their best work.

Marcus Buckingham and Ashley Goodall, in their excellent *Nine Lies About Work*, reviewed what we know about positivity with this striking observation: "Positive attention . . . is 30 *times* more powerful than negative attention in creating high performance on a team. . . . [If] all our efforts are directed at giving and receiving negative feedback more often and more efficiently, then we're leaving enormous potential on the table. People don't need feedback. They need attention, and moreover, attention to what they do the best."[9]

> Positive attention . . . is 30 times more powerful than negative attention in creating high performance on a team.

Other research shows that positive feedback prepares employees to receive negative feedback and helps them make use of constructive criticism. Positivity engenders confidence and psychological safety, which changes the emotional perception of criticism from threatening to helpful.[10]

Our point of view is that feedback should be, at a minimum, five to one positive to negative. Managers should tend toward authentic positive feedback, which is basically a form of recognition. Whether that's in the form of awards or simply conversations, positive feedback should be offered in a dedicated recognition program, which in the daily flurry of e-mails and messages offers an oasis of goodness and positivity.

Fast and Frequent

Peter Cappelli, director of the Wharton School's Center for Human Resources, and Anna A. Tavis of New York University have written that the agile organizational model demands more frequent performance assessments. When employees' work becomes project-based, in flexible teams with different leaders and facing different challenges, the notion of a single annual review makes little sense. Instead, individuals can get multiple feedback from many sources covering a wide range of activities, throughout the work year. Cappelli and Tavis cite giant companies in retail, pharma, insurance, finance, and other industries as successfully transitioning to a continuous feedback process.[11]

Giving and receiving feedback is a place where the tenets of the human enterprise converge with the need to be more agile and flexible. Frequent feedback addresses recent performance, which is clearer and fresher in the mind of both giver and receiver. It can come from one individual manager or a team of peers. It can change emphasis, for example, emphasizing Six Sigma quality on one project and rapid development on another. Even if a person's job tasks remain the same, fast and frequent feedback is more discreetly focused on the most critical parts of the job; the reviewer doesn't have to attempt a full review of every bit of performance, just the most critical. If people are trying to improve performance in one area, they don't have to wait a year to get feedback. Instead, they can try a new technique, and if no improvement appears, the review can empower them to try something else. That mirrors the fast development and iteration cycles of an agile business.

Research firm Gartner suggested ways in which new forms of performance management are evolving from older ideas like cascading goals (setting goals from the top down) and management by objectives. In a 2018 report, Gartner researchers wrote of continuous improvement measures, including frequent check-ins, the use of key results for more frequent goal management, and performance management linked to learning management systems.[12] They also wrote that learning systems need to be more user-controlled, with employees deciding what they needed to learn and shorter learning content and study cycles. They added, "A key use case we see is to link a recognition platform to the performance management process so that any recognition is visible and recorded as part of the employee record." Learning and developing one's skills deserves recognition as much as hitting a goal, because in an agile organization, learning is central to success.

EXPERT INSIGHT

"Leaders can become nervous about performance conversations out of fear of hurting people. They shy away from being fully present. But when we come to the conversation with more mindful presence, with compassion, it can transform the nature of how we communicate. Then, it isn't just about how someone needs to change, but how can I enable that change. What do they need from me as a leader that supports the change and helps them perform better? This mindful perspective can alter the entire experience for both parties in the conversation."

—Marissa Afton, US Director and Global
Accounts Lead at The Potential Project

It's All About the Learning

In Chapter 1, we discussed the ways in which a human enterprise adjusts to a changing environment. Change requires employees and teams to master new capabilities, and this means that learning is inseparable from performing well over time.

In the 30 years since MIT professor Peter Senge popularized the term *learning organization*, his proposals such as personal mastery and team learning have become so widely accepted that it's hard to remember that traditional corporate structures were once designed to restrict the flow of information, protect expertise, and hoard power. Traditional corporate learning was built around a model of preparing select individuals for promotion and advancement into leadership; others would stay in their place.[13] The human enterprise rejects that limiting view. It embraces learning because it confers competitive advantage and also opens a path to greater job satisfaction and even happiness.

Learning should be part of most employees' goals for reasons beyond job mastery. Humans are curious. Learning is energizing and satisfying. Employees with a range of skills are more flexible when the team or organization has to adjust to change.

Employees who grow and expand their opportunities are more likely to stay with the organization. The feeling of achievement and self-esteem that accompanies learning raises the overall positivity of the culture. A company need not require every instance of microlearning to justify itself in a direct return on investment.

Companies that offer online courses can spread responsibility for the learning function from a centralized training department out to the individual. Employees can choose courses that they believe will best supplement or expand their skills and take those courses on a just-in-time basis. They become accountable for their development. When employees and managers then rate courses for their usefulness, a customized "curriculum" can become widely known and adds to the crowdsourced narrative of what works best for that organization. Online learning developers are making this more convenient by presenting brief, "microlearning" courses that teach a specific skill. A junior manager, for example, can become better at planning work by studying the basics of project management software without having to complete the entire certification course required by the Project Management Institute.

Formal learning systems like these are one component of a culture of learning and growth, but they are not the most powerful component. The ultimate learning technology is *conversation*.

THANK **TALK** CELEBRATE

Vikki Sly, chief people officer at Blue Prism, a 2,000-employee visual analytics firm, believes frequent, authentic conversation is a central part of performance management. Speaking to Workhuman in 2018, when she was VP of Global Talent at Qlik, she said, "Conversations® (the performance management component of Workhuman Cloud) works because it's fueled from a source of positivity. It's changed the conversation from evaluative and backward-looking to one that is future-oriented. We are able to proactively implement learning solutions before a knowledge gap arises."[14]

Ongoing communication among all members of the human enterprise weaves learning into the flow of work: Conversation between manager and employee. Conversation among peers. Conversation with far-flung members of the company who might otherwise never meet or exchange ideas.

We are talking about the conversations that solve a problem, cross-pollinate ideas, create serendipitous connections, and challenge someone to see situations from a new angle.

In the human enterprise, everyone is a student, and everyone is potentially a coach. Employees anywhere are surrounded by an invisible network of skills, ideas, reactions, insights, and life experiences from others. A culture of learning, of giving and receiving, and of reaching out for help makes the invisible network visible. It's impossible to know in advance what benefits will appear, but it's certain that they will.

EXPERT INSIGHT

"Leaders commonly say, 'We only hire A players. We don't tolerate B players.' The reality is that B players can become A players if you treat them in a way that makes them feel truly grateful."

—Adam Grant, Wharton professor
and author of *Originals*

The Performance Management Network

Continuous learning means feedback can come from anywhere (Figure 9.1). Picture a network of resources surrounding a single employee. The employee in the center of this network is responsible for reaching out and actively learning—self-management. That can only happen in a culture of trust. If you reach out, the resources will be there. Recognition and social connection help build the trust that encourages this kind of initiative.

Figure 9.1 A Feedback Universe
Employees are surrounded by potential feedback. Trust is the key to openly seeking and receiving it.

Imagine how that simple statement upends the old paternalistic corporate model. The days of top management selecting elite employees early in their careers and putting them on a predictable track up the ladder are long gone because the ladder has been replaced by a lattice. As any HR professional or career counselor knows, most careers now resemble a mosaic of job positions, employers, and job status (full time, freelance, etc.). With new opportunity and new instability in the job markets, employees must decide what they do best, what they value most, and how they can advance in the direction they choose.

This change in career management has been going on for at least two decades, and in recent years organizational management has converged with the change. Instead of job goals cascading down from on high, goals and projects rise up from the front line of employees, where creative inspiration and new innovations germinate.

THANK **TALK** CELEBRATE

People find their work more meaningful when they understand the connection between what they do and the bigger purpose and strategic goals of the organization. Helping employees understand how their personal priorities and goals line up with and support the organization's strategic goals should be a top-priority conversation in goal-setting one-on-one meetings.

Let's take a deeper look at the levels of performance management feedback in Figure 9.1.

Self-Management

Self-management means an employee takes the initiative by setting goals in consultation with a manager, directly connecting the goals to a team-level and enterprise-level priority.

Recognition has a role to play in self-management. As people receive recognition with detailed descriptions from another point of view, they develop greater awareness of how their actions affect other people and shared goals.

The Manager as Coach

The next level of performance management feedback resides with the manager, who is more coach than commander. Gallup suggests the importance of continuous feedback between manager and employee. Both the quantity and quality of their conversations need to improve: "Employees need to talk with their managers about their progress more than once or twice a year to effectively improve performance. As is often the case, communication is crucial for that relationship to succeed. Employees who strongly agree they have had conversations with their manager in the last six months about their goals and successes are 2.8 times more likely than other employees to be engaged."

Unfortunately, Gallup also reports that most organizations are a long way from achieving this ideal state: "While the frequency of these conversations must increase, the content of these ongoing conversations also needs to feel purposeful. Currently, most managers are not providing the type of feedback necessary to drive better performance. Only 23% of employees strongly agree their manager provides meaningful feedback to them, and 26% of employees strongly agree the feedback they receive helps them do better work. Those who strongly agree with these feedback elements are more likely to be engaged than other employees (3.5 times and 2.9 times, respectively), demonstrating the need for managers to learn how to coach their employees more effectively."[15] That sort of developmental conversation ought to be really happening every six to eight weeks, with operational check-ins happening on a weekly or biweekly basis.

Workhuman surveys show an overwhelming employee preference for continuous check-ins, whether the conversation is purely positive feedback or constructive and developmental feedback (Figure 9.2).[16]

This preference is the reason we emphasize conversation and check-ins as an essential part of a continuous performance management practice. If it's an authentic conversation happening between manager and employee, it's more an ongoing conversation than a formal, structured meeting. Our teams at Workhuman strive for an authentic, honest flow of conversation, and we find that developmental feedback happens quite naturally in that context. When manager and employee have mutual respect for each other, mutual interest in each other's development, and mutual interest in moving forward together successfully, continuous performance management becomes completely different from the obsolete rank-and-comment system.

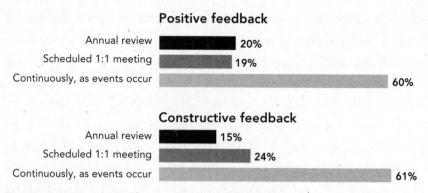

Figure 9.2 People Prefer Continuous Feedback
Workhuman surveys show that employees prefer feedback of any kind to be delivered continuously.

THANK **TALK** CELEBRATE

It's hard to trust someone you don't know. The best way to get to know people better is by talking together more often. At work, where we all have priorities and to-do lists, encouraging those conversations is important. Recent research conducted by Workhuman showed workers who check in with managers at least weekly as opposed to never are more than two times as likely to trust their manager, nearly two times as likely to respect their manager, five times less likely to be disengaged, and nearly two times as likely to believe they can grow in the organization.[16]

Being a manager is about being a leader. Leaders have different styles, but based on all the evidence we've seen in today's multigenerational, global workforce, the most successful mindset is coaching-oriented. It's also highly efficient on a team basis because when you model that kind of developmental dialogue, team members learn to do it among themselves. Continuous learning and striving for improvement become cultural assets.

The frequency of performance discussions is central to the manager-employee level of feedback, and the simple operating rule is, More is better. Research shows that 54 percent of high-performing organizations provide feedback at least quarterly, compared with 35 percent of all others. Of those high performers, more than 30 percent require performance discussions on a monthly or even more frequent basis.[18]

Does coaching work if an employee is highly introverted? Jenessa Disler of Bell Flight has run into that and similar problems. She says:

> When a person just simply doesn't communicate in my style, I have to adapt my approach. You can't train for every situation, but you can think about how you might communicate differently. If I notice that I'm not getting a lot of input, or not having any influence in a typical performance discussion, I'll ask more simple and focused questions, and we'll keep the focus on the project, not the person.
>
> Sometimes we don't talk at all about work. Instead, I engage in more casual conversation, just to build trust and comfort with that person. If you're reading between the lines and shifting your approach appropriately, you can move on later to that more rich conversation.

Frequent performance discussions are key to establishing priorities, which begins with an employee initiative in naming them and continues with a deeper discussion of how an individual's most important tasks align with the priorities of the organization as a whole. At this time, managers lead with questions like, "How does that result in our need to control costs?" and "If you have to choose just three of these priorities among your tasks, what are they and why did you choose them?" Managers help employees relate their work to organizational values as well, and because these are part of the performance discussions, they restate the importance of values more emphatically than any poster on a wall.

Frequency also fosters comfort with asking for feedback. It is less formal and more flexible than administrative-driven performance reviews, and because it happens frequently, the focus is on achievement and progress, without the compensation question hovering over the discussion. When most of the feedback is positive, developmental feedback feels more constructive than critical.

THANK **TALK** CELEBRATE

Can anyone be a good coach? The basic qualities of a good coach are clear in any field, whether that's business, sports, or life skills, and they can be learned. Coaching is an ongoing conversation among team members, led by the leader whose job it is to make people perform at their maximum potential. Coaches:

- Are sharp-eyed observers of each individual's strengths and weaknesses
- Balance and adjust teams for maximum effectiveness and change the mixture according to the project or situation
- Communicate the individual's contribution to the shared goal
- Guarantee that team members have what they need to get the job done—equipment, practice, knowledge, time
- Show team members how to coach each other
- Pause the action frequently enough for everyone to understand the situation
- Strengthen connections among the team and the people outside the team with whom they work
- Communicate the team's progress wherever it needs to be shared

We think of these frequent, focused, and less formal performance discussions as check-ins, similar to project status meetings, but concentrating on continuous improvement for the employee. As more jobs trend toward interacting with data and applications, and the life cycle for both becomes shorter and shorter, check-ins help adjust the dynamic flow of work. What emerges is less a checklist against a job description than a "job canvas," which Deloitte describes as a job that takes a more expansive, meaningful view of what needs to be done.[19] The job of any coach is to help people perform; in an ever-changing work environment, the job of the coach is to help people change.

EXPERT INSIGHT

Cy Wakeman, a perennial favorite speaker at Workhuman Live, shares this pithy advice for both sides of the performance discussion:

- "Most of the evidence on happiness shows that a majority of your current happiness level is not driven by circumstances; it's driven by the accountability you take for your circumstances."
- "Keep things conversational *so they never need to get* confrontational."
- "The *traditional* performance review . . . is like a punch in the face to the ego.
  - The power of a leader is not what you tell people; it's what you get people thinking about.
  - The best formula for growth is short, factual feedback and great assignments.
  - Work as hard to find out how feedback is true as you do to find ways it isn't true."
- "The ability to take any feedback without defense frees you up to learn so much about yourself."

The Team and the Crowd

We've noted that high-performing teams of today behave more as a network than a hierarchy, with shared authority and shared goals. Team members know each other's strengths and where they need to be supplemented. Skilled teams collaborate inside and outside their boundaries, and functioning teams even manage conflict in a healthy way that moves their shared goals forward. Teams can be the front line of performance management.

IBM uses team feedback in its agile environment, which is so fast-moving and changeable that monitoring progress from above is almost impossible. In daily team check-ins, members can identify issues, suggest solutions, and keep tabs on the many moving parts of an agile project. Their feedback to one another is captured in a summary app, which anyone—including managers—can use to know what's going on. A good quality of this transparency is that it tends to make feedback constructive and forward-looking and discourages engaging in corporate gamesmanship or undercutting colleagues. (Bad organizational behavior rarely thrives in the open.)[20]

Organizations that rely on more frequent performance reviews are more likely to use peer feedback.[21] This might come from the immediate team or from the network of peers outside the team.

Social recognition that includes these conversations is the ideal platform for tapping the resources and power of the network. The managers don't see everything . . . not even close. And they shouldn't need to see everything when trust is woven into the culture. Team feedback through social recognition means everyone is empowered and accountable for the team's success.

Recognition broadens individual development to become group development. Each recognition moment forges stronger relationships among the team and between the team and others in the organization—and when the recognition platform maps that activity, the manager can see a map of those relationships. Facilitating deeper connections increases departmental and interdepartmental flow of information. It engenders trust between departments.

Leaders can pool data on team members to get a sense of where their department might have weaknesses or soft spots. Say, for example, a department of engineers is getting a lot of recognition for quality, but few for innovation or risk taking. That might indicate a need to take a few more chances on product ideas or to reach out to other departments or resources to cross-pollinate ideas. Perhaps a marketing organization is often recognized for its creativity but rarely noticed by people in sales. Making time to build relationships between the groups can result in new ways they can work together.

THANK **TALK** CELEBRATE

We've adapted another feedback shorthand for managers from our customers at Baker Hughes: *Continue, Consider, Celebrate*. They are three different conversations, so separating them keeps the message simple and memorable:

Continue means a quick check-in that confirms that an employee is on the right track. Here we confirm the actions and information that are delivering desired results and say, "OK, let's keep doing this."

Consider means imagining if something can be done better, or whether a course of action should be abandoned because it isn't delivering value. This is a great weapon in the fight against bureaucracy, as in, "Do we really need to fill out a form to make a $25 purchase?" It also puts the burden of critical thinking on the employee: "We know you're making enough calls, but how can we raise your engagement rate?"

Celebrate might be the most powerful of the three, because celebrating anything—closing a sale, giving a great presentation, learning a new skill—tells everyone what's valuable. Public recognition of even small successes creates positivity and connection among team members. When you celebrate a nonwork event, like someone running a half-marathon for the first time or being named a trustee of the town library, those human connections grow stronger, more open, and are . . . just more *human*.[22]

Data and Conversations

Stacia Sherman Garr of RedThread Research says artificial intelligence applications are on the verge of providing simple, real-time coaching to supplement manager or crowdsourced feedback. "It might come in the form of nudges and suggestions in the flow of work we're doing, helping us make better decisions."

For example, natural language processing can analyze the text of a manager's performance reviews to find inconsistencies in language used for coaching men versus women (more on that in the next chapter). AI can monitor a team's progress on a project, compare milestones and conversations, and suggest more efficient or innovative actions at just the right moment.

Dr. Jesse Harriott, who leads the Workhuman research team, notes that recognition and collaboration applications can use AI to confirm one person's judgment about performance with that of the crowd. Let's say Steve gets recognized a lot for the quality of innovation. Ten people have cited innovation in his social recognition record, but that data point doesn't say *how* Steve does it. Natural language processing can examine the text of all 10 recognition moments. Perhaps it reveals that Steve's innovative ideas all come at the beginning of a project and are focused on reimagining the process or path by which something gets done. Even Steve might not be aware that this is his strength, and that awareness can magnify his effectiveness, because once it's noticed, Steve's gift for reimagining processes can be brought to other teams' work.

Harriott points out that we're still relatively new to this kind of analysis, but the promise of AI to work in partnership with humans to manage performance can hardly be overstated. When designed with care to protect people's privacy and autonomy, AI could help organizations leave the old performance management systems—and the bureaucratic thinking that created them—as a relic of the past.

The promises of AI and continuous conversation are central to a new form of performance management. They challenge us to shake up bureaucracy. And in the next chapter we'll see how AI, conversation, and personal courage can advance a critical HR issue for the twenty-first century: advancing the cause of diversity and inclusion.

Adam Grant: Reward People for Failing

"One of the mistakes that I think too many leaders and too many organizations make is they essentially reward and punish based on results. And what that means is that people feel, 'I'm going to be recognized and celebrated if I achieve my goals, and I might pay a penalty if I don't.'

"That creates a serious culture of risk aversion where people don't want to do anything that would even open up the possibility that they might fall short of their key results and objectives. It's deadly to innovation, which is all about taking risks and running experiments and trying things that haven't been tested or proven yet.

"When you shift accountability to both process and outcomes, there are four potential scenarios: 1) Good process and good results—that's success. 2) Bad process and bad results—that's failure and you learn from it. 3) Bad process and good results—that's luck, and you should be careful about rewarding luck because it's not repeatable. 4) Good process and bad results—that's really interesting because it challenges your set beliefs.

"The innovation opportunity in a Workhuman organization is to say, 'Let's recognize and celebrate anybody who submits an idea that can be tested. Recognize people who are running experiments where there's real uncertainty.'

"The leading indicator of innovation is not the number of ideas that are successful; it's the number of ideas that are tried."

CONSIDER THIS

The next time you're in a meeting, think about each person in the meeting. What are these individuals contributing to the company? How would they respond if you thanked them two or three times a year for something they did well that had an effect on you? It can be something really significant, like a manager assigning you work that's a big stretch, or something minor, like someone offering an idea you never considered. What if the others in the room considered the same about you, and you received their thanks? In a meeting of six people, that means you'd receive a message of thanks every four to six weeks. How would that affect the way you think of your work and its impact?

10 The Future of Diversity and Inclusion

What Began as a Moral Good Has Grown into a Business Necessity

HUMAN MOMENTS

"In a previous job, I led 'Bring Your Children to Work' Day. One year we had 50 or 60 kids in the big executive conference room, and the kids were black, white, girls, boys, Hispanic, Asian. I had never seen that table surrounded by this beautiful gift of diversity. And I'll never forget the moment that I realized *that these were the children of all the employees but none of the executives.*

"I was the CHRO, and only one of two women on the senior team. I checked the statistics of our workforce and saw the clear pattern: People of all backgrounds rose in responsibility and status but once they hit director level, diversity just fell off a cliff. Then I analyzed what was said in the performance reviews and guess what? At the director level, men got 40 percent more "exceeds expectations" rankings than women. The performance evaluation language was skewing the results of the process, and unconsciously diminishing people. I spent the rest of my time at that company doing something about it."

—Renee Kaspar, Chief People Officer,
Octane Lending

To understand where the practice of diversity and inclusion is going, consider a mystery that began more than 100 years ago.

In 1913, the Queen's Hall Orchestra in London accepted six female violinists. They were the first women to perform in a major symphony orchestra. In 1930, harpist Edna Phillips became the first woman to do so in America, in the Philadelphia Orchestra. The Vienna Philharmonic, one of the world's most prestigious symphony orchestras, did not accept a full female member *until 1997*.

Music had been an essential part of middle-class women's education since the seventeenth century, and their private concerts were standard entertainment in upper-class households. And yet men composed 100 percent of symphonic orchestras until quite recently. Was deliberate bias in classical music that slow to change? The complete story turns out to be more subtle than one of conscious discrimination. Directors of symphony orchestras claimed that music was a purely meritocratic business. Musicians auditioned for their jobs, and talent alone won the day. Men were just better musicians than women, they said, and their auditions proved it.

Then, in the 1970s, some orchestras held blind auditions, in which male and female musicians would play behind screens on stage. Their names were withheld from the judges, and they did not speak. Every obvious clue to a musician's sex was removed.

Yet for several years, men still overwhelmingly won even these blind auditions and continued to claim coveted spots in the world's premier orchestras. Why?

The answer was footsteps. Judges were unconsciously identifying players as male or female based on the sound of their footsteps on the stage. Even though judges thought their decisions were unbiased, their brains registered the clue, and without consciously discriminating against the women, the judges still skewed their decisions toward men. When carpet was added to the stage, so that footfalls couldn't be heard, the likelihood of female musicians being chosen increased by 30 percent.[1] A generation later, almost 40 percent of concert orchestra members are women.[2]

It turns out that unconscious bias is more powerful and pervasive than people realize. It changes our perceptions of merit and achievement. Dealing with unconscious bias is the next great challenge in making a human enterprise.

Diversity and Inclusion—Phase 3

Diversity and inclusion (D&I) are top of mind for every organization sensitive to attracting the right talent and building high-performing teams. Recent surveys find D&I is a top priority for CEOs, for reasons we'll summarize below. We also know D&I is important to employees at large, especially the millennial and gen Z employees who will dominate the workforce shortly.

Diversity and inclusion practices are maturing after three decades of compliance-based efforts. *Phase 1* meant recruiting and retaining a more diverse workforce, and this is where many executives still put their effort. Michelle Grover, the VP of engineering at SAP Concur, says diversity efforts that focus solely on recruiting run into the "pipeline problem."

"When I started in technology 20 years ago, there were a lot of women doing basic programming," she remembers. "But as more and more men moved into technology, and moved up, they tended to hire people who looked like them. Now we say, 'We need more women (or minorities or whomever), let's get them.' But there are only so many people out there. What you need is a pipeline set up for the right people of any kind to be ready for work in your industry—and then you have to have people who want to stay here."

It was that last point—wanting to stay with the company—that led to *Phase 2*, which is inclusion. (Many add the term *belonging* to differentiate between inclusion, which is an organizational effort, and belonging, which is a personal feeling. If people feel they don't belong, inclusion efforts are falling short.) Human resources leaders made the case that recruiting a diverse workforce was futile if you couldn't retain people. You'd always be replacing employees who left for organizations where they felt included. And it turns out that inclusion is a lot harder than recruiting. You can't just invite people in, said HR. You have to hear them, act on their perspectives and contributions, and use their different experiences to change the organization according to its values. In the words of Vernā Myers, VP of Inclusion Strategy at Netflix, "Diversity is being invited to the party; inclusion is being asked to dance."

Inclusion and belonging are "enabling emotions"—they set the psychological stage for top performance. Inclusion means empowerment. Belonging is the feeling that "I am here in my full self, respected and fully engaged, with an equal voice."

"Remember when you were a kid, calling dibs on the front seat of the car?" asks Pat Wadors, CHRO of ServiceNow. "I tell people to think about calling DIBs—Diversity, Inclusion, Belonging—because the Urban Dictionary says it's the most powerful force in the universe, the call to oneself. That's the power of belonging—you can create belonging moments, moments of truth that connect humans through stories. If you create moments like that at work about a human relationship, not necessarily a work relationship, you create a tighter community."

EXPERT INSIGHT

What's the difference between diversity, inclusion, and belonging? Anita Sands, a member of five technology boards of directors and a speaker and author, joined us at our Dublin campus to share this insight recently:

"Diversity is a fact. (Did you achieve your numbers?) Inclusion is a choice. (You choose to include someone or not.) Belonging is a feeling. And a feeling beats a fact or a choice any day of the week."

We know that giving gratitude and recognition creates a more inclusive environment. Our customers at OhioHealth completed an analysis of their recognition data and found that if you plot an employee's feelings of inclusion against the number and value of awards the employee receives, you find a one-to-one relationship. The more connections, the more recognition moments that people receive, the more they feel included (see Figure 10.1). It's one more manifestation of the "new community" idea, that an inclusive and grateful and connected workplace can be a force for good in society and a source of happiness in people.

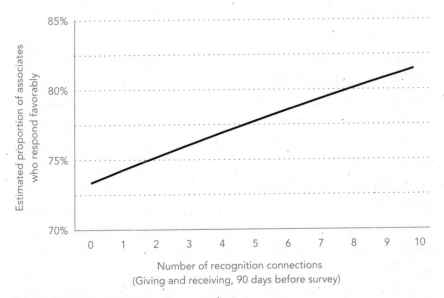

Figure 10.1 Positivity Promotes Inclusion
A greater number of positive relationships leads to a greater feeling of inclusion.

How are we progressing after a generation of D&I efforts? Not fast enough, say CHROs. It's not even a simple matter to quantify how far we've come. For example, even though the companies on the Fortune 500 list are required by law to collect data on employee race and gender, only a fifth release any of that data to the public.[3] Given that diversity and inclusion have been an initiative at thousands of organizations for at least 30 years, why is progress so slow? Can it be possible the overt, intentional discrimination is impervious to all that effort?

We think there's a more subtle dynamic at work in many well-meaning organizations. Like those orchestra judges, employers truly want to approach their work free of prejudices. And like those judges, they mistakenly believe that removing the most obvious bigotry is enough. They don't see the subtle, pervasive internal biases that perpetuate the problem.

Phase 3, which is just in its early stages, is aimed at uncovering and understanding the biases and blind spots that everyone has and making progress toward a broader mindset on everyone's part. There's a saying that you can't change the world, but you can change yourself. The trouble with that saying is that it's extremely difficult to change how you think. In part that's because it comes from your childhood; it comes from how your personality has been wired over your life. In part it's because your life experience is built up in a million interactions: whom you know, what you read or watch, your decisions and their consequences, the ways in which you have learned to take risks, or conversely, to protect yourself. These factors are embedded in everyone's mind so deeply and profoundly that they are hard to change. They only begin to change when they come to light.

In the spring of 2020, the world witnessed a moment we will never forget. The death of George Floyd, an unarmed black man, by a white police officer set off worldwide protests. Our shared pain and despair first led to calls for police reform, and quickly broadened to calls to finally recognize the persistent racism in our society. Calls for systemic change grew. For many white Americans, it was a time of real self-examination. And leaders then and now could finally begin the long work of making the necessary changes to break the systemic racism and injustice, even as the news cycle moves on.

Psychotherapists know that inner change is generally a three-step process: *awareness, acceptance,* and *action.* The process is rarely linear and takes a lot of effort, and it is one of the enduring models of effectively changing one's lifelong behaviors.

In the orchestra example, awareness happened when someone figured out that the different sounds of male and female footfalls were triggering unconscious bias. Acceptance happened when judges said yes, that's actually happening and I'm part of the problem. The action step happened when they eliminated the problem.

Phase 3 is about finding where and when unconscious bias happens, accepting in a healthy and positive way that something can be done about it, and then taking action. This is about activating the change within oneself (by that we mean anyone). Phase 3 is the realization that no matter who you are or how pure your intentions, you are going to have some unconscious bias. And if you want to change that, it would be great to have the tools to help you change at the moment that unconscious bias is triggered.

Again, recognition and data analysis have roles to play here. Before we get to prescribing action, however, we should briefly expand our thinking about diversity and inclusion and understand their importance in a human enterprise.

THANK TALK **CELEBRATE**

An organization can celebrate its diversity in simple ways, says Workhuman CHRO Steve Pemberton: "What's the difference between celebrating St. Patrick's Day, which is a cultural celebration for people of Irish descent, and Juneteenth, an African American celebration, or Diwali [a Hindu festival]? All are chances to say we come from many places and experiences, and all deserve recognition and respect." Even shared holidays can be opportunities to show diversity. For example, someone of Russian heritage can share the traditions (especially culinary) of the Russian New Year's celebration.

When people celebrate a colleague's life event such as a wedding, it's a great opportunity to show diversity as well—sharing pictures of one's own wedding tradition, for example, or giving good wishes in one's native language.

Defining Diversity and Inclusion

The first diversity efforts grew out of the civil rights and women's movements as a matter of righting past discrimination. They focused on both increasing participation in the workplace at large and, in particular, changing the racial and gender (and in some places, religious) makeup of management jobs. The same happened in professions like law and medicine. Incrementally, other broad categories of people, such as LGBTQ or the physically challenged, also raised awareness of their right to equal participation.

The understanding of diverse groups has since expanded to include a variety of formative or defining characteristics, including life experiences. A list of the categories of people who are often targets of discrimination includes:*

- Gender
- Race
- Sexual orientation (LGBTQ)
- Religion
- Age
- Weight
- Military service
- National origin
- Physical disability
- Prior imprisonment status

Studies of the power of diversity at work recommend looking at a larger array of differences that shape who we are as people and what we bring to work, for example:

- Education background
- Economic class or socioeconomic background
- Social membership

---

* This is a list of groups protected by statute, according to the U.S. Equal Employment Opportunity Commission. The EEOC also enforces related prohibitions of discrimination based on pregnancy, sexual or other harassment, and genetic information. Some states protect people against discrimination based on gender identity, political ideology, and service in a state militia. Federal law also prohibits employer discrimination based on black lung disease in coal miners.

- Industry background
- Cultural beliefs
- Family composition or background
- Native language

Now we're getting into the stuff that makes humans really different from each other—and really valuable as contributors to an enterprise.

Anthony Paradiso, an HR consultant and SHRM influencer on D&I issues, takes an expansive view of diversity and inclusion and its effect on employees, saying, "Once, a lot of it was really based on race, but now people see it means dealing with veterans, dealing with disabled people, dealing with people who work remotely, dealing with women, dealing with women who are pregnant, dealing with fathers or soon-to-be fathers or someone who's just come out as gay. It's about trying every day to have everyone feel included." In other words, since you brought these people into the company for their talent, let's remove any invisible roadblocks to those people knowing they fully belong.

"When people feel excluded, they lose their originality," Paradiso says. "They're not being fully themselves. As a gay person who came out in his 20s, I know that living a lie is very, very difficult. You internalize a kind of separation from your surroundings, which prevents you from being fully engaged."

As our understanding of diversity and inclusion expands, it's clear that what began as a moral good has grown into a business necessity. What matters is that people of all kinds bring different capabilities to the organization. Diversity of life experience, opinion, point of view, cultural reference, understanding, talent, knowledge, and temperament magnifies and multiplies your resources. And in a fast-changing, fully connected global market, it's one of the few ways to ensure continuous growth and innovation.

While it's necessary for leaders to foster a climate of inclusion by their own example, it's not always clear how to encourage employees to cultivate and sustain a sense of inclusion through their everyday interactions. This can leave employees uncertain how to navigate social interactions and express cultural differences that enhance feelings of inclusion at work.

Dr. Rachel D. Arnett, assistant professor of management at the Wharton School, partnered with Workhuman to shed light on this issue by testing a counterintuitive hypothesis: that individuals expressing their cultural backgrounds in a rich and meaningful way would actually *increase* inclusive behaviors from others because such rich cultural expressions enable colleagues to form a closer bond, learn from one another, and replace stereotypes with positive attributes. We conducted a study during the Workhuman Live conference in which 118 participants were put in pairs and randomly assigned to answer questions prompting either meaningful cultural expression (such as discussing what aspect of their cultural background is the greatest source of pride or how they have navigated cultural differences at work) or small-talk conversations that may feel "safer" at work (such as discussing a favorite restaurant or actor). Participants who learned about meaningful aspects of their partner's cultural identity felt closer to and thought more highly of their partner, relative to when such identities were downplayed through small talk. Furthermore, participants who were privy to meaningful cultural sharing (rather than small talk) exhibited greater inclusive behaviors: They were more likely to say that they would ask for their partner's professional input, refer their partner for a professional opportunity, and socially interact with their partner moving forward.

Follow-up studies outside of the Workhuman context replicate these findings by showing that cultural minorities (e.g., racial minorities and non-Americans), who may be especially apprehensive about expressing an underrepresented cultural identity, are able to elicit more inclusive behaviors when they open up about their cultural backgrounds to their coworkers.

Studies like Dr. Arnett's suggest that leaders who want to create a more inclusive environment need to provide opportunities for meaningful cultural expression through social interaction—meaningful connections—rather than top-down directives. Like so much that is powerful in human organizations, inclusion benefits from sharing our stories and celebrating what makes people unique in the new community of work, as well as the common values and purpose they share.

Diversity of Thought

"Diversity takes time, and there are steps you can take to change your hiring mindset. One is stop talking about what 'an engineer' looks like. Stop explaining what 'smart' looks like. Smart looks like a lot of different things. Smart people who are baristas who can see patterns and be agile—and they can learn to code. That is actually a thing.

"When I put together my latest team, I changed their interviewing style. And I sat in on their interviews, and I could see we had typecast 'software engineer.' I asked three managers, 'Who is the perfect person for this job?' All three said, 'Somebody like Mark Zuckerberg.'

"I said, 'Well, first of all, Mark Zuckerberg is not gonna work for us. You're describing someone who runs a company. That seems kind of unrealistic, right?' I coach them to skip past the quiz show questions and broaden their horizons. I tell them to have a candidate build something or solve a problem and watch their thought processes.

"There are people who are walking on the street every day who could possibly code just fine, but haven't either been exposed to it, or else they think we're all jerks—and bad interviewing reinforces that. You have to make it OK for people to come in and learn and make mistakes and support them. We're in a talent shortage, so we have to think more carefully about how we find and keep talented people."

—Michelle Grover, VP of Engineering, SAP Concur

The challenge for people in the human enterprise is to broaden their idea of diversity and inclusion while simultaneously learning that it has as much to do with being open to their own shortcomings. Brené Brown offered this candid advice to everyone at Workhuman Live 2019:

Inclusivity, diversity, and equity are big problems in the absence of courage. So, I'm going to give it to you really straight: This is a very easy solution. Brave leaders are never quiet about hard things, and if you have a conversation around race, ethnicity, class, age, gender, sexual identity, if you have that conversation, you will get your ass handed to you and every one of your fears about, 'Oh my God, my words aren't gonna match what I'm thinking about somebody, and I'm going to be called a racist or a sexist.' And all that is probably true. But you do it anyway, because it's the right thing to do. To opt out of difficult conversations about inclusivity and equity and diversity because they make you uncomfortable is the very definition of privilege.

In the interest of being inclusive, we can be tone deaf at times. How often have you heard the statement "I don't see race" or "I don't see gender." This misses the point of inclusion and belonging. In saying "I don't see an essential part of you"—whether that be your gender, your relationship preference, or the color of your skin—we are also choosing to deny a large part of what makes the other people essentially *them*.

Each of us is, yes, more than the color of our skin, or whom we choose to love, or our gender, or our religion, or our ethnic background. Yet all those elements are what make me unequivocally *me*.

People want to be seen for who they are and all that they are.

That's what makes *social recognition* perceived through the Workhuman lens so powerful—it's about recognizing people for what they do *and* for who they are. It's acknowledging that your unique talents, skills, life experience, and perspectives are what enable you to make important contributions and achieve results for organization success. It's about recognizing and appreciating the whole human. It's about truly seeing people as individuals in all their humanity.

Netflix's Vernā Myers explains that embracing inclusion requires "the institution's ability to fully integrate its understanding of and appreciation for the diverse cultures and backgrounds of its employees."

True inclusion sees, welcomes, and respects everything that makes each of us, well, us. And when we're seen for who we are in all our facets, and welcomed anyway, that's how we know we belong.

The Business Case for Diversity and Inclusion

Amy Cappellanti-Wolf, SVP and CHRO of Symantec, describes the multiple ways in which a lack of diversity harms key success factors like innovation:

As companies become more global and more complex, they need people who bring in different experiences and different schools of thought. The customers we have today are very different than the customers many companies had 10, 20, or 50 years ago. If everything in your company is homogeneous, if everything is groupthink and consensus-driven, you're never going to invent solutions that appeal to your wide range of potential customers.

Diversity of thought is so important. I worked at Disney, where in any given moment I was sitting with art directors, show set designers, interior designers, and also estimators, budgeters, project managers. Those roles have very different objectives. The designers were all about experience, about the most amazing theme park ride anyone's ever built. And the estimators and project managers and budgeters were all about, "Let's get it on budget, on time, and durable when we turn over to the parks."

That room would be mostly men, and on the face of it, they may not be as diverse as one might want them to be, but their experiences and perspective on the businesses that they ran were very divergent and different. And that in and of itself was a great display of diversity of thought. So it was less about the gender or the race or where they grew up, and more about the mindsets they brought to bear in terms of left-brain versus right-brain thinking, and the ultimate shared vision of creating an amazing vacation experience for our customers.

The business case for accelerating D&I efforts is so well documented that just a sampling of findings should suffice.

- *Diversity boosts performance.* According to business consultant McKinsey & Company, companies showing diversity in gender are 15 percent more likely to outperform their peers, and ethnically diverse firms outperform by as much as 35 percent.[4]
- *Diversity at the top correlates to better financial results.* For every 10 percent increase in racial and ethnic diversity on a senior executive team, earnings rise 0.8 percent.[5]
- *Diversity aids retention.* This almost seems too obvious to document: If people see other people like them at work and feel like they belong, they're more likely to stay. This commonsense finding has been confirmed in industries from law firms to the food business.[6]
- *Diversity boosts innovation.* A study of 177 firms by the Boston Consulting Group, for example, found a complex and definitive correlation between diverse management pools and innovation. Diverse teams measured 19 percent more innovation (which is why tech firms are among those companies most urgently seeking diversity).[7] Data-obsessed Google found that diversity leads to innovation through a clear, identifiable, and repeatable path.*
- *Diverse teams make better decisions.* One surprising example: A Harvard Business School study of venture capital business, which is overwhelmingly white and male, found "diversity significantly improves VCs' financial performance on measures such as profitable investments at the individual portfolio-company level and overall fund returns."[8]
- *Inclusion accelerates the benefits.* Organizations with inclusive cultures are twice as likely to meet or exceed financial targets, three times as likely to be high performing, six times more likely to be innovative

---

*Google found a number of reasons why more diverse companies and teams succeed. For example, if you are in a more diverse innovation group, you will act differently from the way you'll act in a group where everyone looks like you. You'll feel freer to express different ideas in the former and overemphasize commonality in the latter. See https://rework.withgoogle.com/guides/unbiasing-raise-awareness/steps/watch-unconscious-bias-at-work/.

and agile, and eight times more likely to achieve better business outcomes overall.[9]

Go to the websites of the Society for Human Resource Management, *Harvard Business Review*, Deloitte, Catalyst, or any of a score of think tanks, and you'll find all the evidence you need. D&I is good for business. The real question in front of us today is, What now?

EXPERT INSIGHT

"Bias is not the only challenge to D&I. There is a less malevolent but more universal challenge to D&I: people's natural preference to work and socialize with others like themselves. This is not necessarily because they are biased against any race or gender. Rather, it is motivated by a natural preference for being among people of similar backgrounds.

"Preference is not as serious when an individual has no power or influence. But when managers and leaders act on their preferences to be surrounded only by others just like them, the results can be devastating. Leaders who act on these preferences close doors to talented people who are different from them. They can unintentionally institutionalize racial, religious, or gender discrimination. This is not ethical; nor is it in the best interests of their organizations. Preference bias leads to group think, not innovation. Leaders need to transcend their natural preferences when leading and developing people.

"To transcend or master one's nature takes effort and investment. Building inclusive cultures when it is natural to prefer the company of people like us also takes effort and investment. Acknowledging the effort and investment that inclusiveness demands is precisely the missing piece in the D&I conversation."[10]

—David Lapin, founder and CEO of
Lapin Consulting International and author
of *Lead by Greatness*

Unconscious Bias Is the Next Frontier

The social psychologists Kenneth Clark and Mamie Phipps Clark conducted an extraordinary experiment almost 70 years ago, in the time of segregation. They placed two dolls, one white and one black, in front of African American children and asked questions such as, "Which is the pretty doll? Which is the good doll?" The children inevitably pointed to the white doll. When asked, "Which is the bad doll?" they pointed to the black doll. And when asked, "Which doll is like you?" they pointed again to the black doll. The Clarks' work on the internal effects of segregation was so profound that they were cited in the Supreme Court's *Brown v. Board of Education* ruling. Watching films of the "doll test" today is still a harrowing experience.

Those children were demonstrating an internalized bias (against themselves, tragically) brought on by their environment. It's an extreme example of something that all of us carry: prejudices and assumptions about ourselves or other people based on gender or color or accent or body shape or . . . (fill in the blank). The pain and despair following George Floyd's killing in 2020 was another moment for people to wake up to their conscious and unconscious biases, and to chart a different course for society.

When people in an organization categorize others based on criteria irrelevant to work, that same penchant suppresses their spirit and undermines community.

Some of these biases are obvious, but most are subtle enough to elude our conscious attention. Even the most enlightened people suffer from these internal biases, and they don't know they're exhibiting them. For example, perhaps you grew up overweight and were teased about it. You absorbed society's messages about fat people (undisciplined, indulgent, greedy, dirty) and the importance of not being fat (not just for health reasons but because fat doesn't conform to stereotypical beauty). If you are still overweight, you might internalize these messages into self-criticism. Or you might view overweight people with a full load of irrelevant assumptions about them. Because you don't want to believe you are biased, your subconscious searches for rationalizations like, "She's just not energetic enough for this position."

It's exactly the same double standard embedded in remarks like, "She's just very emotional" or "She's not handling herself with executive presence." It's the same when executives think, "He'll never be a manager with that Indian accent" or "I don't think someone who listens to that music while he writes code is really leadership material."

Unconscious bias has real consequences for people's career advancement, and it often takes place quietly, for example, in a lack of diversity among professional networks. Stacia Sherman Garr of RedThread Research notes, "Exclusion from informal professional networks has been identified as one of the greatest barriers to career success. One multinational study of more than 240,000 men and women found that while 81% of women report some form of exclusion at work—astonishingly—92% of men don't believe that they are excluding women at all!"[11]

We can see internal bias at work with the help of data on hiring, performance management, and other factors in the workplace. In one striking experiment, "white-sounding" names on résumés got 50 percent more callbacks for job interviews than identical résumés headed with "African American–sounding" names.[12] And now that we know these painful legacies exist in our society and in our workplaces, we can't ignore them. We have to raise our awareness of unconscious bias and change our thinking. We have to act.

Finding Unconscious Bias

If we raise awareness of these biases in the moment and accept that they exist, we might be able to disrupt their propagation and act to end them. Maybe we have a hope, over time, of changing those behaviors. In the past, identifying them was a matter of opinion or stupendous self-awareness. But now we have tools that can help do the job.

Workhuman has begun to formulate revealing data queries about some of these micro-biases.

Let's start with the example of gender. We found in our recognition data that women have significantly larger networks at work. They are simply more widely connected than men as a whole. Women's networks are also more gender-balanced. That means that men have smaller networks of relationships at work, and they tend to be more skewed toward men.

When we analyze recognition award data, we find that women receive more recognition awards than men. This might be because they have larger networks, so more people notice what a woman is doing. But the bad news is this: In our aggregated data set, women on average receive 12 percent less monetary value in their awards than men in the workplace.

Put these data together, and we find the contradictions that characterize hidden bias. We see that women, more than men, create the social fabric of our organizations. In fact, they give and receive more gratitude, as evidenced by the fact that they give and receive more awards. But the data shows that they receive less material reward for that gratitude—*even though their networks include more women.* (See Figure 10.2.)

Figure 10.2 Recognition Data Insight—Gender

The data reveals that women receive more recognition awards than men, but at a lower monetary value.

(When we present these data at public gatherings, we get two reactions: Men say, "Wow, that's a profound insight you've achieved." Women say, "It took you 50 million data points to figure that out? Tell us something we don't know!")

Here's why this data matters: because it's based on social recognition, in which peers and managers are making positive judgments about one another. So it's not about structural problems like unequal salaries or promotion opportunities but about moments when enlightened people are congratulating and noticing one another. Right in the moment when people are at their most positive, that unconscious bias is still operating, coloring their judgment.

Unfortunately, we have also identified an even more powerful effect of unconscious bias from race and ethnicity perspectives. Figure 10.3 shows that Hispanic, black, and Asian demographics receive less monetary value than whites overall. Again, this is happening when people are deliberately trying to spread positivity and all the good that goes with it.

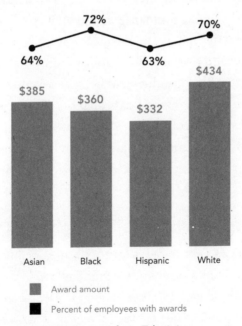

Figure 10.3 Recognition Data Insight—Ethnicity
Large recognition data sets uncover the effect of unconscious bias based on ethnicity.

We see this in our own data, and we realize that companies with such large data sets capturing the composition and behavior of people in the workplace have a moral obligation to do something about what they discover. So, recently we have dedicated a lot of time, talent, and money to thinking about and building on the idea that social recognition can move the practices of D&I ahead.

There are bold efforts to curtail unconscious bias with training, raising employees' understanding and awareness about what bias looks like and when it appears. As Brené Brown notes, however, working on this takes courage. It takes a willingness to be vulnerable when you admit that your judgments about people might be skewed by your experience. We see value in connecting social recognition to this next phase of D&I because it's grounded in positive emotions and actions: giving and receiving gratitude, promoting values, and celebrating individuals.

Organizations can look at the data to identify hidden bias and then do something about it. The action that leaders will take depends on organizational culture and where they are in their D&I efforts. They might look at their D&I training for managers and others, helping them understand hidden bias as well as the business advantages of diversity and inclusion. At least some of the effort can focus on social recognition. The recognition platform helps individuals become *aware* of discrimination; its foundation in nonjudgmental data analysis encourages *acceptance* of unconscious bias; it provides one *action* step—bringing recognition to the workforce in an impartial and positive way. In this context we can say again: S*ocial recognition can help fix the problems it identifies.*

Natalie Egan—Listening to Your Unconscious Bias

Natalie Egan is a CEO who knows a lot about change. She founded her second company, Translator, about the time she began her transition from male to female. And during this time, she says, "I was starting over in a lot of ways—starting over in a new gender of course, and I was also starting a new company.

"A lot of managers and executives are very threatened by the idea of evolving their style. They think, 'My way of dealing with people got me this far. Why should I change? How can I change? I got investors, I got stockholders, I can't take the chance of changing our culture.'

"Translator's mission attracted a very diverse group of people, and that was deliberate. But even with all the changes I'd experienced, I led the company in the style I'd learned growing up in a very forceful, typically 'masculine' mindset. That style didn't work at Translator and people let me know, fast. They said, 'This is what you did, this is why it upsets me, this is what you need to do in order to accommodate my X, Y, Z learning styles, or my personal issues because of trauma that I've experienced in my life.'

"Once, during an acquisition process, I talked aloud about 'acquiring people.' Someone spoke up and said, 'Maybe that's not the best language to use.' And I replied, 'Hey, we acquired this company because of its talent, and we own them for as long as they work here.' To me that was just logical, but now I can only imagine what that sounded like to an employee.

"As sensitive as I try to be, I can still have a very condescending tone. I can talk in a very assertive, kind of controlling, way. And sometimes I would come on too strong, and degraded people's work, and didn't give them credit for what they had done. I judged them as people instead of talking about the work. That's an unconscious bias driving that thought process. But this culture we're building helps me see that, and Translator's in a better place because of that.

"We all have different privileges, and once we understand our privilege the question is: Are we going to use it just for ourselves or to raise up other people? It's not always as obvious as being born white, cisgender, and male. Privilege is literally height. Privilege is voice. Privilege is where you were born, and when you were born, and what kind of resources you grew up having. We don't notice it because we never saw it that way. But now we can learn."

A Social Recognition Scenario

Since analyzing recognition data can identify hidden bias, it's a starting point for raising consciousness in the workplace, and an advanced analysis tool accelerates that journey through awareness, acceptance, and action. Exciting possibilities appear when you add natural language processing to the mix, because it creates teachable moments right in that positive context, when people are most receptive to making things better.

Let's say Brad nominates Barbara for a teamwork award. He'll go select "Teamwork" as a company value in the recognition platform and choose an award level at the middle point, which in Brad's system is called a Cheer award and has a value of 2,500 points. He then writes up a nice message to Barbara for all to see.

An inclusion awareness function uses natural language processing and a bit of artificial intelligence to check all the metadata around this award before Brad sends it, to see if there's something to reflect on.

Brad gets a message that shows his award with two sentences and the award level underlined. That's a signal to Brad that there might be an issue he hadn't thought about. He clicks on the underlined phrase where he wrote, "You seem to grasp all the technical details." It's being flagged as having a dismissive tone.

The natural language processing system caught the faint praise in "you seem" and is suggesting to Brad that he consider revising it.

Brad realizes that Barbara is in fact a technical expert, and he used language he probably wouldn't use with a male employee. Brad has a small moment of self-awareness, a tiny teachable moment in which he reflects on his tone with the women on his team. The system is not condemning him—it's helping Brad move in a direction he wants to go. He changes the message to "You have an amazing technical grasp of the details and you impart that to us."

If a D&I trainer had been with Brad in the moment he wrote the initial award, that trainer would have seen that teachable moment and said, "Brad, that sounds like faint praise. If that's what you mean, go ahead, but take one minute to think if that's exactly the message you want to send." It's a subtle lesson because it's a subtle issue—but addressing the issue right then can make the difference between an award that lightly perpetuates a stereotype and one that recognizes Barbara for her unique talents and contribution.

A D&I trainer can't monitor every award (and we wouldn't want that); but Brad can get the same benefit of that teachable moment because the system can give him a little nudge in the right direction. The system improves Brad's award to Barbara, and it also gives Brad a little moment of consciousness-raising at the moment he was expressing gratitude. It's not punishing Brad; in fact, it helps him feel better about the award.

Unconscious bias is somewhere in everyone, even the most enlight-ened people. The goal of this system is not to command people to adopt a uniform language or change them in some regimented way. The goal is to help individuals change a little and therefore change the organization as a whole.

This gentle positivity overcomes a big obstacle that HR people know in D&I training: As people move along the path of understanding their hidden biases, with a dedication to changing, they can feel shamed or embarrassed at the extent to which their preconceived notions about others shade their judgment. That creates denial or resistance. Brad has no reason to feel that way because the system is coaching him to change himself.

Here's another example. Grace is giving an award to a team mem-ber who created a new script for the customer service team. When that employee brought the script to the team meeting, everyone offered com-ments and praise because the script had a lot of sharp insights. During the meeting, the writer sat silent, barely looking up from his screen.

Grace writes up a recognition award for the excellent work and includes a little bit of coaching for the writer. "Your script is really bril-liant, as everyone in the meeting said. Don't be shy. We want to hear what you think." In her enthusiasm, Grace isn't considering that this employee is a deep introvert. Grace's language, meant to encourage this person, is just not optimal. But Grace is a powerful extrovert and carries an unconscious assumption that someone who is quiet feels not fully part of the team. She's misinterpreted the writer's affect.

When she checks the award before sending it, Grace gets a bit of coaching herself: It says, "Avoid terms that might seem to mandate one work style. Consider how your colleague would receive this award." If Grace is happy with the wording, she can send it along. But the system has caught a common problem—assuming everyone has to communicate in the same way—and hinted to Grace that she might reconsider. Grace might rewrite that part of the message to say, "It's always good to hear what you think, so don't ever hesitate to run ideas by me or other team members in a meeting, in email or whatever form is most comfortable for you."

One of the most common questions that come up in recognition awards is the amount of reward value to choose for a particular award, and large data sets can offer assistance here as well.

When people send a recognition award, they choose an amount based on the degree of achievement. Sometimes they are unsure which amount to choose or want to confirm that the scale of the award is in line with the accomplishment. There's a degree of human judgment at work here. But if they wish, they can also compare that award with others. The system will look at parameters of the award usually around project scope, level of effort, contribution, time invested, and result achieved and will compare it with activity in the company, or the country, or 50 million awards in the recognition database.*

The system will offer its analysis in an infographic comparing that award with others. And that's the moment that it can also reveal unconscious bias, because it can compare the chosen award level between, for example, women and men. It might note the data point we mentioned earlier: "Women receive more recognition than men, but the awards are lower in value." It might show that for the demographics, there is a discrepancy in the global data on the award amount. Or it might zero in right on that person giving the award and note, "You tend to give higher

---

* The system makes adjustments based on cost-of-living calculations, inflation, currency fluctuations, and other data.

point values to men than women"—another private, personalized, and low-stress teachable moment in the D&I journey.

Companies have made progress against discrimination with training and teaching and role playing in the last generation. We still have a long way to go toward creating work environments where all the employees feel like they are treated fairly and they belong. Dealing openly and fairly with unconscious bias is the next step, and if we are committed to justice in our society and our companies, there's no going back to the way things used to be. Social recognition and big data analysis can bring coaching into a new era of awareness, acceptance, and action.

The next 50 million rows of data can be 50 million teachable moments in the world. If we create the technology to latch onto them, and disrupt them, and help correct them over time, even enlightened people will find they can use a bit of positive help.

TIP SHEET

10 Ways Human Applications Help Diversity and Inclusion Initiatives

Human applications like Social Recognition® and Conversations®, our continuous performance management product, and the data analysis that underlies them, promote all the goals of diversity and inclusion initiatives.[13] Human applications:

1. Amplify positive human interaction in THANK, TALK, CELEBRATE moments.
2. Promote equality—thanks from the new line worker appears next to congratulations from the CEO for all to see.
3. Connect people and networks that might otherwise never meet, especially in a large or multilocation enterprise.
4. Democratize feedback, illuminating areas and people that are otherwise hidden.
5. Help employees be proactive about their own development, requesting and receiving positive feedback and coaching from all

corners of the organization. People can actively seek mentors and sponsors from anywhere.

6. Raise awareness of unconscious bias with data analysis, reminders, and coaching based on natural language processing.

7. Flag potential problems quickly and privately, enabling people to self-correct their diversity and inclusion efforts. This can also prevent small problems from escalating.

8. Help peers and managers support each other. Recognition, feedback, events, and celebrations all show peers that they are seen and appreciated, reinforcing the critical feelings of emotional support and group inclusion that are the heart of a D&I culture.

9. Build empathy and humanize people who share wisdom, congratulations, and support.

10. Align everyone across personal differences by emphasizing shared purpose, goals, and values.

CONSIDER THIS

This exercise can be confidential or shared with a trusted friend or colleague. Consider if a hidden bias might affect your working relationships. One way into this uncomfortable subject is to think of someone whom you find difficult and ask yourself, "What would I change about this person?" Would you change the person's behavior, physical appearance, or way of communicating?

Then in writing:

1. Identify the person by name (or use a pseudonym if you wish).
2. Describe the quality in that person you find difficult.
3. Describe your reaction to that quality in detail. Are you annoyed? Threatened? Disgusted?
4. Describe why that quality is relevant to the person's performance at work.

The purpose of this exercise is not to make you feel guilty or ashamed but to become aware of the complex emotional reactions we have that might affect our judgment.

You might follow up this simple exercise by participating in Project Implicit, a series of tests created by a consortium of top universities. It identifies potential implicit biases in more than a dozen categories. The test can be taken here: https://implicit.harvard.edu/implicit/takeatest.html.

11 | Redesigning Rewards

Give at Least One Penny of Every Payroll Dollar to the People, to Give to Each Other

HUMAN MOMENTS

"The first thing companies need to be aware of is that there is a folly in telling people, 'We want you to team up, we want you to work well together,' and then rewarding them only as individuals. It's asking people to live with an inherent contradiction and that's obviously not easy. Any time rewards unduly favor individual achievement at the expense of collaborative achievement, you will get behaviors around competition and withholding that you don't need and don't want.

"How to do that is just make sure that, first, a substantial portion of the reward system is based on collective performance: How did our unit do? How did our project do? How did our company do? And second, make sure there aren't direct contradictions built into the reward system: like we want you to work together but then we're going to force rank you."[1]

—Amy Edmondson, Novartis Professor of
Leadership and Management, Harvard

"I've done compensation design for 39 years and I guarantee you, we don't know what motivates you ... but I'm certain that *you do* know what motivates you." This startling statement was made at Workhuman Live 2019 by Peter Newhouse, executive vice president of Global Rewards for Unilever, the 160,000-employee consumer products company. Newhouse went on to describe Unilever's reengineered compensation plan, which enables employees to design their own mix of fixed compensation (salary and benefits) and variable compensation (bonus and co-investing in Unilever shares). The idea is to put greater compensation choice in the hands of the employees individually, so they can design their total rewards according to their needs, because each person knows best what part of total rewards motivates him or her.

Not every organization can engineer such a sophisticated program, but Newhouse makes an essential point: Compensation that is stuck in century-old models of salary and bonus is inadequate in a world where products and services of all kinds are personalized. Why should a person saving to buy a house be compensated with an identical salary, or benefits, or bonus structure as a person getting ready to retire? Shouldn't employees be empowered to choose how much of their compensation they receive in company stock plans? Within the limits of equal treatment, it makes sense for some part of compensation to be variable, including an element of consumer choice.

We have long advocated a policy of variable compensation that includes some portion based on crowdsourced pay. Total compensation for most employees can be envisioned thus:

Base salary + benefits = fixed compensation
Bonus/commission + crowdsourced rewards = variable compensation
Stock/profit sharing* = variable ownership equity

Since that proposal, evidence has accumulated that crowdsourced rewards in the form of social recognition are a substantial improvement over the traditional salary-benefits-bonus formula.

To understand the importance of crowdsourced rewards, we first need to understand how today's business environment has changed employee perceptions of value.

The Problem with Pay Today[†]

How we attract and manage talent is evolving. Shouldn't the way we compensate and reward that talent evolve too? In the past, compensation and benefits teams worried that pay-for-performance models might be too radical or risky for anyone but top executives. Employment expert Josh Bersin says, "Our most recent research showed that only 42 percent of companies believe their reward strategy aligns with their business strategy. C'mon, that's way too low!" He suggests HR needs to apply the creative thinking that has changed performance management:

> We are now embarking on continuous performance management with feedback taking place almost all the time. Why do you have to wait until December to get a raise or bonus? And why do we all get the same benefits as each other?
>
> I believe HR leaders are risk-averse. Many of them are beholden to the CFO because they are being asked to hold down costs. They often don't understand that paying people more money can actually reduce overall costs. For example, higher pay

---

*In the case of publicly held companies or privately held partnerships, e.g., LLCs.
†For simplicity, this chapter will use the term *pay* when referring generally to a system of total rewards.

*for top performers results in higher overall corporate productivity.
We also have basic cost pressures. Today the cost of employee
healthcare is around 32 percent of pay, [and] companies are
worried about these fixed expenses. And companies now have
dozens of benefits available. Even though many of these are
rarely used, there is a fear of taking them away.*

*We need to move to a world where pay is highly tailored
to each individual and we treat everyone like a potential high-
performer. Right now, managers just don't have the tools,
education, or authority to do this, so we tend to pay everyone
equally.*[2]

Today's leading companies understand that variable pay is an essential component of an attractive and fair compensation system. Fast business cycles, the gig economy, and the personalization of everything have
employees thinking differently about pay. Sheila Sever, senior manager
at Deloitte, shared current statistics that explain the shift in employee
mindset: 40 percent of workers are now employed in a work arrangement
different from traditional full-time employment, and 64 percent of millennials have a "side hustle" that supplements income.[3]

"Ideally," says Bersin, "each employee's reward program should be
customized to that individual."[4]

Variable pay offers the easiest transition path to customized pay
design, but the infrequency of traditional variable pay in the form of
annual and quarterly bonuses dilutes its effect. They aren't awarded close
enough to work behavior to be motivational or psychologically linked to
that behavior. Even if they are KPI- or performance-based, they end up
being seen as entitlements.[5] Research shows that pay motivates employees best when it comes as soon as possible after the accomplishment(s)
being rewarded.[6] Infrequency also makes bonuses high risk since they
are "all or nothing," instead of incremental rewards from multiple sources
that might even out over time, mitigate bias, and reduce the stakes.

In Chapter 8 we noted that the psychological benefit of receiving
an annual bonus lasts about a month, and that the same benefit can be

extended with many rewards spread out over a year. Figure 11.1 illustrates another way of looking at the relative effect of an annual bonus versus a recognition award. Even though the psychological boost tapers off (38% of survey respondents say the positive feeling lasts about a week), the recognition award costs a fraction of the annual bonus, so it can be repeated many times.

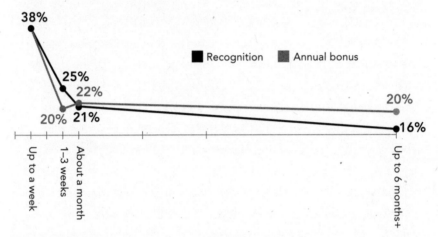

Figure 11.1 Recognition and Annual Bonus Compared
Despite a lower investment, recognition awards generate a feeling of positivity lasting similar durations to annual bonuses.

Another problem with annual bonuses is that they are too predictable. Because of their regularity (and in many companies, ubiquity), bonuses become transactional. They rarely make an impact as a true incentive to drive satisfaction or behavior. However, this expectation and predictability produces a reverse incentive when bonuses are withheld. The decision whether to withhold a bonus threatens to introduce real or perceived bias. For example, despite evidence to the contrary, men (and in particular fathers) are still widely seen as primary breadwinners who would suffer disproportionately from loss of a bonus.[7]

In an agile environment, annual bonuses are also too inflexible. Pay scales based on organizational structures don't account for the fast-moving nature of business today. They support the bureaucratic structure and macro-accomplishments, but as a standard part of a pay package in one or another salary range, they don't recognize the broad differences in achievement among individuals.

Differences matter to employees, and making a distinction among people based on their performance is a matter of fairness as well as good motivation.

EXPERT INSIGHT

"Fundamentally, our systems of work today were all designed around the idea that work is a contract with the employee. But all the data we have about employee experience suggests that employees experience work more as a relationship. They expect the same things out of work that they do of any other significant relationship in their life. They want to feel valued and appreciated, and cared for, and trusted, and included, and connected.

"Our job as leaders is to create a work experience that feels like a healthy relationship for the employee because when we can do that, people will start showing up more fully. They'll be more committed. Everything else is secondary to that. Until we solve that issue, everything else is shuffling deck chairs."

—Jason Lauritsen, author of *Unlocking High Performance*

Variable Pay and Equity

Pay equity is a critical issue in the human enterprise. If people are not paid a fair and equal wage for equal work, every other effort to promote human values is delegitimized. Today, when talent is highly mobile and compensation is easy to research, an organization that tolerates unfairness in money matters will simply not hire or hold the best employees. As we've seen, success depends on a workforce that is engaged and energized enough to keep moving ahead through rapidly changing times. How can employers ensure that all their employees are rewarded fairly, and without bias, for fulfilling their minimum job requirements and also for the discretionary effort they expend?

There is no simple solution for mitigating the bias that can lead to pay inequity, but a total rewards strategy that empowers employees is a smart step in the right direction. Here again, a social recognition platform that combines authentic human appreciation and careful data analysis benefits employees and the organization at the same time.

Pay equity is often conflated with pay equality, and not everyone uses these terms the same way. We define *pay equality* as the assurance that everyone is provided the same pay rate for the same work, and we define *pay equity* as giving everyone the same opportunity to be rewarded for superior performance—regardless of gender, race, age, disability, color, creed, national origin, religion, sexual orientation, or other differences.

The conversation about pay equity has recently become part of the discrimination conversation—where white men still outearn most other groups.[8] Pay equity has become part of the #MeToo conversation[9] as systemic gender discrimination has been highlighted as a source of workplace harassment.[10] SHRM has predicted that employers in the United States should be prepared for sweeping pay equity legislation at the federal level.[11]

Companies are taking a closer look at incentive systems—things like annual, quarterly, and even spot bonuses—and seeing significant flaws and failures to achieve the intended results:

- *Incentive systems exacerbate existing discrimination.* They are usually tied to salary rate: Bonuses are often given as a percentage of annual earnings, which means someone with an unequal wage to start with will earn a similarly disparate bonus. According to Goldman Sachs, the average bonus for a woman is 72 percent lower than it is for a man, largely due to the smaller percentage of women in high-earning pay brackets.[12]
- *Incentive systems have a single-source bias.* When bonuses are tied to reviews or manager discretion, they are at risk of becoming a single point of failure.[13] If a manager carries a bias (conscious or

unconscious), employee equity will suffer. Earlier, we saw how real and unconscious bias can poison diversity and inclusion efforts, and bias in compensation is toxic. Pay inequity based on gender and race bias, for example, creates significant gaps in trust.[14]

Reward systems that include crowdsourced recognition can advance fairness and equity against each of these flaws. While many companies are working hard toward equity through assessment, recruitment, and promotion, recognition can quickly add balance to even entrenched disparities in traditional pay. Where bias has existed or its remnants remain, social recognition creates a counterweight that can promote equal opportunity.

Crowdsourcing rewards through social recognition expands the single manager's perspective to reflect an employee's performance from many viewpoints, which helps to mitigate bias.

The Power of Unselfish Expression

Social recognition gives peers the power to affect compensation. It's hard to overstate the power of that cultural statement. We like to say, "Give at least one penny of every payroll dollar to the people, to give to each other."

As small as that percentage of compensation is, it's enough to break through the cynicism surrounding so many compensation systems. Peer-to-peer awards build trust in the fairness of the system because they are based in trusted relationships. The effects can be dramatic. Through a peer recognition program, an outstanding employee in a lower-earning role has the potential to earn the same total reward as an employee in a higher-paid position—or perhaps even more.

Although crowdsourced rewards tend to be smaller and more frequent and to be given over time, they have the power to add up to something more significant than a bonus, because they come with all the psychological and community advantages that we've discussed earlier, including gratitude given and received. Rewards based on social recognition are authentic and given in real time from peers and managers based on real accomplishment, so they reinforce a message of equity.

From an impact perspective, we're often asked if many small recognition awards can affect even highly compensated employees. We recently spoke to leaders in a large bank, and they said, "Oh, that wouldn't work here. People make too much money. What are they going to do with a $50 award?"

We replied, "If your mom gives you a $50 sweater, aren't you going to feel good about that? You won't say, 'Gosh, Mom, this is a cheap sweater.' You'll say, 'Oh wow, that's a lovely sweater. Thank you!' If a friend brings a vase of flowers to your house, do you say, 'Actually, I only like the bigger, more expensive arrangements from the hotel flower shop.' Of course not. You say thank you, and you feel gratified at your friend's thoughtfulness."

Even for highly compensated individuals, there's magic in the act of a colleague who has no vested interest taking the time to write a sincere message of thanks, attaching an award to give it a bit of extra weight, and recognizing them. Colleagues aren't required to take on extra work creating a moment of unselfish expression—they do it in a spirit of generosity. In fact, we'd argue that in those businesses where the daily money metric has an outsized cultural impact, a moment of unselfish expression is all the more meaningful.

Ultimately, the company that dedicates a portion of payroll to a completely voluntary system of recognition is taking a leap of faith. Of course, a recognition system must have security and governance built in, but peer-to-peer recognition means leadership is truly putting confidence in the power of gratitude.

Crowdsourced Compensation

Crowdsourced variable pay can be implemented by dedicating a small portion of the overall payroll budget to social recognition. The social platform we described earlier is effective and efficient because it empowers everyone in the organization to award part of that variable-pay investment to multiple employees many times a year. Such a system creates a greater impact than lump-sum bonuses given annually.

> The notion is that "coworkers know who the top performers are, and crowdsourced pay can encourage collaboration and teamwork."

Think of recognition as giving employees the power to grant each other micro-bonuses (in the form of points that can be redeemed for goods or experiences), which are always accompanied by a statement of why the recipient merits the bonus. "Coworkers know who the top performers are," says George Benson, director of the master's program in human resource management at the University of Texas at Arlington. "And crowdsourced pay can encourage collaboration and teamwork."

Why award redeemable points instead of cash? "Goods and services are far more reinforcing than cash," says Jim Brennan, a compensation consultant in New Braunfels, Texas. A crowdsourced pay system streamlines the process. "It's nimbler than cash compensation," says Brennan, "and 'redeemable points' enable an employee's entire family to help choose a reward, magnifying the reinforcement impact. The faster the consequence, the stronger the impact on the recipient—that's human nature. The speed of the reward determines the intensity of the response."

It puts choice in the hands of the recipient, who can redeem points for a near-term reward (like high-end travel gear) or accumulate them over time for a bigger reward (like a luxury hotel stay). That kind of choice renews the good feelings of community and gratitude once when the award is received and later when the recipient experiences the reward. Every time someone uses that cool high-end luggage that she would never have bought otherwise, she remembers the good feelings engendered by the TALK, THANK, CELEBRATE moments that accumulated to let her indulge herself.

This is backed by experience as well as data. An analysis of cash versus noncash recognition at Corning yielded the surprising finding that $500 in noncash recognition (points accrued by individuals, to be redeemed in goods or experiences) was associated with a 58 percent decrease in turnover, compared with $500 in cash recognition. The psychological benefits of such crowdsourced compensation include greater feelings of belonging and social cohesiveness among employees.[15]

Benefits Matter More Than Ever

Gabrielle Thompson of Cisco shared how and why her company rethought benefits, to play a differentiating role in the total rewards structure: "Cisco's culture puts such a heavy focus on our people because our people are the ones who make this company great. Benefits are an example. Years ago, benefits didn't really matter much in attraction and retention of talent. It was something that companies put in place essentially to be on par with others. But today benefits are such the differentiator; they are the connection for employees to the culture—what message do the benefits offered say about the culture of the company? We don't really care what other companies are doing (other than if they're doing something really cool that we think would be great for our employees). What we do care about is what our employees need and want and ensuring that we're providing that.

"We instituted 'becoming a parent' and 'emergency time off' as new benefits because when you're adding a family member through birth or adoption, we want you to take the time in those early days for the child and parent to bond. It doesn't matter if you're male or female—if you are the primary caregiver you get 13 weeks of paid time off. If you're a secondary caregiver, we still want to make sure you have a chance to have that early bonding experience. So, we have another four weeks off for that secondary caregiver. We even have three days paid leave at the birth of a grandchild.

"Emergency time off is flexible. Companies typically have an official bereavement policy that might say you can take three or four days off with pay. We think that's terrible! We want you to take whatever time off you need. So our policy allows you to take up to four weeks of paid time off to deal with emergencies that happen in your life. If you need more time than that, you can talk to your manager and determine what additional time you need."

Three Tiers of Reward

As part of a total benefits package, crowdsourced reward systems can be considered in three general forms. Most companies will use them as a powerful complement to an already robust compensation and incentive system (which might still include bonuses), helping to make them more equitable.

The most basic form is often called *micro-bonuses*, which set aside a percentage of the total compensation budget to be offered as recognition for discretionary effort. Continuous, small, but valuable incentives serve as persistent reminders to employees that their contribution is appreciated, improving job satisfaction. As we've noted, the best practice for such programs is to set aside at least 1 percent of payroll as a bare minimum, to enable everyone in the organization to both give and receive rewards and recognition. It's possible to construct a reward program with less, but in our experience 1 percent is a significant threshold to realize the benefits we've described. That threshold is certainly vital to achieving benefits like identifying conscious and unconscious bias described in Chapter 10.

Some companies have gone to the next tier, past micro-bonuses to what we call *macro-bonuses*: transferring money that would normally be given as larger bonuses into crowdsourced rewards. These "pay-for-performance" bonuses take the place of typical annual or quarterly bonuses. The total allocation for these programs can reach 5 to 20 percent of salary. While micro-bonuses tend to be accrued in points, merchandise, or gift cards, macro-bonuses will usually include some cash component. Like micro-bonuses, they feel more authentic, specific, and fair because they come both from leaders and from colleagues who can see and appreciate their work, firsthand. Because they are linked directly to behavior and real outcomes, they have more power to act as an incentive to future discretionary effort. Because they do not rely solely on initiation by a manager, a single point of failure is removed that could otherwise create or be perceived as bias.

The highest tier of crowdsourced incentive is probably the least likely to be seen in an enterprise setting but is nevertheless common in certain industries. This tier bases all—or a significant majority—of pay on crowdsourced rewards. In many ways it is not yet practicable in most workplaces, but in some professions it is already the norm. In hospitality or any industry where a majority of salary comes from gratuities, staff are effectively being rewarded based directly on performance. A similar pay dynamic is happening in the gig economy (although countervailing forces like price pressure are also taking place as a few companies compete for dominance).

A continuous flow of income, in direct proportion to work and effort, and crowdsourced from peers (or gig customers), can be seen as the most equitable pay solution available—provided care is taken to ensure the system is not abused. The system is entirely merit-based and holds the potential for high gain for employees who put forth large amounts of discretionary effort, which can in turn result in high levels of productivity for organizations. Because it can be seen as competitive to the extent that it draws from a finite source, this pay type works well for industries or departments that are engaged in "cooperation."

While crowdsourced pay may be a bridge too far for many organizations, even investing a small percentage of payroll through rewards programs can have a significant impact on pay equity. Rewards will directly address equity by compensating those who deserve it. The data gleaned from crowdsourced rewards and recognition—when triangulated against pay and performance data—renders deep insights into potential equity problems. Tackling the gender pay equity gaps begins with awareness and education through empirical data.

By looking at who is receiving rewards and why, you can spot high performers through the eyes of their peers and highlight them for development or promotion. You can use this data to compare against salaries and performance ratings, audit for equity in pay, and spot possible areas of manager bias. Those employees who are reviewed highly but have fewer rewards might be lacking in social capital. This offers an opportunity to balance the scales or integrate them more into your culture and work community.

Might the crowd carry unconscious or overt bias into a new rewards structure? Pay equity already struggles with manager and institutional biases that impact not only pure compensation but also hiring, promotion, and development. If we add to that the potential for peer-to-peer bias, you can see the potential for rewards to go disproportionately to popular people, similar people, or those in support roles.[16]

That's why crowdsourced pay must be recorded and analyzed. Combined with other quantitative data, such as an internal labor market audit and pay equity analysis, recognition data will measure and benchmark performance against pay. If you are aligning your employee reward program with your cultural values, you might consider adding a cultural value that aligns with equity, such as diversity, inclusion, or equal voices. This can be a powerful tool both to remind the givers of the rewards that they should be thinking about equity and to create a moment of self-reflection for those giving awards. This kind of self-reflection is also powerful in molding behavior and learning,[17] research has shown. In this way, reward programs can also be used as a tool to create equity and reduce the biases that exist in the organization. This is a positive step toward connecting your people to your purpose and vision as an organization.

Change is always challenging, so we don't recommend you go from big quarterly bonuses straight to a 100 percent pay-for-performance reward model. But we do recommend that you benchmark where you stand now, and then allocate at least 1 percent of your payroll to "anyone-to-anyone" recognition and rewards.

The 1 Percent Threshold

Earlier, we proposed 1 percent of payroll as a benchmark for a strong recognition program: "Give one penny of every payroll dollar to the people to give to each other."

Our customers have learned that 1 percent is a jumping-off point for getting the momentum that makes recognition self-sustaining. If an employee making $60,000 a year is getting 1 percent of his compensation in the form of recognition awards, that's $600 a year or a $50 award once a month. That's a sustainable cadence, and it's hard to quantify the benefits of the program at a frequency of less than that. After 1 percent, the benefits are linear; you get double the results in terms of retention, for example, by going to 2 percent of payroll, and that linear correlation continues as you increase recognition. At our company, which of course has recognition on our minds all the time, we're up to 8 percent, and in the annual Great Place to Work® survey, 99 percent of Workhuman employees said they wanted to remain with the company.[18]

The 2018 SHRM/Workhuman employee recognition survey found that programs funded at a minimum of 1 percent of payroll are 86 percent more likely to be rated as good or excellent by employees than e-thanks programs (ones that have no monetary investment). A majority of the latter programs (58 percent) were rated as poor or fair.

Evidence from outside Workhuman correlates to the 1 percent threshold. Organizations that invest more in recognition are more likely to be award-winning workplaces. The difference is striking: "Best work-places" cultural awards were earned by 55 percent of companies investing 1 percent or more, while only 22 percent of those making zero investment earned that distinction.[19]

Another way to think of the investment in crowdsourced pay is found in Workhuman's real-world data. Employees who are recognized five or more times in a year are two times less likely to leave the organization. The average award in 2018–2019 ranged between $75 and $100. So the investment in people recognized averages about $500. What other investment costing $500 per person can drop the turnover number like that?

> Organizations that invest more in recognition are more likely to be award-winning workplaces.

That doesn't mean, however, that a crowdsourcing pay investment begins by allocating $500 per employee. In the real world as seen in Workhuman data, the number of people who receive five or more awards starts out as a minority as people implement the new system and make a cultural and psychological shift toward giving and receiving gratitude at work.

After an organization reaches the 1 percent threshold, a flywheel effect starts to take place. Gratitude inspires more gratitude. Calling out great performance and company values reinforces "what works" in an employee's mind. Building a narrative of performance through stories in a social media–styled system helps people stop for a moment and remember that great thing someone else did and follow suit.

Investment Plan

Chris French, Workhuman's EVP of Customer Strategy, shared this sharp analogy for determining the level at which to fund a recognition rewards program: "If you had $1,000 to invest and you know you'd get a 30% return on your investment, would you put $10 into that investment and celebrate that you got $3? And then keep the other $990 in a bank account making half a percent?

"Of course not. So why would you want 10 percent of your workforce receiving crowdsourced pay that boosts productivity, decreases turnover, inspires loyalty and goodwill? If you're serious about saying, 'People are our most important asset,' make sure that you reach a threshold where everyone is participating in the program."

When you reach and pass that 1 percent threshold, you start to gather enough data in the system to accomplish other benefits we've discussed. It's only through repeatable actions that you can know you are making a positive impact on strategic goals like discovering unconscious bias, improving performance management, growing a diversity and inclusion practice, comparing your organization against industry benchmarks, and mapping the informal networks that tell you how the company is really operating. You can identify factors that turn a star performer into a flight risk. When you have enough throughput in the system, you can become proactive.

For example, if you have 15 percent turnover in the IT department, that causes huge headaches throughout the organization. You set a goal to get that turnover down to 5 percent. Crowdsourced pay through recognition can identify patterns and suggest actions, such as getting to a point where everyone in that department is receiving 12 awards a year. Why isn't everyone getting that number? That's where you look deeper: Is everyone trained and habituated in giving and receiving gratitude? Is there a flaw in the hiring process? Is the manager's assessment of an employee in conflict with the crowd's assessment? Is the IT department a positive or negative place to be, and why? A recognition system will help narrow down the possibilities so HR or senior leadership can take action.

Recognition Punches Above Its Weight

Business media stories about pay are frequently accompanied by a chart showing its breakdown into different components. For example, a story about tech will show the average pay package for a programmer comprises 75 percent base salary, 15 percent stock bonus, and 10 percent cash bonus. On Wall Street, bonuses typically make up a greater share of pay.[20] Some companies have intricate pay formulas to encourage high performance, retention, and long-term value creation for stockholders, customers, et al.

Here's the striking thing: If you chart these compensation designs, 1 or 2 percent dedicated to social recognition *would barely show on the chart*. Recognition's documented effect on business outcomes is dramatically higher than its relative cost; it's what ringside sportswriters call "punching above its weight."

One percent of payroll is the threshold at which the benefits become self-reinforcing and self-sustaining. The benefits of social recognition don't stall out at 1 percent, however. Getting to 2 or 4 percent magnifies the positive effects of crowdsourced pay.

So how do you get there?

Variable Pay Ways and Means

Every budget allocation represents a priority and a trade-off, and though the case for social recognition as a fundamental part of a human organization is strong, we're often asked how HR or executives should frame the decision to dedicate a percentage of payroll to peer recognition. Given that leaders must always tailor their budgets to the unique circumstances and culture of the organization, we can suggest several ways of looking at the money question.

Social recognition is an investment with quantifiable returns that we detailed earlier:* increased engagement, productivity, quality, and profitability; decreased turnover and absenteeism. One way to view the investment is to measure it against the opportunity cost of *not* improving those numbers. If you calculate the cost of turnover at your company, what savings does dropping that number by 30 percent or 50 percent represent?

Merit pay increases have stayed in the low single digits for some time, despite record unemployment. SHRM reports that actual year-over-year increases were 3.1 percent in 2018 and 3.2 percent in 2019, and it projects an average growth of 3.3 percent in 2020 (barring an economic slowdown).[21] We've shown that the positive psychological effect of getting a raise lasts about a month, then tapers off quickly. How much more effective would it be to take some portion of that merit increase and dedicate it to a regular cadence of recognition awards?

That suggestion is sometimes met with the concern that people expect a merit award every year and decreasing it might be demotivating. The response to that is to contrast the possible negative effect of a somewhat smaller merit increase, given with little difference between exceptional performers and average performers, and a plan that directs more rewards, democratically given by peers, to the most productive and positive employees. Taking the negative option, we have seen, is a bureaucratic method of avoiding the fact that some people contribute more to both profitability and culture. We think that greater contribution should be met with greater rewards, both material and psychological.

---

*See Chapters 3, 7, and 8.

Adding crowdsourced pay to compensation structures doesn't necessarily mean increasing a company's total payroll budget, says Jim Brennan. "Crowdsourced variable pay can be self-funding. It will come out of productivity improvement, which makes it easy to sell to management."

Human resources budgets have a lot of components, and we've seen companies just starting on their recognition journey successfully take an incremental approach by drawing a small amount from a number of substantial budgets to get to that 1 percent threshold. Some call this their "cheese slicer" approach, and it's a good way to get initial spending approved so the program can have time to show its results with a minimum of gross new budget.

EXPERT INSIGHT

"How can social recognition be used to determine someone's compensation? It's become less of a top-down decision and more of a peer-based, group consensus. What is your value to the team, to the organization? Can we take the information that's derived from employees—your peers and my peers—and use that to determine your compensation? The peer-to-peer approach is becoming more and more important as organizations become larger and more complex—it's much easier to gather information from multiple sources, i.e., your peers, to determine a more comprehensive and more holistic assessment of contribution and performance."

—Dave Bond, Director, Talent Management
and Total Rewards, The Minto Group

One model that's working in forward-leaning companies is to create a "power curve" allocating a percentage of the variable pay budget for peer-to-peer awards. This causes variable pay and bonuses to migrate toward high-performance, high-potential employees regardless of their seniority or position.

Figure 11.2 shows an example in which variable pay is 10 percent of compensation, with 8 percent going to the top 20 percent of employees via standard bonuses and incentive programs (with some of this bleeding in "the mighty middle").

The rest (totaling 2 percent of compensation) is given to both the middle and top performers as micro-pay from peers across the organization via crowdsourced recognition. This real-time model of continuous rewarding leverages the "crowd" to determine where the money flows, matching reward with performance to unify and direct people toward company priorities. Naturally, the bonuses are weighted more heavily toward the top performers. Over time, as more people are recognized and understand more fully how their contributions make a difference, people will deliver more and perform at a higher level, ultimately increasing the volume of high performers.

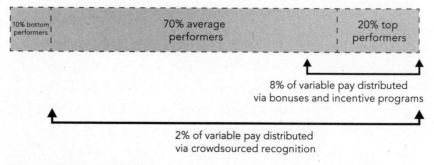

Figure 11.2 Power Shift
Dedicating 2 percent of payroll to recognition from a model 10 percent bonus pool extends its reach to far more employees.

The ways and means of funding a crowdsourced variable pay option are process questions, distinct from the decision to direct some portion of rewards toward creating a more human enterprise. Human resources leaders will adapt total rewards to the new realities of the workplace as part of a long-term cultural evolution to making work more human.

CONSIDER THIS

Think back to your first job. Did you and your peers feel that the rewards system was fair and equitable? How transparent were the various reward arrangements among functional areas and levels in the organization? Did you have any input into your compensation? Write a short paragraph beginning, "The reward system was fair because . . ." or "The reward system was unfair because . . ."

Next, imagine that you and your peers had the power to distribute at least 1 percent of the total payroll to one another based on social recognition of outstanding performance. Estimate how much that 1 percent would be. For example, if average compensation is $75,000 per employee, consider the effect of peers awarding each other $750 per year in recognition in 10 awards averaging $75 in value each. Appreciation and gratitude would be given and received among peers, along with material reward, on an average every five weeks. What would that do to the perception of fairness? What would it do to the perception of employee power to make a difference in the culture?

Finally, imagine you are a manager constructing a pay package offer for a candidate you really want to hire. Would lowering the base pay offer by 1 percent break the deal? We doubt it. But would demonstrating that the candidate would be working in a culture of inclusion, gratitude, and goodwill be worth that 1 percent? We think it would.

12 | Leading Humans

Advice from Leaders About Working Human

Our favorite part of every Workhuman Live event is meeting with the people who attend. Sometimes that's by the stage after an inspiring keynote, and sometimes it's just a momentary conversation on the way from one workshop to another. And every year, we're asked one question more than any other: "What do I do now?"

This is a question that open-minded leaders ask. They want to create a more human organization. They want to build a workplace where ideals like gratitude, purpose, fairness, equality, and transparency are put into practice at every level of the organization.

Our answer: By listening to these speakers and participating in these workshops, you've already started. What's needed now is the energy and courage to lead change, because once you leave this conference, you'll go back to a world that is crying out for these ideals to become reality but fearful of change. Once you find the courage to make that change, the rest is just hard work. And nobody who wants to change the workplace is afraid of hard work.

At Workhuman Live (and a number of smaller gatherings throughout the year), we find inspiration from people who have invested their hard work, intelligence, and even careers in the study of organizations. In this chapter, we share advice and experience on leadership from 10 leaders who have pointed the way. They represent a fraction of the people who lend their insight and experience to the cause of making work better for everyone. We offer these voices as a thought-provoking chorus of leaders talking about leading humans. We introduce each of them with a short note.

KAT COLE
What Is Your Water?

Speakers at Workhuman Live often tell us about turning points in their thinking about leadership. Sometimes this comes from data or from a teacher. Sometimes it comes from an unexpected source, like a village leader in East Africa. Kat Cole, COO and president, North America at FOCUS Brands, told us this story in 2019. In meetings at Workhuman, we still ask, "What is our water?"

I've done humanitarian work in eastern Africa for more than a decade. I was sitting in a village in Ethiopia on the Somali border with a group of friends, some of whom had never been to Africa, and I had been many times before. We were there to participate in what's called village transformation, where we help villagers who are in conflict zones learn to support their families because, if they can't support their families, they're going to do whatever someone says that promises them money, food, and resources— including terrorist organizations. But if they can support themselves, the world is a safer place.

We asked, "What are your priorities? How can we help you?" And one of the village leaders says, "Well, our number one priority is water. We need to get it to the places it needs to go to water our farms and vegetation, and we need to sanitize it so we can drink it and have proper nutrition and hygiene." And so *my friend writes down, "water." Then he asked, "What are some other things you're focused on? What's your number two priority, your number three, your number four?" And our translators, speaking Amharic, repeated the questions.*

Their response needed no translation because it was laughter. Then they said, "Our number two priority is water. Our number three priority is water, and our number four priority is water. You can build us a school if you want, but if we're sending our children to go get water, they won't be in the classroom. And you can teach us about hygiene and nutrition if you want, but if we can't get water where it needs to go, it will be meaningless."

As we were engaged in the conversation, I had an out-of-body leadership experience. It was as if my mind floated up and observed us, and I thought, "Wow, they're so clear on their priorities. If I could only be that clear. In my business, with my teams, in my personal life. If I could only be that clear!"

When I returned, I told this story to our teams at FOCUS Brands, and I said, "From now on I'm going to ask you this question: What is our water? What is the one thing to do right now so that everything else would get better on its own?"[1]

NATALY KOGAN
Why Gratitude?

Nataly Kogan is the founder of Happier @ Work and an expert on the surprising science of happiness. She says that happiness is not an emotion but a learnable skill. In a recent interview, Kogan shared the importance of practicing gratitude to counteract the neurochemical effects of stress.

Stress is the new constant at work, and we're all trying to deal with it. Research has brought us some good news about resilience and dealing with stress: gratitude.

Gratitude is the magic pill we're all searching for. We have it for free; there are no side effects; you can practice it anytime. And research shows that the moment you begin to think of something you are grateful for, your brain is firing dopamine. Practicing gratitude actually creates new neurons in the brain. Our brain's priority is not to feel good; its priority is to protect us from danger and conserve energy. Gratitude helps us avoid that, to overcome the negativity bias in the brain's natural adaptability.

Gratitude has also been shown to be one of the greatest forces of resilience. Research has shown consistently that when you practice gratitude during times of challenge or stress, it is a significant source of resilience. There was a study in Florida that followed hurricane victims—people who had lost everything. Those who approached that dire situation with some sense of gratitude actually rebounded faster than others. They would say, "It's obviously awful, we lost our home, we lost our car . . . but I'm so grateful that our dog survived, or that we survived, or that our neighbors are OK." They did so much better than families who only focused on what they lost.

Those are the two reasons that gratitude is nonnegotiable for emotional health. It helps to counteract the true natural tendencies of the brain, the negativity bias and adaptability. And it's a huge source of resilience during times of stress. And stress is the new constant.[2]

SHAWN ACHOR
Social Bonds Make Us Resilient

Shawn Achor has delighted Workhuman Live participants for several years as he relates the latest research in the science of happiness to real-life situations. Known for his popular TED Talk about happiness, Shawn has also joined us in deep studies of how creating community at work increases both traditional performance metrics and engagement.

As soon as you separate meaning and happiness, you've already made a mistake because you can't actually have happiness for very long if it's not ending up being meaningful. And people that try to live a meaningful life without that fuel coming from the positivity can't actually sustain it for very long as well. What we need to do is to be able to link them back together, to feel that joy as we move toward our potential.

We were working with Orlando Health. We went out to a level-one trauma hospital and got them at their staff meetings where they're doing life-or-death decisions to start the meeting. The very first task on the meeting docket was to go around the room and have every person say one thing that they were grateful for as quickly as possible so they could do it in less than a minute or two so they could get back onto the resource allocation.

Two years almost to the anniversary of this training, the Pulse nightclub shooting occurred three blocks away. And all the victims of the second largest shooting in U.S. history came to the teams that we had been working with and researching with.

The very next morning they started with gratitudes again because that's their work routine, and what they were grateful for is that for the past two years they weren't just doing work together; they were actually deepening their social bonds. Having those social bonds is one of the greatest predictors of resilience and grit.[3]

SIMON SINEK
Playing the Infinite Game

In 2018, Simon Sinek challenged Workhuman Live participants to rethink the role and purpose of human resource work. He conceives of successful business as an infinite game, not with fixed players, rules, and endpoints but constant change. His bestselling book *Start with Why* emphasizes the critical roles that purpose and inspiration play in business.

You can choose to live by the rules of the finite game, which means trying to get ahead faster and make more money and *accumulate more power than anyone you know. Or, you can choose to live a life based on the infinite game, which is not about how much you can gain, but how much you can help others gain. The infinite game is about the impact you can make in the lives of others. When others say, "I am who I am today because of you. This organization is what it is today in part because of your contribution," then you are playing the infinite game.*

The entire discipline of human resources should be the best example of what it means to play the infinite game. You are responsible for the lives of human beings; what impact are you having on them? Are you creating an environment in which they can work at their natural best? Are you working to create environments in which people feel they can be themselves?

When your people feel someone is watching out for them, they will be smarter, happier, and also more likely to give everything they've got to the organization. They'll use their talents to make the organization grow and thrive. That's what it means to live an infinite life.[4]

SUSAN CAIN
What Do Leaders Look Like?

We see it in the bookstore at Workhuman Live every year: People pick up a copy of Susan Cain's *Quiet: The Power of Introverts in a World That Can't Stop Talking*. They start reading it, and a look of relief comes over their face. Cain's deeply researched book reveals how introverts are the (literally) unsung heroes of the workplace. At the register, they tell us, "That's me!" Cain asked a ballroom full of managers to look beyond their preconceptions at Workhuman Live in 2017.

You might be familiar with the research on which Jim Collins's Good to Great was based. Studying exceptional companies, he found that every single one had a remarkably similar CEO: Number one, these people had a fierce sense of will and dedication to their companies. And number two, they were described by their peers and employees, and so on, as quiet, unassuming, low-key, soft-spoken, and even shy.

That's a whole constellation of traits that, if we're being honest, we normally do not associate with inspired leadership. And so, what could possibly explain these results? Well, it's actually not as mysterious as it might first sound.

The thing about introverts is, they tend to get really passionate about one or two things in their lives. And so, if you get introverts who are passionate about their work, about their company, about the thing they're doing, they will get really into it. They'll start building alliances and acquiring expertise and inspiring trust, and they'll end up ascending to leadership positions, not because they were seeking to be leaders in the first place, but just through this channel of really caring about what they are doing. Their leadership happens almost as an incidental.

I would love for each of you right now to think about someone you know in your workplace who is really talented and really committed and who would not strike you as a so-called natural leader in the conventional sense of that word. Think about what you could do to groom that person, to help them realize the gifts that they have for themselves and for your organization.

As soon as you get back to work, see if you can sit down with that person and figure out what is their one-year plan, what's their three-year plan, what's their five-year plan. How can you help them get there by drawing on the strength they already have and stepping outside their comfort zones strategically?[5]

AMY CUDDY
Personal Power

Harvard Business School professor Amy Cuddy's discussion of "power posing" is one of the all-time favorite TED Talks. At Workhuman Live, she went deeper into the social and biological reasons that such a simple-seeming behavior can be transformative to one's outlook in a stressful situation.

When we are present, when we're showing up as our authentic selves, we're basically putting this trustworthy side of ourselves forth. We're saying to people, "I'm gonna show you who I am." We're being vulnerable. It allows other people to do the same.

They can meet you where you are. They're not scared. They feel comfortable, they feel safe, and when you can do that, you have opened up this whole conduit of influence, of communication, of connection.

We can't all have social power all the time in every situation, but we can all have personal power. We all can access those skills, those core values, the best parts of ourselves, [and] it's true for women and men. [Our research] has found that humans who have more power and feel more powerful, have higher testosterone and lower cortisol. And those people are rated as better leaders by the people who work with them. They're seen as confident and strong but also as tuned in to other people's needs. They're able to put the interest of the team ahead of their own interests.

We have this idea that power is all about the self, that power is selfish, and leadership is all about being dominant. It's not. It's about being able to connect and being able to be strong, being able to listen and being strong.[6]

ADAM GRANT
Inviting Other Voices into the Conversation

Professor Adam Grant of the Wharton School is the author of *Originals*. As a social scientist, Grant often questions common wisdom and devises databased research to test the assumptions that business leaders make. Grant chaired a landmark panel discussion at Workhuman Live 2018, talking about the #MeToo movement with Tarana Burke, Ashley Judd, and Ronan Farrow. In 2017, he talked about the importance of raising voices that haven't typically been heard in the workplace.

We found that when women spoke up in meetings with ideas and suggestions, they were either barely heard or judged as too aggressive. Men who came with the same ideas were celebrated and rewarded for it. And in the data, this was actually really worrisome not only because of that but because on average women had more creative ideas. When you separated whose idea it was from the idea itself, women's ideas were rated as more novel, more useful than men's. And yet they were more likely to be silenced. And later we found the same patterns for members of multiple racial minority groups, both black and Latino, consistently. So when you think about cultural contribution, recognizing demographic diversity as a source of insight, as a different way of solving problems, is something so critical for us all to do.

If we really want diversity of thought in organizations, if we really want original ideas, we need more white men to step up and use that privilege that exists to make sure that the ideas of people who are underrepresented are heard. That might be women. It might be racial minorities. It also might be skill minorities. How many tech companies devalue salespeople and marketers? How many organizations dominated by extroverts ignore introverts? And I think the best thing we can all do if we really want to build a truly human workplace—if you believe that the work environment should be a place where we don't check our values and our identities at the office door—the best thing we can do is figure out whose voices are not being heard. And then invite those voices into the conversation.[7]

CHRISTINE PORATH
The Conversations That Change Us

Christine Porath is a professor of management at Georgetown University and the author of *Mastering Civility: A Manifesto for the Workplace*. Her research focuses on civility in organizations, and she is a frequent contributor to the *Harvard Business Review* and many other publications. Her TED Talk on civility in the workplace proves why being respectful in the workplace is good for business. She spoke with us in August 2019 for this book about making civility happen.

> How can we encourage civility at work? One way is building expectations and norms for how people are going to treat each other with respect. Another would be role modeling—leaders need to model civility and encourage it. And the third would be holding people accountable. You do that by gathering feedback about how people are treating each other. If there are reports of people who mistreat others, whether that's being rude, harassing, or bullying, then leaders have to take action: Meet with the person; provide coaching; provide resources. Sometimes there may be a gap where it's simply not going to be possible to deliver, whether that's because of a different generational expectation or different cultural norms. Ultimately there may be consequences if people don't change.
>
> It's in leaders' and organizations' best interest to create workplaces where people can thrive. Organizations are starting to separate themselves by being known for their culture. And hopefully others try to follow suit and raise the bar.
>
> The important thing, especially for managers and leaders, to realize is civility is subjective. It's all in the eyes of the beholder. If you want people's best work, however, you need a grasp of what they feel. I think it's always helpful to gain a realistic perspective of where a person is coming from, and to tweak your behavior accordingly because it can make a huge difference.

Feedback is useful information because so much of the problem of incivility stems from a lack of self-awareness. So if we can provide feedback to them, that's really a gift.[8]

GARY HAMEL
Leading with Love

Gary Hamel is one of the world's most influential business thinkers. His iconoclastic articles and books envision a world in which organizations break away from their old bureaucratic ways of thinking and acting, and his blog, http://garyhamel.com, offers practical and provocative ideas for "creating work environments where human beings are free to flourish." Shortly after the death of Southwest Airlines' CEO Herb Kelleher in 2019, Hamel used Southwest as an example of a culture where humans thrive.

Everybody who works at Southwest Airlines believes they're doing God's own work. They believe they are letting all of us be able to afford to fly. Everyone there shares the same financial data. Every employee knows exactly what drives the airline's profitability, knows how they're doing month to month, knows how many seats you have to fill for a flight to be profitable. There's very little hierarchy; every decision is consultative and talked about and worked through. Every job is deemed as important as every other job. There's a huge emphasis on families getting to know families and connecting not just as employees but with their families together. People are encouraged to bring their personal struggles to work. If you're going through a divorce, if you're struggling with a child with an addiction, if you recently lost a parent, if you're up against a difficult medical decision, you need people to talk to. If you have to go for 8 or 10 hours of the day and those people are not around you, I can tell you that you are not going to be at your best and neither will your business. That's why Herb Kelleher, founder of Southwest, said a company is stronger if it's bound by love rather than fear.

Let me ask you, when was the last time in a meeting in your company you used the word love to talk about your culture. When was the last time you heard your CEO say, What we really need is a little bit more love? Our organizations have become so inhuman that we can't even use the language that matters to us most. Herb Kelleher had it exactly right; he said the tragedy of our times is that we've got it backward; we've learned to love techniques and use people. I couldn't have said it any better than that.[9]

BRENÉ BROWN
Changing Yourself

Brené Brown's invitation to lead with a "strong back, soft front, and wild heart" strikes a deep chord at Workhuman Live. In recent years her books and a Netflix special brought Brown's bold and vulnerable vision to a wider and wider audience. But as HR professionals, and as humans, we still think of this researcher/executive/consultant/speaker/author as "one of us."

If you're brave with your life, you're going to know failure. You're going to know disappointment. You're going to know setbacks. If you love somebody, you're going to get your heart broken. That's why I think the heartbroken are probably the bravest among us, because they had the courage to love.

If you set up a culture within your organization where there is no tolerance for vulnerability, where there's no tolerance for uncertainty, no tolerance for failure, do not expect people to be innovative and creative. Period. No vulnerability, no innovation, no creativity. It just doesn't work.

Trust is built in tiny small moments every day. A metaphor we use is marbles in a marble jar. Trust is built every day in the smallest of moments, in the recognition moments, but also in the

"Hey, Sue. Good to see you. How's your dad's chemo going? How was the soccer tournament? How are you feeling? What's going on with Steve's job search?" moments. Those are the moments trust is built in.[10]

A Call for Change

Each of these speakers, and the thousands of others we have met at Workhuman Live, is allied in a noble purpose. We are all working to make organizations more human. Whether they are organizations small or large, businesses or nonprofits, even universities, schools, and other places where people come together, they are all part of a growing movement and determined to change the world for the better. We are grateful for their leadership and participation in the cause that defines our business and our Workhuman community.

We'll continue to invite voices, including yours, into the Workhuman Movement. In the final chapter, we'll describe another way that we can all make our workplaces—our new communities—more human.

CONSIDER THIS

At the end of every Workhuman Live conference, people ask, "What can I do? Where do I start?" We hope this book has offered some answers.

The answer to making a human enterprise isn't found in a single formula or a single strategy. A human enterprise is, in Simon Sinek's term, an *infinite game*. There will always be new challenges to face and progress to be made.

Work will become more and more human as individuals everywhere wake up to the obsolete behaviors and habitual thinking that characterize far too many of our organizations. This is not a project with a defined end, but a process that continues for as long as humans work together.

In the final chapter of this book, we describe a new idea that Workhuman is pursuing—Workhuman Certified—and the ways we are making that idea a reality.

The last writing exercise for readers of this book is simple: If you truly wish to make work more human, what can you do today?

And what will you do tomorrow?

13 | A Call to Action

We began this book with a call for a new charter of human rights focused on employees, and we end by calling on you, the reader, to take action. Employees have the right to a human workplace. Leaders have the power to create one. What will you, a leader at any level of your organization, do with your power? Will you spend your career in the twilight of the bureaucratic corporate model, or enlist in the movement to make the workplace better?

Creating a human enterprise is a big job, and it could be the most important work you do in the coming years, because the human enterprise is both a sustainable business and a servant of society. What better mission can you undertake at work than creating that?

Every organization has a culture. Consider yours for a moment. All too often, it simply exists as a by-product of neglect, bureaucratic inertia, or through the relentless drive to make the latest quarter's numbers rather than purposeful direction. There is a big difference in such organizations between the appearance of change and actually doing what it takes to put human-centric behaviors and policies into practice. It's no longer a matter of checking boxes; it means sparking real change.

Here's the good news: You are not alone. Companies and professionals around the world are eager to discover ways to optimize employee efficiency and performance, foster a happier workforce, promote fairness and equality, and still create profits that sustain and grow healthy economies.

At the end of every Workhuman Live event we find ourselves exhilarated by the power of these ideas and by the energy of thousands of people coming together to make work more human. We've talked to hundreds of business leaders, given keynote presentations, and listened to brilliant business leaders like those quoted in Chapter 12. And on the final day, attendees have one concern greater than any other. They ask, "How do I get started? What are the most important guidelines for making my workplace more human?"

To answer that concern, we created the *Workhuman Charter of Workplace Rights* described in the Introduction to this book. Then in 2020 we created a process to attest that a company believes in those rights and is on a journey toward implementing them. By putting a stake in the ground and committing to the rights, they can be *Workhuman Certified*.

Workhuman Certified is an opportunity for both companies and individuals to join our movement and be recognized as champions of human-centric work environments and practices. As an international seal of recognition for organizations that are helping lead the movement, it celebrates the power of humanity in the workplace *and* testifies that human workplaces are better than the traditional bureaucratic model in every way. These organizations and individuals share a collective goal of fostering strong cultures, maximizing human potential for exemplary work and personal growth, and discovering shared mission and purpose around which people can rally.

Our aim is to make Workhuman Certified a standard of recognition and commitment to progress for cultivating human-centered workplaces—those in which people are supported to do the best work of their lives.

We know many worthy organizations with ideas about making workplaces better. But none of them focuses on the relationships we see connecting human happiness, gratitude, performance and feedback. None of them has a database containing millions of moments of values-based recognition, or an objective method for uncovering unconscious and conscious bias. With that focus and that data, we realized we were uniquely positioned to cast the vision, bring the community together, and facilitate progress, as we have done with our Workhuman Live event and movement.

That realization became a responsibility that now guides all the work we do.

The Workhuman Charter of Workplace Rights is our call to action, and the journey of becoming Workhuman Certified guides that action. We designed these rights because it's not enough to say, for example, "Everybody's voice matters here." All too often, companies look at workplace rights as a checkbox item, not as a core part of their mission and their brand. And all too often, they view noncompliance with those rights as a public relations problem instead of a moral or ethical problem.

Why Do We Call These Rights?

Why do we call these "rights?" *Because employees do.* Something big happened in the last 30 years, as the old psychological contract between corporations and employees dissolved. Once, most employees tolerated bureaucracy, inequality, and inauthenticity in exchange for job security. As job security disappeared, people became more mobile out of necessity. They found they had more choices of where and how to work, and who to work with. The most talented, who had the most choices, saw that they didn't have to leave their principles or personalities at home when they went to work. Leading companies learned that culture was the most important factor attracting talent.

Today competitive pay, decent benefits, and OSHA compliance are no more than table stakes. Workhuman Certified shows next-level commitment to delivering what employees want and demand in a great workplace: cultures that authentically deliver meaningful work, gratitude, growth, a sense of belonging, work-life harmony, opportunities to be heard, and the twin expectations of accountability and equality on behalf of every employee. It shows commitment to a stronger, more diverse, and equitable workplace.

Equality means all employees have the right to reward based on their accomplishments. A fair meritocracy, based on equal opportunity and free from unconscious or conscious bias, is part of a human workplace. In fact, this is one of the strongest arguments for crowdsourced pay—by giving part of a reward system to the crowd, organizations are committing to a more just distribution of resources. Great workplaces aren't afraid of striving toward equality of opportunity while simultaneously giving rewards based on individual accomplishment.

Workhuman Certified is different from checkbox surveys of compliance. It's not an assessment of your organization's HR practices, but a declaration of your organization's commitment, plans and actions taken to create a work environment that serves the changing needs of a modern, globalized workforce. Laws protecting employees and HR practices designed to attract and retain the most talented are necessary but still fall short of delivering the employee experience that will be required to remain competitive in the future.

How Change Happens

Changes like those we envision don't happen overnight, but there is reason to believe that the time is right for workplace rights to become commonly accepted. In August 2019, the Business Roundtable, for the first time in 41 years, redefined the purpose of a corporation. Instead of insisting that public corporations exist primarily to serve shareholders, 181 CEOs joined the Roundtable's statement that corporations exist to benefit all stakeholders—customers, employees, suppliers, communities, and shareholders.[1] It's fair to view such declarations with both optimism and skepticism, but they are another step in the right direction for workplace rights.

Before COVID-19, Workhuman called workplaces the new community. Then, during the early months of the pandemic, the ways in which people reached out to support their coworkers and neighbors confirmed that belief for us. Purpose, meaning, and gratitude came to the forefront of our workplaces as crisis showed us what was really important.

It won't end when we take off our masks. Speaking at Workhuman Livestream in May 2020, Simon Sinek shared this advice: "I've been in a go-mode, mission-focused mindset since the start of COVID-19, but when I called a friend in the military and jokingly asked when it's all going to hit me, he cautioned that there's no such thing as compartmentalizing trauma. When things return to normal, we'll still have to process those emotions."

As of this writing, we don't know exactly what the workplace will look like when the pandemic ebbs. Neither do we know how worldwide calls for racial justice will change our work cultures. We do know that those who are called to reinvent work will be energized by purpose, meaning, and gratitude. Even in the next "new normal"—purpose, meaning, and gratitude guide us to make work a better place.

As we asserted in Chapter 1, the future of business depends on work becoming more human, and that's a powerful impetus toward progress. As the business writer Daniel Pink recently observed, "Individual companies are waking up to the fact that they need talent more than talent needs them."[2] The best employees have a choice of employers and, economic cycles notwithstanding, we believe this trend will continue.

Companies have had to make the case that they are a superior place to work, but society has evolved faster than most company culture. People see diversity, inclusion, and racial justice as fundamental human rights, and those whose talent gives them a wide choice of employers will choose accordingly.

When social standards change, some influential companies take the lead, and signal a tipping point in corporate behavior. For example, Apple established standards of environmental responsibility that are now proliferating through the technology landscape. Apple publishes an annual supplier responsibility progress report, mapping the progress of its suppliers. For example, 100 percent of final assembly plants for most Apple products are UL Zero Waste Certified.[3] Again, changes like this don't happen overnight, but they happen a lot faster when large enterprises put their financial power behind them. Apple is highly conscious of this effect, and part of its program is to enable its suppliers, in turn, to be role models and leaders in their own industries and locations.

A new charter for workplace rights like Workhuman Certified tells people which organizations truly share their values—not only in words but in deeds. As those companies influence their vendors and suppliers, we believe more and more organizations will become places where every workplace right is respected, promoted, and celebrated.

Most movements start small. Environmentalism was considered a fringe issue by most businesses in 1960. Fifteen years later it was a mainstream concern, and today the conversation about climate change has brought an unprecedented urgency and global efforts by corporations to address the climate crisis. Activists started the movement, and government responded as well, but widespread change became inevitable when business embraced the principles.

We think the Workhuman movement is following a similar and accelerated trajectory. Technology, social media, and global connection speed up change, including change for the better. For example, Workhuman Live 2018 speaker Tarana Burke began working with victims of sexual harassment and assault in 1997. She coined the term *Me Too* in 2006 to mobilize people against sexual harassment and assault. In 2017, the #MeToo movement became a social tsunami as widespread allegations about serious workplace misconduct involving high-profile business leaders spread on social media and in the press. Companies that had previously just "talked the talk" took a hard look at their practices, and things changed. They are still changing. Now, sexual harassment is an unavoidable issue for organizations large and small. We believe that the full range of workplace rights is poised to become part of the public consciousness.

Join Us!

The Workhuman Charter of Workplace Rights, and the Workhuman movement, are not focused exclusively on profit-making businesses. Schools, higher education, and nonprofits—they should be part of this movement as well. They are also places where people come together to accomplish common goals—to work, to learn, to serve a mission. They too are part of the new community we defined in Chapter 2.

Ultimately, it's the daily actions and beliefs of individuals that comprise Workhuman Certified. We are also creating a way for individuals to begin their own personal journey. We are developing short modules of training across all the charter themes that will allow individuals to sign up to the charter, express their aspirations, and then take some practical steps to widen their knowledge and align their behaviors with their beliefs. In Chapter 10 we noted that everyone has unconscious biases and assumptions. Making progress toward our better selves means changing ourselves for the better. The training is designed to meet that need and encourage those folks on the journey to put their aspirations for a more human workplace into practice.

Collectively, the learning and certification modules will comprise what we are calling the Workhuman Hub, in which all the topics discussed in this book—performance management and feedback, diversity and inclusion, purpose and meaning, recognition and the rest—contribute to the growth of individuals in the workplace. We hope that a comprehensive approach to training in the charter's principles will equip both individuals and organizations to navigate the disruptions roiling the modern workplace while still making progress toward a more human-centric workplace culture.

If at the end of this book, you ask, "Where do I start?" we answer, "Here's a practical next step that you can take: Workhuman has a road map for becoming a more human workplace. Share evidence of your commitment to making work more human, and if you still have progress to make (which we all do), we'll help you find your way."

This book is just a beginning. As this book is being completed, the Workhuman movement will continue to grow in the months and years to come. If you agree that the time has come to make your workplace more human, and if you embrace the vision to build our shared beliefs into a common cause, join us at **workhuman.com**.

NOTES

Introduction

1. Heather E. McGowan and Chris Shipley, "Future of Work: Learning to Manage Uncertainty," August 27, 2017, https://www.linkedin.com/pulse/learning-uncertainty-imperative-heather-mcgowan/.
2. Peter F. Drucker, *The Essential Drucker: The Best of Sixty Years of Peter Drucker's Essential Writings on Management*, pp. 14–16.
3. "The Future of Work Is Human," Workhuman Analytics & Research Institute 2019 International Employee Survey Report.

Chapter 1: The Human Enterprise

1. 2019 Edelman Trust Barometer, top-10 findings.
2. "The Financial Impact of a Positive Employee Experience," IBM Smarter Workforce Institute and WorkHuman Analytics & Research Institute, June 2018, p. 5.
3. "Towards a Reskilling Revolution: A Future of Jobs for All," World Economic Forum/The Boston Consulting Group, January 2018, p. 3.
4. Josh Bersin, "LinkedIn 2019 Talent Trends: Soft Skills, Transparency and Trust," https://www.linkedin.com/pulse/linkedin-2019-talent-trends-soft-skills-transparency-trust-bersin/?trk=eml-email_feed_ecosystem, accessed January 31, 2019.
5. Seamus Heaney. Here's his Nobel lecture, https://www.nobelprize.org/prizes/literature/1995/heaney/lecture/.
6. "The 5 Trademarks of Agile Organizations," McKinsey Agile Tribe, December 2017.
7. Twitter, @AdamMGrant, November 2, 2018.
8. "Navigating the Future of Work," *Deloitte Review*, No. 21, July 2017, p. 132.
9. Ibid.; also see Z. Ton, *The Good Jobs Strategy: How the Smartest Companies Invest in Employees to Lower Costs and Boost Profits* (New Harvest, 2014).
10. "The Future of Work: Capital Markets, Digital Assets, and the Disruption of Labor," MIT Initiative on the Digital Economy (report), 2018. p. 5

Chapter 2: The Future of Work Is Human

1. "Eight Futures of Work: Scenarios and Their Implications," white paper, World Economic Forum in Collaboration with The Boston Consulting Group, January 2018, http://www3.weforum.org/docs/WEF_FOW_Eight_Futures.pdf.
2. Josh Bersin, "Catch the Wave: The 21st-Century Career," *Deloitte Review*, No. 21, July 2017, pp. 70–71.
3. Cathy Engelbert and John Hagel, "Radically Open: Tom Friedman on Jobs, Learning and the Future of Work," *Deloitte Review* special report, July 2017, p. 103.
4. Bersin, "Catch the Wave," pp. 69–70.
5. David M. Mayer, Madeline Ong, Scott Sonenshein, and Susan J. Ashford. "To Get Companies to Take Action on Social Issues, Emphasize Morals, Not the Business Case," *Harvard Business Review*, February 14, 2019.
6. 2019 Edelman Trust Barometer, top-10 findings.
7. Interview with Gabrielle Thompson, SVP Acquisitions and Total Rewards, Cisco, June 26, 2019.
8. Vivek Murthy, "Work and the Loneliness Epidemic," *Harvard Business Review*, September 2017.
9. Shawn Achor, Gabriella Rosen Kellerman, Andrew Reece, and Alexi Robichaux, "America's Loneliest Workers, According to Research," *Harvard Business Review*, March 19, 2018.
10. 2017 Deloitte Millennial Survey, p. 15. See chart.
11. Interview with Susan Cain, November 15, 2019.
12. "Social Impact in the Human Workplace," Workhuman Analytics & Research Institute, 2018.
13. "Social Impact in the Human Workplace," Workhuman Analytics & Research Institute, 2019.
14. Adapted from "6 Megatrends Changing the Face of HR and Business," Workhuman white paper.
15. Adam Satariano, "Amazon to Retrain a Third of Its U.S. Workers as Automation Advances," *New York Times*, July 11, 2019.
16. https://www.leanproduction.com/kaizen.html.
17. Globoforce interview with Josh Bersin.
18. "6 Megatrends Changing the Face of HR and Business."

Chapter 3: The Employee Experience

1. Nina McQueen, "Workplace Culture Trends: The Key to Hiring (and Keeping) Top Talent in 2018," LinkedIn blog, June 26, 2018.
2. "The Financial Impact of a Positive Employee Experience," IBM Smarter Workforce Institute and Workhuman Analytics & Research Institute, 2018, p. 2.
3. Interview with Daniel Pink, October 24, 2019.
4. Gary Hamel keynote, Workhuman Live 2019, March 19, 2019.

NOTES 243

5. From "6 Megatrends Changing the Face of HR and Business," Workhuman white paper.
6. "The ROI of Recognition in Building a More Human Workplace," WARI report, 2016.
7. "Teams Are Key to Organizational Progress: A Q&A with Amy Edmondson," https://resources.globoforce.com/globoforce- blog/teams-are -key-to-organizational-progress-q-a-with-amy-edmondson, accessed May 20, 2019.
8. "WHO Redefines Burnout as a 'Syndrome' Linked to Chronic Stress at Work," NPR, May 28, 2019, https://www.npr.org/sections/health-shots/ 2019/05/28/727637944/who-redefines-burnout-as-a-syndrome-linked-to -chronic-stress-at-work, accessed May 28, 2019.
9. "Teams Are Key to Organizational Progress."
10. Christine Porath, "Creating a More Human Workplace Where Employees and Business Thrive," SHRM Foundation's Effective Practice Guidelines Series, 2016, sponsored by Globoforce.
11. Zeynep Ton, "Why 'Good Jobs' Are Good for Retailers," *Harvard Business Review*, January–February 2012.
12. 2019 Deloitte Millennial Survey, p. 15.

Chapter 4: What Do Employees Want?

1. Nataly Kogan, Workhuman presentation, March 19, 2019.
2. "State of the Global Workplace, Executive Summary," Gallup, 2017, p. 6.
3. See Charles Duhigg, *The Power of Habit: Why We Do What We Do in Life and Business*, Random House, New York, 2012.
4. Jonathan Gottschall, *The Storytelling Animal: How Stories Make Us Human*, Houghton Mifflin Harcourt, New York, 2012.
5. Rita Gunther McGrath, "Management's Three Eras: A Brief History," *Harvard Business Review*, July 30, 2014.
6. E. Lesser, J. Mertens, M. Barrientos, and M. Singer, "Designing Employee Experience: How a Unifying Approach Can Enhance Engagement and Productivity," IBM Smarter Workforce Institute, 2016.
7. "The Employee Experience Index Around the Globe: How Countries Measure Up and Create Human Workplaces," IBM Smarter Workforce Institute and Workhuman Research Institute, 2017.
8. "The Financial Impact of a Positive Employee Experience," IBM Smarter Workforce Institute and Workhuman Analytics & Research Institute, 2018, p. 2.
9. "The Overlooked Essentials of Employee Well-Being," *McKinsey Quarterly*, September 2018, p. 7. Pfeffer is also the author of *Dying for a Paycheck: How Modern Management Harms Employee Health and Company Performance—and What We Can Do About It*, HarperCollins, New York, 2018.
10. Workhuman Live keynote address, 2018.

Chapter 5: Purpose, Meaning, and Gratitude

1. Simon Sinek, *Start with Why: How Great Leaders Inspire Everyone to Take Action,* Portfolio, New York, 2009, p. 95.
2. Maria Semykoz, "How to Manage the AI Disruption: A Culture of Purpose," Gallup, August 3, 2018.
3. 2019 Edelman Trust Barometer, Trust in Technology, p. 34.
4. Valerie Keller, "The Business Case for Purpose," *A Harvard Business Review Analytical Services Report, Harvard Business Review,* 2015.
5. 2019 Edelman Trust Barometer, pp. 28–33.
6. 2019 Edelman Trust Barometer, p. 34.
7. Imperative/NYU Workforce Purpose Index, 2015, p. 13.
8. Vincent Jelani, "Avoiding Staff Burnout Through 'Meaningful Work,'" Harvard University, 2017, https://scholar.harvard.edu/vincentjelani/publications/avoiding-staff-burnout-through-%E2%80%9Cmeaningful-work%E2%80%9D, accessed June 5, 2019.
9. WorkTrends™ 2016 Global sample for the IBM/Workhuman Employee Experience Index Study. Figures in the chart show the percentage contribution of each of the six human workplace practices identified as drivers of a positive employee experience.
10. "The Employee Experience Index Around the Globe: How Countries Measure Up and Create Human Workplaces," IBM Smarter Workforce Institute and Workhuman Research Institute, 2017, p. 6.
11. "Bringing More Humanity to Recognition, Performance, and Life at Work," Workhuman Analytics & Research Institute 2017 Survey Report, p. 6.
12. 2019 Deloitte Millennial Survey, pp. 26–27.
13. https://www.mercer.com/content/dam/mercer/attachments/global/Career/gl-2018-talent-trends-2018-infographic-usa-mercer.pdf, accessed June 5, 2019.
14. Mercer Global Talent Trends 2019, p. 2.
15. "Leading the Social Enterprise: Reinvent with a Human Focus," *Deloitte Insights,* 2019, p. 6.
16. State of the Global Workplace, Executive Summary, Gallup, 2017, p. 7ff.
17. Interview with Nataly Kogan, July 9, 2019.
18. Summer Allen, "The Science of Gratitude," a white paper prepared for the John Templeton Foundation by the Greater Good Science Center at UC Berkeley.
19. Ibid., p. 48ff.

Chapter 6: Human Moments That Matter

1. Paul Leonardi and Noshir Contractor, "Better People Analytics—Measure Who They Know, Not Just Who They Are," *Harvard Business Review,* November–December 2018.
2. "Q&A with the Co-founder of *Wired,* IBM.com, https://www.ibm.com/watson/advantage-reports/future-of-artificial-intelligence/kevin-kelly.html, accessed June 5, 2019.

3. https://www.icims.com/hiring-insights/article-employee-turnover-statistics -and-what-it-costs-companies.
4. https://news.gallup.com/businessjournal/189875/amid-rapid-fire-workplace -change-pulse-surveys-emerge.aspx.
5. http://scholarworks.sjsu.edu/cgi/viewcontent cgi?article=8101&context=etd _theses.
6. https://www2.deloitte.com/content/dam/Deloitte/mx/Documents/about -deloitte/Talent2020_Employee-Perspective.pdf.

Chapter 7: Recognition: The Heart of Working Human

1. findings-from-the-2018-shrm-globoforce-employee-recognition-survey -designing-work-cultures-for-the-human-era.pdf.
2. "Thanks, but No E-Thanks," August 28, 2019, https://www.workhuman.com/ resources/papers/thanks-but-no-e-thanks.
3. https://www.workhuman.com/resource-center/#ufh-i-416750193-2018 -shrm-workhuman-employee-recognition-survey.
4. https://news.gallup.com/reports/199961/7.aspx.
5. Karen Higginbottom, "Employee Appreciation Pays Off," *Forbes*, March 3, 2017, https://www.forbes.com/sites/karenhigginbottom/2017/03/03/ employee-appreciation-pays-off/#39462bec6ddc, accessed July 19, 2019.
6. Christine Porath, "Creating a More Human Workplace Where Employees and Business Thrive," SHRM Foundation, 2016, p. 9.
7. Ibid., p. 3.
8. Jim Harter, "Employee Engagement on the Rise in the U.S.," Gallup, August 26, 2018.
9. https://resources.globoforce.com/papers/the-employee-experience-index.
10. "The 4 Es of Employee Engagement," Workhuman e-book, 2019.
11. Ibid., p. 3.
12. Ibid., p. 4.
13. ROA: return on assets; ROS: return on sales, IBM/Workhuman Analytics & Research Institute, March 2019.
14. 2019 Edelman Trust Barometer Global Report, p. 33.
15. *Success Magazine* interview with Shawn Achor, November 3, 2016.
16. Charles Duhigg, *The Power of Habit: Why We Do What We Do in Life and Business*, Random House, New York, 2012, p. 255.
17. "Bringing More Humanity to Recognition. Performance, and Life at Work," Workhuman Research & Analytics Institute, 2017.
18. Thomas F. Mahan, Danny Nelms, and Christopher Ryan Bearden, "2018 Retention Report: Truth and Trends in Turnover," The Work Institute, 2018.
19. Shawn Achor, "The Benefits of Peer-to-Peer Praise at Work," *Harvard Business Review*, February 19, 2016.
20. WARI study conducted June 2017–May 2018.
21. WARI Ohio Health study, 2019.
22. For an excellent case study, see Charles Duhigg's telling of the story of Paul O'Neill at Alcoa in Duhigg's *The Power of Habit*.

23. WARI study conducted, June 2017–May 2018.
24. Interview with Stacia Sherman Garr, March 27, 2019.

Chapter 8: Recognition: Basics and Best Practices

1. Interview with Christina Hall, October 21, 2019.
2. Chris Pang and Melanie Lougee, "Use Recognition and Reward Programs to Boost HR and Talent Effectiveness," Gartner Report, August 16, 2018.
3. E. Diener, E. Sandvik, and W. Pavot, "Happiness Is the Frequency, Not the Intensity, of Positive Versus Negative Affect," in E. Diener (ed.), *Assessing Well-Being*, Social Indicators Research Series, Vol. 39, Springer, Dordrecht, 2009.
4. "Connect People and Transform Culture," Cisco case study, Workhuman, 2019.
5. Mercer estimated that in 2018 US companies had a voluntary turnover rate of 16 percent. https://www.imercer.com/ecommerce/articleinsights/North -American-Employee-Turnover-Trends-and-Effects, accessed July 24, 2019.
6. Jim Harter, "Employee Engagement on the Rise in the U.S.," Gallup, August 26, 2018.
7. Human Capital Management Institute Productivity Linkage Analysis, 2018.

Chapter 9: Performance Management

1. Marcus Buckingham and Ashley Goodall, "Reinventing Performance Management," *Harvard Business Review*, April 2015.
2. "Why Performance Management Isn't Working," Gallup, https://www.gallup .com/workplace/215927/performance-management.aspx.
3. Peter Cappelli and Anna Tavis, "The Performance Management Revolution," *Harvard Business Review*, October 2016.
4. Gary Hamel, speaking at Workhuman Live 2019, Nashville, TN.
5. Cappelli and Tavis, "The Performance Management Revolution."
6. Dr. David Rock, speaking at Workhuman Live 2018, Austin, TX.
7. https://news.harvard.edu/gazette/story/2013/05/winfreys-commencement- address/.
8. Ken Segall, *Insanely Simple: The Obsession That Drives Apple's Success*, Portfolio, New York, 2012, p. 17.
9. Marcus Buckingham and Ashley Goodall, *Nine Lies About Work: A Freethinking Leader's Guide to the Real World*, Harvard Business Review Press, Brighton, MA, 2019, pp. 117–118.
10. Eloïse Marthouret and Sofie Sigvardsson, "The Effect of Quick Feedback on Employee Motivation and Performance," research paper, Linköping University, Spring 2016.
11. Peter Cappelli and Anna Tavis, "HR Goes Agile," *Harvard Business Review*, March–April 2018.
12. Chris Pang and Melanie Lougee, "Use Recognition and Reward Programs to Boost HR and Talent Effectiveness," Gartner Report, August 16, 2018.

13. Marthouret and Sigvardsson, "The Effect of Quick Feedback on Employee Motivation and Performance."

14. "How Qlik Successfully Transitioned to Continuous Performance Development," Workhuman case study, 2018.

15. State of the American Workplace, Gallup, 2017, p. 80.

16. "Bringing More Humanity to Recognition, Performance, and Life at Work," 2017 Survey Report, Workhuman Research Institute, https://www.workhuman.com/wp-content/uploads/2017/10/WHRI_2017 SurveyReportA.pdf.

17. "The Future of Work Is Human: Findings from the Workhuman Analytics & Research Institute Survey," 2019 International Employee Survey Report.

18. "Four Essentials of Effective Performance Development," Brandon Hall Group Research Team, 2018. Figure includes an option to choose "as frequently as needed."

19. "Leading the Social Enterprise: Reinvent with a Human Focus," 2019 Deloitte Global Human Capital Trends, p. 32.

20. Cappelli and Tavis, "HR Goes Agile."

21. 2018 SHRM/Workhuman Employee Recognition Report.

22. "6 Megatrends Changing the Face of HR and Business," Workhuman Executive Forums; see also Leonardo Baldassarre and Brian Finken, "GE's Real-Time Performance Development," *Harvard Business Review*, August 12, 2015.

Chapter 10: The Future of Diversity and Inclusion

1. Claudia Goldin and Cecilia Rouse, "Orchestrating Impartiality: The Impact of 'Blind' Auditions on Female Musicians," *American Economic Review*, Vol. 90, No. 4, September 2000, pp. 715–741.

2. https://www.classicfm.com/discover-music/when-did-women-join-orchestras/.

3. Grace Donnelly, "Only 3% of Fortune 500 Companies Share Full Diversity Data," *Fortune*, June 7, 2017. Race and gender data is reported privately to the Department of Labor.

4. Vivian Hunt, Dennis Layton, and Sara Prince, "Why Diversity Matters," McKinsey, January 2015.

5. Ibid.

6. Karen Brown, "To Retain Employees, Focus on Inclusion, Not Just Diversity," *Harvard Business Review*, January 4, 2018.

7. Rocío Lorenzo, Nicole Voigt, Miki Tsusaka, Matt Krentz, and Katie Abouzahr, "The Mix That Matters: Innovation Through Diversity," BCG, April 26, 2017; also "How Diverse Leadership Teams Boost Innovation," January 23, 2018.

8. Paul Gompers and Silpa Kowali, "The Other Diversity Dividend," *Harvard Business Review*, July–August 2018.

9. Juliet Bourke and Bernadette Dillon, "The Diversity and Inclusion Revolution," *Deloitte Review*, January 2018, p. 82ff.

10. David Lapin, "The Missing Piece to D&I," Workhuman, December 5, 2018.
11. Stacia Sherman Garr, "Women, Networks, and Technology: Premise," January 19, 2019.
12. Marianne Bertrand and Sendhil Mullainathan, "Are Emily and Greg More Employable Than Lakisha and Jamal? A Field Experiment on Labor Market Discrimination," *American Economic Review*, September 2004.
13. Adapted from "Accelerate Diversity and Inclusion Initiatives: 10 Ways Human Applications Can Help," Workhuman Analytics & Research Institute, 2019.

Chapter 11: Redesigning Rewards

1. Emily Payne, "Teams Are Key to Organizational Progress: Q&A with Amy Edmondson," Workhuman, January 30, 2018.
2. Dan Miller, "Rearchitecting Pay: Exclusive Q&A with Josh Bersin," Workhuman, July 9, 2018.
3. Sarah Payne, "Total Rewards 2019 Recap: Disruption Is Here to Stay," report of activity at the WorldAtWork Total Rewards Conference, May 9, 2019.
4. https://resources.globoforce.com/globoforce-blog/rearchitecting-pay-q-a-josh-bersin.
5. https://www.shrm.org/resourcesandtools/hr-topics/compensation/pages/performance-based-bonuses.aspx.
6. Gerald E. Ledford, George Benson, and Edward E. Lawler III, "Cutting-Edge Performance Management," WorldatWork Research, August 2016.
7. https://www.pewresearch.org/fact-tank/2017/09/20/americans-see-men-as-the-financial-providers-even-as-womens-contributions-grow/.
8. https://www.pewresearch.org/fact-tank/2016/07/01/racial-gender-wage-gaps-persist-in-u-s-despite-some-progress/.
9. https://resources.globoforce.com/globoforce-blog/hr-metoo-where-we-stand-one-year-later.
10. https://money.cnn.com/2018/01/04/pf/pay-gap-sexual-harassment/index.html.
11. https://www.shrm.org/hr-today/news/hr-news/conference-today/pages/2018/employers-should-plan-for-stronger-pay-equity-laws.aspx.
12. https://www.washingtonpost.com/news/business/wp/2018/03/26/wall-streets-average-bonus-in-2017-three-times-what-most-u-s-households-made-all-year/?noredirect=on.
13. https://hbr.org/2017/08/when-employees-think-the-boss-is-unfair-theyre-more-likely-to-disengage-and-leave.
14. https://sloanreview.mit.edu/article/getting-the-short-end-of-the-stick-racial-bias-in-salary-negotiations/.
15. Payne, "Total Rewards 2019 Recap: Disruption Is Here to Stay."
16. https://www.forbes.com/sites/georginagrant/2018/08/07/similar-to-me-bias-how-gender-affects-workplace-recognition/#52c494b3540a.

17. https://www.researchgate.net/publication/23784531_Readiness_for_self
-directed_change_in_professional_behaviours_Factorial_validation_of_the
_Self-reflection_and_Insight_Scale.

18. Dan Miller, "Globoforce Rearchitects Company Compensation Through
Social Recognition," Case Study, 2018.

19. "Designing Work Cultures for the Human Era," SHRM/Workhuman, 2018.

20. Barry Ritholtz, "Wall Street Bonuses Aren't Really Bonuses: Deferred Profit-
Sharing Is the Better Way to Think of the Annual Payouts," Bloomberg
Opinion, March 27, 2019.

21. Stephen Miller, "2020 Salary Budget Growth Expected to Notch Just Above
3%," SHRM, August 15, 2019.

Chapter 12: Leading Humans

1. Workhuman Live keynote address, 2019.
2. Interview, July 9, 2019.
3. Workhuman Live keynote address, 2018.
4. Workhuman Live keynote address, 2018.
5. Workhuman Live keynote address, 2017.
6. Workhuman Live keynote address, 2016.
7. Workhuman Live keynote address, 2017.
8. Interview, August 8, 2019.
9. Workhuman Live keynote address, 2019.
10. Workhuman Live keynote address, 2018.

Chapter 13: A Call to Action

1. "Business Roundtable Redefines the Purpose of a Corporation to Promote
'An Economy That Serves All Americans,'" Business Roundtable, August 19,
2019.
2. Interview with Daniel Pink, October 24, 2019
3. "Supplier Responsibility 2019 Progress Report," Apple.

INDEX

ABOUT THE AUTHORS

ERIC MOSLEY
Cofounder and CEO, Workhuman

Eric, a visionary for the future of leadership and the modern workplace, is the acclaimed author of *The Crowdsourced Performance Review* and coauthor of the award-winning book *The Power of Thanks*. Eric is a regular contributor to *Forbes* on the topics of recognition and humanity in the workplace, and a frequent contributor to publications including *Fast Company* and *Harvard Business Review*.

As CEO and cofounder of Workhuman, he is a pioneer of the Workhuman movement and its annual conference, Workhuman Live, which has grown into thousands of attendees leading the charge to dismantle old HR processes and challenge organizations to build new ways to connect the modern workforce. Eric guides some of the most admired global brands in the world on how to create more human-centric workplaces that leverage the way people work today, focusing on employee development, social connections, and organizational communities and teams.

Eric has long believed that employees achieve their fullest potential when they feel appreciated, connected, and empowered to be who they are in the work they do.

DEREK IRVINE

Senior Vice President, Client Strategy and Consulting, Workhuman

The renowned coauthor of *The Power of Thanks,* Derek is one of the world's foremost experts on social recognition, continuous performance management, engagement, and the future of work, guiding business leaders to elevate their vision and ambitions for their company culture. A celebrated speaker, Derek teaches HR leaders how to make work more human by proactively nurturing and shaping company culture.

His writing is regularly featured across major HR publications including *HR Magazine, Human Resource Executive, HR Zone,* and *Workspan.*

Derek is also senior vice president, client strategy and consulting, Workhuman, where he leads the company's consulting and analytics divisions. Derek helps customers—such as Cisco, P&G, Merck, JetBlue, and LinkedIn—leverage proven strategies and best practices to build employee engagement, increase retention, and improve bottom-line results.

WORKING HUMAN IS

more than just words on a page